The Providence of God

BOOKS BY G.C. BERKOUWER

MODERN UNCERTAINTY AND CHRISTIAN FAITH
RECENT DEVELOPMENTS IN ROMAN CATHOLIC THOUGHT
THE TRIUMPH OF GRACE IN THE THEOLOGY OF KARL BARTH
THE SECOND VATICAN COUNCIL AND THE NEW CATHOLICISM

STUDIES IN DOGMATICS SERIES —

THE PROVIDENCE OF GOD
FAITH AND SANCTIFICATION
FAITH AND JUSTIFICATION
FAITH AND PERSEVERANCE
THE PERSON OF CHRIST
GENERAL REVELATION
DIVINE ELECTION
MAN: THE IMAGE OF GOD
THE WORK OF CHRIST
THE SACRAMENTS
SIN
THE RETURN OF CHRIST
HOLY SCRIPTURE
THE CHURCH

Studies in Dogmatics

The Providence of God

BY
G. C. BERKOUWER

PROFESSOR OF SYSTEMATIC THEOLOGY,
FREE UNIVERSITY OF AMSTERDAM

WM. B. EERDMANS PUBLISHING COMPANY
GRAND RAPIDS, MICHIGAN

© Copyright Wm. B. Eerdmans Publishing Co. 1952
All rights in this book are reserved

Reprinted, May 1983

Translated by Lewis B. Smedes from the Dutch edition,
De Voorverziening Gods,
published by J. H. Kok N.V., Kampen, The Netherlands
ISBN 0-8028-4814-1

PHOTOLITHOPRINTED BY EERDMANS PRINTING COMPANY
GRAND RAPIDS, MICHIGAN, UNITED STATES OF AMERICA

Contents

1. THE CRISIS OF THE PROVIDENCE DOCTRINE IN OUR CENTURY 7
2. THE KNOWLEDGE OF PROVIDENCE 31
3. PROVIDENCE AS SUSTENANCE 50
4. PROVIDENCE AS GOVERNMENT 83
5. A THIRD ASPECT? 125
6. PROVIDENCE AND HISTORY 161
7. PROVIDENCE AND MIRACLES 188
8. THE PROBLEM OF THEODICY 232

CHAPTER I

The Crisis of the Providence Doctrine in Our Century

ONE cannot give thought to the Church's confession of faith in Providence without very soon being impressed by the distance between this confession and modern thought. Though it is not our intention to discuss the modern mind, we cannot close our eyes to the increasingly noticeable, almost vibrant intensity of thought in the background of the modern scene. Contemporary scientific and philosophical thought — as well as that of the ordinary man — is engrossed in the question of the meaning and purpose of the world and its history, of human life.

A long series of revolutionary and catastrophic events has made an almost undeniable empirical fact of the meaninglessness of human life. Not only has this century been ravaged by global wars of incalculable destruction but, with the descent of peace, new tensions and new fears have possessed our tired generation. Can life, then, still make sense? Dare one call this life meaningful? This is now a pre-eminently existential question whose persistence we cannot avoid. The time of tragedy has visited individual and social life, and appears to have come to stay. The situation is mirrored in the abundance of "declarations of decline," now often bearing an even more radical stamp than those which appeared after the first World War under the influence of Spengler's *Decline of the West*.

The optimism that keynoted the eighteenth and nineteenth centuries has made room for a hard and often ruthless realism. Even the best intents to give some perspective to the changing scenes of human life and a fundament to history have seemed impotent to withstand the almost supra-personal destructive forces of our time. We need not be surprised that just in this age men are again talking seriously about demons, about their influence on life in all its aspects; about crisis, chaos, decline, nihilism — words that are finding a strikingly prominent place in modern man's vocabulary. Humanism, it is true, has not died out completely since the war. Yet, we may speak of a profoundly shaken outlook on life, of a suspicion that casts a shadow on the whole of life.

Can we not hear today a lamentation over man? Are not the terror and alarm of countless tragedies — tragedies which still lie at least on the border of our lives — still fresh in our memories? Shall not the twentieth century, though productive of much that is good, always remain the century of the concentration camps and the pogroms, of war and hatred, of attack on the worth of humanity itself? And must we not bate our breath for what is to come?

The turn from optimism to pessimism does not by any means always wear a radical character. Even where the lullaby of gradual improvement is changed to a cry of despair and where the facts of experience prove too bitter for restful optimism, there is still a notable absence of talk of a profound and radical revolution. There is talk of demonizing and corruption, but the main motif of many confessions of modern life is better characterized as tragedy than as repentance, as despair than as conversion. We hear of sorrow and desperation, of distress and estrangement, of fate and death. The old optimism has made room for a new realism; but this new realism by itself is not the *real* crisis of the awareness of and confession of guilt.

The real crisis lies in the meaning of the reality of God to this shattered world. Does the Gospel have meaning and worth for our time? Does the church have the courage and the right to preach the living God in the midst of *this* senseless world, this world of the twentieth century which seems to have room for only one realistic world and life view: nihilism? Is not the present situation in the world a clear proof that at least on this side of life there is no perspective beyond the burden and the darkness? And is not all this irrefutable evidence that there is no God? Does not atheism seem now to be the only logical and permissible conclusion to draw from the reality of our century?

Indeed, to many, this has been the only conclusion. The turn from optimism to pessimism has brought no change in this. Modern realism is at bottom just as atheistic in its acceptance of reality as was optimism in its avoidance of reality. It was, in fact, empirical reality which seemed to *force* men to atheism. With an eye to the facts, man could not — in honest resignation or honest revolt — flee anew to the supersensible world or to a hereafter in which all the raw distress of this actual world would be soothed away. If what Berdyaev writes is true,[1] that catastrophe often forms a goad to speculation, then one must admit that it can also lead to a rejection of the "speculation" of the Christian faith. In the speculation of which Berdyaev speaks, man will not flee. He chooses *consciously* for the existential reality of today and tomorrow, even though the last word in this reality must be meaninglessness and absurdity. It is a choice against the traditional confession of the Church, the confession of God's Providence over all things. This total and universal aspect of the Church's confession renders it unacceptable to many as too simple an answer to the urgency of our times. Can all this, all this that fills men's hearts, fall within the circle of a Divine Providence? Can man with honesty and clear conscience still believe it?

It seems as though this confession — God's rule over *all things,* more than other confessions — were thrown into the

---

1. N. Berdyaev, *The Meaning of History,* 1945, p. 1.

crucible of the times. This does not mean that in fairer days the Providence of God was never doubted or denied. Even in eras of peace and quiet, when man still had confidence in the inevitable gradual improvement of life, there were burning questions to disturb the honest mind. The lot of man in sickness, suffering, and death has always raised questions about God's Providence. But the question forces itself far more directly and disturbingly upon us in times of all-embracing crisis, in times when nihilism has become a fad.

These are times in which the Church of Christ must ask herself whether she still has the courage, in profound and unshakable faith, in boundless confidence, to proclaim the Providence of God. Or is she possessed of secret doubts fed by daily events? Can she still speak of God's rule over *all* things, of His holy presence in *this* world? Can she yet proclaim confidently His unlimited control over the world and life — war and peace, East and West, pagans . . . and Jews? Dare she still, with eyes open to the facts of life — no less than those who *from the facts* conclude an imperative atheism — still confess her old confession?

* * *

It is necessary to pause over this question, the more since God's Providence seems to be one of the most self-evident articles of the Church's confession. The confessions of the churches contain a common witness to the Providence of God over "all things," those of the Roman Catholic as well as those of the Lutheran and Reformed churches. In Protestant confessions there is a remarkably uniform definition. In the handbooks of theology, too, the definitions and distinctions appear in striking consensus. We read in all of them of sustenance and rule, and of God's embracing in His prescient government all that occurs in the universe.

Many of the treatises give little if any attention to crisis phenomena. The doctrine of Providence is discussed usually in general and timeless terms. We receive the impression that a finished definition has been reached, that we may now content ourselves with a repetition of the many lucid declarations of the Church. Thus, this article of faith for a long period failed to arouse the same kind of opposition as did, for instance, the doctrines of substitution and satisfaction. When the person and work of Christ was in the center of dispute, the Providence doctrine had not yet became a serious stumbling block. Providence seemed to be a "truth" which could rely upon universal assent — in distinction from other truths like the virgin birth, the resurrection, and the ascension, which were the *scandalon* of the nineteenth century. Anyone who accepted the existence of God usually believed as well that He sustained and ruled the world. The Providence doctrine was often used as another way of stating man's belief in progressive evolution. God was discernibly leading the world to His own benevolent end. Not only the maintenance of the world, but the sequence of historical events appeared to confirm the confession of the Church. Of course, the Church did not speak of evolution. But it did speak of fulfillment and purpose; and was not *purpose* a catchword in the optimism of the last century — and, for that matter, in the preaching of the kingdom of God?

All this in our century is radically altered. The friendliness of God, which man thought he saw reflected in the stream of history, has become increasingly disputable. In truth, has it not been disproven by historical reality? Do not the researches of such men as Spengler, Lessing[2], and Toynbee[3] underscore it? In all this, the reality of God, His guidance and purposeful management, has today become a profound problem — *the* problem for persons who have never even considered it before. Many feel themselves forced into agnosticism or atheism. The facts of experience which used to be the most striking illustrations of God's Providence have

---

2. Theod. Lessing, *Geschichte als Sinngebung des Sinnlosen*, 1929.
3. A. J. Toynbee, *A Study of History*, 1946.

become an even more convincing counter-argument. Everywhere profound doubts have risen as to the reality of God; men not only deny Providence over *all things,* but ridicule the idea by pointing to the reality around us. True, the confessions of the Church also speak of human suffering and grievous distress. They avoid adversity no more than prosperity, and embrace barren with fruitful years, sickness with health, and "all that can yet come over us." They even include the evil that God in His *pity* sends.[4] But the proportion of this evil has become so great and frightful that the word *pity* must, it seems, be forced to take on a new meaning.

* * *

We can perhaps thus frame the contradiction which life poses: the comfort of the old confession of God's Providence versus the *dread* that rises from the events of our century. Dread has now become the essence and intensification of the unrest and concern latently present in all times. "In a period in which the problem of man is anew considered and argued, with the authority of the traditional constructions rejected, dread — a dread which invades the essence of man — arises anew in all her nakedness and primitive strength."[5] Dread may be considered the result of man's being more or less ruthlessly snatched out of an old and trusted order and forced into a strange, hostile world. We may say that the trusted order out of which man is plucked is the order of Providence. But the causes of man's radical displacement and estrangement are complex. Various forms of philosophical thought, for instance, have seeped into the life outlook of the average non-philosophic person. Existentialism, in particular, has pointedly forced the problem of dread to our attention. Heidegger spoke about "anxiety as the essence of existence," about the "primariness of dread as existential phenomenon," and

---

4. Heidelberg Catechism, Question 26.
5. W. Banning, "Overwinning van Angst," in *Angst en Crisis der Moraal,* 1949, p. 81.

about "existence unto death."[6] Heidegger's existentialism has been of profound influence in modern philosophical and non-philosophical thought. And what Heidegger called "the suspension of existence within nothingness"[7] corresponds with modern man's dread.

There are few who would still insist that the cultural phenomenon of dread is exclusively social in nature, that we can overcome dread by way of the social sciences. Communists still tell us that we need an authoritative power to root out the misery of a social dread. It is, they say, a kind of freedom which is the cause of mass dread. But dread clutches man too tightly and involves him too deeply for him thus to be cured *en masse*.

In this situation the confession of God's Providence over all things seems the last thing which could justly pretend to answer the basic question of human existence. The confession of God's Providence has become, now more than ever, a stone of stumbling.

The conflict between the confession of God's Providence and the modern mind poses a threat which the Church should understand. And the Church will understand it so long as she truly lives out of the Word of God. For it is the Word which points most clearly to the deep distress which rises from life's displacement into a hostile order. It shows us how seriously the influence of sin and enmity against God and man alienates and displaces man from the fellowship of God, the fellowship which casts out dread.

This is the light that the Scriptures cast on dread. They do not isolate one or more aspects of the phenomenon, but reveal the radical estrangement which is the cause of dread. The Scriptures diagnose the sickness unto death at its source, and thus explain its effect on the whole complicated human situation. That is why the believer knows that the problem of

---

6. M. Heidegger, *Sein und Zeit*, I^4, 1935, pp. 191ff., 184ff., 252ff.; cf. Heidegger, *Was Ist Metaphysik?* 1929, pp. 18ff.
7. *Was Ist Metaphysik?* p. 23.

estrangement is the problem of his own relationship to God. He is shown how in man's estrangement empirical reality seems to speak with final authority and brings on a crisis of belief in God's Providence. Thus, this belief can never be the consequence of empirical considerations and reasoned conclusions. It is, rather, that the displacement and dispersement are overcome from above. The Church knows that this victory is not the crown of autonomous thinking, but a gift of God's grace. In this victory the Church must, in humility and courage, go *through* the world and through the crisis of our time. She knows from Scripture and experience how often her faith has been tried by the riddles of history, by the terrifying enigmas of experience. She knows, too, that in her own past the timid question provoked by a failure to understand has often crescendoed into a revolt of doubt and faithlessness. The Bible does not hide from us the fact that questions born in fear and uncertainty can whelm up with remarkable force in the hearts of believers. Recall the illustrations in Scripture: in the Psalms, the Book of Job, and Ecclesiastes — illustrations which contradict all rational self-evidence.

In the Psalms we face the problem of the prosperity of the ungodly. This prosperity — a contrast to the suffering and oppression of the believer — repeatedly awakens doubt, not out of selfish envy, but from a desire to believe in God and to walk in His Light. Asaph, in Psalm 73, tells of a crisis in his thoughts about God's sovereignty. "But as for me, my feet were almost gone; my steps had well nigh slipped" (Ps. 73:2). He fails to understand God's ways with men. "How doth God know? And is there knowledge with the Most High?" (Ps. 73:11). He wrestles with the facts of daily experience, inexplicable in the light of God's presence and goodness. He tries to resolve the presence of God with the suffering and darkness of life. But it was a torment for him (Ps. 73:16). We need not dwell here on how he transcends the tension by entering God's sanctuary. We need only observe the revolv-

CRISIS OF THE PROVIDENCE DOCTRINE 15

ing of a serious crisis in the torment, embitterment, and irritation of the writer — of the believer (Ps. 73:21). It is true that in this same Psalm we hear Asaph confessing his guilt in humble lament over his foolishness. But the lament accents the more sharply the gravity of the crisis, the crisis of belief in God's Providence.

When Israel in the midst of darkness hears the voice of the people: "Who will show us any good?" she answers in her prayer: "Jehovah, lift thou up the light of thy countenance upon us" (Ps. 4:6). The "good" is not defined in their prayer. This is because that good lies *in* the light of God's countenance. But a crisis still arises for Israel when she sees so many "goods" in the life of the proud as their grain and wine multiply (Ps. 4:7) and instead of judgment, they receive extraordinary prosperity (Ps. 73:4, 5). Happily, the crisis is overcome when God answers her prayer and teaches her to discover the hand of God. But we see here how the Scriptures frankly reveal that the Providence doctrine is not set in a mold, is not a calm and tensionless constant. They tell us how this belief can go through the crucible, even be lost for a time and be rediscovered in the way of prayer and confession of guilt.

In Job, too, we meet a deep lamentation which reveals a crisis in his faith. Job is not concerned about the problem of human suffering in the abstract. This dilemma, large as life itself, faces him: his pious walk before God and the destructive calamity that scourges his life. The catastrophe that threatens his life is from God. Job cannot believe that his distress has any other source. The Lord has taken away (Job 1:21). He has caused the crisis in Job's life. This is the reason why Job's mouth is filled with complaints against his Maker and against the terrors risen in force against him. Job speaks for all to hear: *God* has crushed him in the storm! God has increased his wounds *without cause* (Job 9:17). The why of this tortured life grows to a complaint, a charge: God's goodness and wisdom come into controversy.

Again in Ecclesiastes we encounter crisis-phenomena, and again in connection with the apparent purposelessness of life's maze. Vanity of vanities! In the "all is vanity" God's presence, God's rule, seems to be at stake. Ecclesiastes has often been interpreted as Eastern fatalism, as the "Autumn Book," the book of withered leaves, the cry of the senselessness of existence. But this interpretation is contradicted by the words of the Preacher himself. He reveals a vertical perspective within the closed-circle of experience. But the upward look is revealed only against the background of a vicious life-circle, of the hard facts of life and the world, of every day's injustices that find no retribution (Eccles. 7:15-22).

That such a book as this could find its place in Holy Scripture shows how earnest the question of God can be, and how seriously such questions are considered *within* revelation. How real, precisely in the crisis, becomes the warning to fear God, who shall bring every work into judgment (Eccles. 12:13, 14). Scripture never avoids the problematic. It bares the problem in all its oppressive urgency, so that *in* the oppression the light of revelation may fall, anew and startlingly, on life. The Church in our time may well remember how the believers of Scripture recalled *in* their victory and subsequent praises the distress of the temptation. And it is good, too, to remember how sorely man's distress required a physician. This Scriptural realism should warn us against all over-simplification which offends the raw reality, as the over-simplification of Job's friends aggravated the distress of his life. Scripture warns us with many examples not to disguise the facts of life but to face them in all earnest, and not to observe the crisis of doubt with the aloofness of pious pride. The Church, herself involved in the duress and misery of this life, must witness to the living God — the God for whom the Old Testament saints cried, not content with sham comforts, unable to rest until they had seen Him with their own eyes (Job 42:5 and Ps. 73:23 ff.)

This is a warning for the Church not to lift herself out of contact with those who, in storm and night, in distress and fear, feel the ground shaking under their feet, a warning for the Church to witness, not *to* the night, but *in* the night. With one eye to the failures of the Church in the past and the other on our confession in God's Providence, we have reason to call ourselves again to watchfulness and prayer.

* * *

The same questions about God's Providence that swell in the hearts of Bible saints may be observed rising perpetually in the history of the Church. When God's hand presses hard on man's life, when the richness of life seems to evaporate into vanity, then the question of God becomes eloquent. In days of crisis and persecution the murmur swells: Why? Why? And yet how long? Where is God? Why should God permit us to be thus tortured? *Everything* depends upon this, whether man can through faith transcend, while not escaping, crisis — through faith, the perspective that overcomes the world and fills the heart with honest, though mysterious, repose.

This is the question that defines everything in our time. It is the question that pierces the phase of estrangement in the world. We cannot here fully discuss this alienation of man from his trusted order, but we can clearly see some of the factors that have helped create and mature man's feeling of being a stranger in the world. The estrangement comes from secularization. God is estranged from man; and man becomes a stranger in His world. We may delineate three motifs that have played an important role in secularization: the scientific-, the projection-, and the catastrophic-motif. Let us address ourselves briefly to each of these.

1. *The scientific-motif*. We mean here to investigate, though not exhaustively, the influence of modern natural

science on man's faith in God. Natural science has been the bridge on which many have crossed over to unbelief. As nature has been consistently reduced to natural causes, the "hypothesis" of God's preservation and rule of the world has been rendered less necessary. The enlightened scientific mind has come to look on the Providence doctrine more or less as a bromide convenient for pre-scientific naivete, but now rendered unpalatable by the "deeper insights" of the scientific method. The thought of a world locked up in natural cause has acted as a power of suggestion on the modern mind. Now that nature has given up her secrets and man has seen through what used to be called supernatural, the world has been relieved of God. The naive may still find correspondence between the "flame of the Lord" of Psalm 29 and the "work of God" in nature and in history, but the enlightened know only the lightning, nature, and the process of generation. Such thoughts as these of Addison:

> *The spacious firmament on high,*
> *With all the blue ethereal sky,*
> *And spangled heavens, a shining frame,*
> *Their great Original proclaim*

may grace the patterns of naive desires, but must be sloughed off now that man has learned to know and rule the ways of nature. True, the conviction is growing that man in his manipulation of nature has set himself on paths on which he no longer holds himself and his safety in his own hands. But this does not minimize the fact that for man under the spell of popularized natural science the reality of God has been deftly relegated to the irrelevance of the pre-scientific age. Though many are beginning to talk again about the limitations of the scientific method and though one hears occasional murmurs against its imperialism, the inevitable conclusion of modern science is that it has left no room for God. This is one of the sources of the crisis for belief of our times. We shall return to it in another connection.

2. *The projection-motif*. With this second motif we arrive in a terrain that is likewise closely related to the question of God's Providence. It has become popular to speak of religion as nothing more than a projection of human subjectivity. This criticism of the meaning and truth of religion is perhaps the most radical possible. It not only discards the truth-character of religion, but appears to give a very plausible explanation of its tenacity.

This "explanation" runs like a red thread through the thought of the nineteenth and twentieth centuries. It appears in the thought of many influential figures: Marx, Ludwig Feuerbach, Nietzsche, Freud, et al. Already in Marx we find the projection theory in fairly well defined form. Dissecting religion, he described it as a chimera created by man to make an unbearable life bearable.[8] Oppressed by miserable reality, man created in religion all sorts of "illusions" whereby he could escape his misery. Hence the Marxian formula: religion, the opium of the people. Reacting to Hegel's optimistic view of history as the self-development or objectivizing of the Spirit, Marx insisted that history be interpreted out of the historical process itself. He saw this process as indissolubly related to the involvement of the very essence of human life in the social problem. Thus, he came to the absolute priority of the actual here-and-now economically-defined life. Marx, in the phrase of Troeltsch, economized the Hegelian dialect. The whole superstructure of life in law, state, fidelity, duty, and religion was construed as resting on the foundation of economics. Marx saw religion as turning this scale of being upside down. Considering the idea that religion is a matter of eternal and universal truths as a fatal projection of the human spirit, he fought ferociously against all forms of it. This projection, he thought, was an anesthetic, a stupifying palliative that turns man's

---

8. Cf. his *Zur Kritik der Hegelsche Religionsphilosophie*, 1844.

thought away from the earthly, actual life and leaves him unable to revolt against its injustices. The true reality of life in all its terrible significance must be unveiled before man again. And for this, the blindfold of religion must be removed from man's eyes.

We find the same projection theory in just as sharp a form in Ludwig Feuerbach. He explained religion as subjective, egoistic wish-projection. Analyzing religion empirically, Feuerbach came to the conclusion that the gods were nothing but objectivized, projected wishes. Man, he said, was the beginning, middle, and end of religion; theology was anthropology.

These and similar ideas were supported in no small way by Nietzsche's emphatic rejection of Christianity. Nietzsche saw Christianity as "Platonism for the people," faith as man's projection of an ideal, supernatural world which devaluated earthly reality.

In the psychoanalysis of Freud, religion receives similar treatment. Freud, like Feuerbach, explained the phenomenon of religion as a projection of man surrounded and menaced by the powers of nature. Defenseless against these threats, man groped and searched for places of refuge. A world of imagination was thus conjured out of the sheer necessity of making human helplessness endurable. The Providence of God, rewards, and hereafters were products of such imaginings. The gods were given the task of absorbing the shocks of nature and of redeeming man from his unhappy fate. "We tell ourselves that it is very beautiful indeed that there is a God, Creator of the world, a kind Providence, a moral order, and a life hereafter — but it is very striking that all this is exactly as we should wish it for ourselves."[9] Providence, moral order and a hereafter — beautiful ideas all, but alas, only religious fancies. Thus, religion answers to no other reality than the psychic creation of man in distress. Freud was con-

---

9. S. Freud, *Die Zukunft einer Illusion*, 1928, p. 53.

fident that the illusion would be gradually dispelled through science. This would, he prudently admitted, have to occur gradually; no one, he said, can shake off a narcotic in a moment. But, once rid of the illusion, man would understand that he is not committed to God and His Providence, but to his own strength.

This, briefly, is how the projection motif tries to explain the origin and tenacity of religion. We can see how the views of Marx, Nietzsche, Feuerbach, and Freud form an important factor in the present crisis of the Providence doctrine. In their "clarification" they make clear the expendability of religion. Belief in Providence becomes, in fact, a very dangerous affair; it is nothing but the other side of a lust for safety and protection against the threats to our existence. It is a symptom of a bourgeois escapism in which man seeks to banish, above all things, fear.

In contrast to this, man must, when he sees religion for the fiction that it is, be reared to sobriety and realism. He must be taught to accept life for what it in reality is, void of illusions. As for the fiction of Providence, we have no more need of it. It must make room for an uncertain, hazardous, and dangerous life, full of risk and experiment. Thus shall man be released from his bonds; thus shall he be set on his own resources to face the reality of today and tomorrow. He shall in freedom find his own way.

We find a connection between the projection-motif, with its idea of freedom, in modern, atheistic existentialism. Here, too, man creates his own freedom without consideration for a power that might surround his life with blessing and security.

3. *The catastrophic-motif.* We encounter in the third motif the idea of catastrophe as a refutation of the Church's confession of God's Providence. The experience of the meaninglessness of human life in the present crisis seems to cut off every perspective that reveals purpose. Humanism tried to instill sense of purpose into life and culture, but failed, for

the most part, to awaken any real sense of meaning in modern man. With the collapse of humanism, there arose a nihilistic attitude to life. Man either spends his years in orgy, continues his tedious way in boredom, or bows his head in submission to the tyranny of a pitiless fate. In any case, the Providence doctrine fails to give an explanation of the gruesome reality that holds life in its grip. Faith says life has meaning and purpose. But where can one point to purpose or reality in the radically ungarnished life of our times? Already in 1921, Karl Heim referred to "the notion of fate as expressing the modern quest for meaning" and, under the influence of Oswald Spengler, observed "the weary spirit of world decline."[10] Though Spengler may have later insisted that he by no means intended to be a propagandist for pessimism, many of his readers looked in terror to the irresistible power of fate that manifested itself in every historical development and in every culture, including our own. The idea of fate aroused the feeling that man is utterly powerless. Human life, it appeared, is so closed-in and so inescapably defined that flight is impossible. Man's reaction can be only desperation, dread, or dull resignation.

The voice of Job can be heard in our own harassed life: "Why was I not stillborn . . . ?" A dismal thing this, life without perspective: total imprisonment of life, in the hands of the powers of destruction. Heim, in connection with the idea of fate, has said that in this situation man must find a release in another world. In the notion of fate we stand before the door that opens into the inner chambers wherein God is to be found. Impressed by man's imprisoned existence, Heim sees two alternatives: nihilism or discovery of God. But he realizes that the latter possibility comes only through a gift of grace, the grace of revelation. In our time we see the first alternative conspicuously realized: desperation and

---

10. K. Heim, *Glaube und Leben*, 1928, pp. 406ff.

CRISIS OF THE PROVIDENCE DOCTRINE 23

nihilism. The confession of the Providence of God scarcely finds a sounding board.

Raw reality assaults this comforting and optimistic confession. Could the catastrophic terrors of our century, with the improportionate sufferings they inflict on individuals, families, and peoples — could these be a reflection of the guidance of God? Does not pure honesty force us to stop seeking escape in a hidden, harmonious super-sensible world? Does not honesty tell us to limit ourselves realistically to what lies before our eyes, and, without illusions, face the order of the day? How can we overcome the catastrophic by a return to a confidence in the meaning of life, when the possibility of meaning itself is in question? Realism and a facing of facts have come to fetter the human heart. The beautiful story of Providence and the Hand of God, it is said, is a religious fancy, and belief in it an illusionary escape from reality.

* * *

Though modern life has thus been caught up in a strident process of secularization, the image of our times is not uniformly clear. While we receive the impression that modern man has radically broken with the Providence doctrine, and is, furthermore, heroically prepared to live without recourse to any ideology of comfort and security, we can also observe a certain amount of hesitation to burn every bridge that forms a link with the other world. Having found that life without a vertical perspective is cold and comfortless, a world without windows, man attempts to regain a perspective beyond the confines of empirical reality. Faith in the Providence doctrine having been outmoded, this perspective is being sought in such occult sciences as spiritism, astrology, and, more recently, para-psychology.

Since para-psychology presumes to be a new science, we may by way of parenthesis take note of it here. Though para-psychology defines as its field psychic phenomena which are beyond the ken of ordinary psychology, it often ranges out into metaphysical matters. It embraces phenomena, we are told, which include contact with the dead, or with other psychic beings. Its occult tendency is also revealed in its interest in horoscope and the prognostication of the future. It seeks, in fact, to get at the essence of the human soul and thus provide a new theory of the essence of man. It claims that man is able in principle to predict his own future, and thereby it seeks to demonstrate that an immortal essence lies at the root of our empirical personality. In para-psychology man is assured of his own immortality, is given some certainty of his future, and thus is offered a new perspective in his otherwise meaningless life. It is the pretension of para-psychology that it enriches man's life at its center.

The prediction of the future, which para-psychology claims is possible, reveals a remarkable trend in modern thought. Man has rejected the Providence doctrine as a threat to human freedom and human autonomy. But now that man fears his own autonomy, determination appears again. Though its essential content is changed, even the word predestination is heard in the circles of para-psychology. For only if the future is in some way determined can it be prognosticated. The possibility of error is conceded, and it is said that, beyond a certain number of years, only a general trend can be prognosticated. This possibility of error is related to the question of determinism. Some within para-psychological circles wish to retain a place for indeterminism and freedom so that man may have an opportunity to change his course, having seen, via prognosis, the general lines of the future of his present life. Thus, there is enough determinism to allow for prognosis and enough indeterminism to allow for human initiative in the light of the prognosis. At any rate, there is a line that ties the future to the present. In fact, para-psychology claims to have given an entirely new outlook on the idea of time, on the relationship between future and present.

The fact that para-psychology revives interest in immortality and determination gives the impression that it offers something basically significant to man in his modern impasse. But man's estrangement is not thus relieved. This vacuum cannot be filled with an empty belief in immortality any more than by nihilism, realism, or absurdity. A hope that man may survive the shock of death provides little real confidence and security over against the judgment of the living God who encounters us, not only at the end of life, but at every point within it. Nor can a determinism without God open a window to a new world. Thus, though man rejected Providence as a projection of human wishes, he is again attempting new projections that seek to reach out to the other side of the grave. The crisis of the Providence doctrine runs itself out in these projections.

* * *

Perhaps, if we search, we may be able to find historical causes and occasions in the past for the crisis in man's trust in Providence. It is not inconceivable that previous unfortunate readings of the confessions of Providence have been a cooperative factor in its rejection in favor of the modern ideas of fate, tragedy, futility, and doubt. It is, in fact, quite possible to indicate such causes.

We may point, for instance, to the watering down of the Providence doctrine, perhaps best typified as the humanizing of the God-concept. The modern crisis of faith has been in large measure defined by this humanizing of God. The living God, working and ruling in majesty, was portrayed as a shrewd and calculating craftsman, carefully and intelligently managing his affairs. Deism, remarkably, was very influential in the creation of this concept of God. It is a mistake to call eighteenth century deism merely a new form of Epicureanism with its teaching of a God who never bothered himself with the trivial affairs of this world. This notion certainly plays a role in deism but it was deism which particularly wished to *relieve God of all traces of anthropomorphism*. It sought a purification of the God-concept. And this brought it into headlong opposition to the traditional idea of God. The upshot of its attempt to dis-anthropomorphize God was that only the thin God-concept of natural theology was left — empty, without content, glory, or comfort. This corrupted God-concept, though casting its spell on many, divorced itself totally from the God of the Word and from the living, majestic, overpowering, Divine working in judgment and grace. Deism, then, in trying to de-humanize God, ironically succeeded only in picturing Him as sterile human intellect.

In reaction to this barren intellectualism, the coin was turned to reveal the other side. In place of Intellect, God became Love. The God-concept was still humanized, but God was made in the image of human love. Ritschl, for example, saw the idea of wrath in God as a complete misunderstanding by those who had not yet learned to know the true God. He set about to rectify the error by presenting a God incapable of wrath. But armed with such a milked concept of God, man could hardly erect a defence against the coming storms of the new era. It has become patent that the terrorizing world with its demonic appearance cannot be explained by an eternal, self-evident philanthropy, by this grace without judgment. Relations between this "god" and this world became increasingly strained. In times of quiet prosperity the rose-colored light of the providence of this "god" may have appeared to fall over the world. But in catastrophe, in the trenches, the caves, and the concentration camps of this world, the eternal Philanthropist was exposed as a delusion. This was the beginning of the crisis of faith in our day. This view of Providence can command no argument against the plausible criticisms of the three motifs discussed earlier. This preaching no longer jibes. This "god" may still be eulogized; but he inspires no confidence. But when this God-concept fell, the confession of the Church seemed for many to fall with it. Disfigured even in church and theology, the real confession of the Providence of God was and is by many unknown or misunderstood.

We may, then, take some pleasure in knowing that this God-concept, from which so many have been repelled because of its tragic contradiction of reality, is far removed from the Biblical witness. Nothing is clearer than that the Bible witnesses to another God, a stranger to this gentle Philanthropist. The Bible writers were not so advanced as the optimists of the eighteenth and nineteenth centuries, and could not so neatly explain the world in terms of such a humane love-concept. The Bible does not present Providence as an obvious reflection of repose, evolution, and security. It witnesses to the Lord of Hosts, to His judgment and grace, to the clouds shrouding His throne (Ps. 97:2).

A one-sided, optimistic God-concept is in absolute contradiction to the God-picture of, for instance, Psalm 46. This Psalm certainly sings jubilantly of the protection of God, of God as refuge and strength. But it also breaks through all over-simplification and sings of the Lord of Hosts who devastates the earth and makes an end to wars. He breaks the bow, splits the sword asunder, and burns the chariots with fire (Ps. 46:9). At the center of the Biblical message lie salvation and redemption, unmotivated and inconceivable philanthropy (Titus 3:4), but the comfort that comes to us in this gospel is first seen against the background of real wrath and real judgment. The comfort is revealed in this, that Jesus Christ saves us from that wrath (I Thess. 1:10).

Mere optimistic love lacks, in the first place, the Biblical tension. It is an abridgment, a minimizing, and therefore a vitiating, of Biblical preaching. The era following the Enlightenment is pre-eminently the era of the humanized God. At bottom its quiet continuity is static, the consequence of its break with orthodoxy, that is to say, with the Church's dynamic confession of the corruption of human nature and redemption through the cross. Released from the bonds of the

Gospel, the Enlightenment could produce only what someone has called its "genial Providence." This geniality was stubbornly maintained for a surprisingly long period. The earthquake of Lisbon, Voltaire's taunts, Kant's broadsides, all, though causing doubts, failed to discredit it completely.

This genial Providence, this grace without judgment, this love without justice, this forgiveness without redemption, forms the background of the crisis of our century. Modern man has intuitively felt that this teaching of a smiling Providence rested on an unreal simplification, and offered no foundation in times when the firmament itself trembled. The idea of a genial Providence is only a disfigured remnant of the doctrine of universal Providence. It runs parallel with the vague belief in immortality which is an unfertile residue of the Church's eschatological confession. When the suppositions of this humanized God-concept — peace, security, and development — fell, the God fell with them leaving in the modern consciousness a dangerous vacuum.

Now, in the twentieth century, we are witnessing a sharp reaction to the humanizing of God. It is manifested, for instance, in a turn from evolutionary to eschatological thinking. The sharp protests began after the first World War. Men such as Rudolph Otto and Karl Barth cannot be understood apart from the cataclysmic changes of the time. Both of these theological revolutionaries developed the theme of the non-human in God. He is the wholly-other God, full of majesty and holiness, the Unapproachable, the Unaccountable, dwelling in unapproachable light. It was Barth particularly who laid great stress on God's transcendence and on His judgment, and who labored in his earlier years over "The Righteousness of God." He broke with Schleiermacher and Ritschl, and sounded again the reality of God's wrath.

Chaos and threatened destruction, war and nihilism, no longer loomed as contradictions of God and His holy presence in the world. On the contrary, they were a striking witness

CRISIS OF THE PROVIDENCE DOCTRINE 29

to the sovereignty of God's rule revealing itself in wrath and judgment. There was no more talk of genial Providence. This was a call to a recognition of Divine, sovereign working in judgment and grace, full of tension and seriousness, challenge *and comfort.*

The question of theodicy was placed in a new light.[11] The justification of God by human thought was no longer the proper intent; another justification, that of man with his guilt and corruption, his revolt and fall, became the problem of theology. From theodicy, the justification of God, to the justification of the ungodly! No wonder that attention was again addressed to the confession of the Church. There was a leap back over the Enlightenment into the embrace of sixteenth century theology. There was no humanizing of God in the Reformation. Its concepts of history and Providence were completely other than the genial Providence notion of the eighteenth and nineteenth centuries. In confronting the Reformation understanding of the Gospel, we stand, with the Church, before questions that will henceforth in this volume occupy our attention. The Church has been warned — even by history. She has been taught how totally a shrunken and unbiblical Providence doctrine is rooted out in the storm and tempest of reality. The question of today is the *content* of the message of the Church.

We can speak less than ever today of Providence as a confession commanding more or less universal agreement. In this situation, the Church must not lose her courage, nor the strength of her witness. She is called to clarity and fidelity of Scriptural confession. We must be conscious that our own reflections will never have the power to overcome the crisis involving the doctrine of Providence. But as the Scriptures rule our thinking and speaking, as they measure the preaching

---

11. We think here of the first phase of Barth's theology, particularly of the *Römerbrief*, 1922. But the line of development runs throughout his exposition of free grace and predestination in Christ. Cf. the final chapter of this volume.

of the Church, so the Word of God will speak to the distressed and disordered life of our times. The man of the twentieth century will be called out of his self-made refuge, called — not to spineless resignation, not to fatalistic capitulation — but to the doing of the Prophetic Word: "Jehovah of hosts, him shall ye sanctify; and let him be your fear, and let him be your dread. And he shall be for a sanctuary" (Is. 8:13, 14).

CHAPTER II

The Knowledge of Providence

IN TIME of crisis this question thrusts itself before us in bold relief: how do we *know* of the reality of Providence? Is there a reliable basis for this knowledge? Is it possible for us to know of an absolute certainty in life, a certainty that can command resistance to all the attacks and temptations that lie implicitly within every scientific-, projection-, or catastrophic-motif?

To pose such questions does not mean that we should seek a rational basis for our belief in God's Providence — as though this belief is at bottom dependent on human thought or science. In that case science would have to determine for us whether we may or may not even speak of Providence. When we ask about the basis for our faith in Providence we are asking simply for an analysis of faith itself, of that faith which rests in God's revelation of His Providence, and of that faith which finds in that revelation its complete confidence. Nevertheless, the analysis of this faith and its relation to knowledge is significant, if only because here we enter the dangerous context of modern crisis thought. And history reveals too clearly how foreign influences can, within the Church, menace and darken the trust of believers in God's Providence. With persuasive voices on all sides casting serious doubt upon and attacking the guidance of God in the world, it can hardly be otherwise now than that believers should be called back to the question of their final and unshakable certainty in life.

During the last war, Christians were often embarrassed by the question: What does your faith mean now in the obviously senseless and perspectiveless treadmill of this life? Or, what do your prayers mean now in these "mysteries" of God's rule? The reality of God's guiding hand and of His hearing of prayer became for countless persons the most existential question of their lives. The confession of God's Providence was snatched out of the sphere of theoretical reflection and confident clichés. The question of Psalm 42:4 became acute again: "Where is thy God?" That is to say, what is the basis for that miraculous faith which lives in spite of scoffing questions? (Ps. 42:10). "Why art thou cast down, O my soul? And why art thou disquieted within me? Hope thou in God; for I shall yet praise Him . . ." (Ps. 42:5, 12). Where lies the spring of this confidence in God's guidance, of this certainty that our life is not a victim of comfortless destiny and fitful chance — that the hand of God is in our life from day to day?

We may remind ourselves, first, of the clear voice of the Church. She has spoken most emphatically and positively of the indisputable reality of the Providence of God. Reading superficially in the confessions one may receive the impression that he is again in touch with a "genial Providence." In a number of our confessions, it is true, an atmosphere of quiet trust and tranquil confidence prevails. It is as though the formers of the confessions were unmindful that terrible contradictions are continually storming the restful citadel of the Providence doctrine. We read of a universal perspective, of perfect harmony, and of a final equity in the light of which all present tensions are relativized. The confessions tell us with some force that there can be no surprises or accidents in history or in our individual lives. All the apparent surprises and accidents fall within the wide circle of God's providential order. We are told that the Father of Jesus Christ, through His eternal counsel, sustains and rules heaven and earth and all things in them. Further, He cares for all the needs of body and soul. And all the evil that comes to us in this valley of sorrows will, in the end, work to our good. It is confessed that God's power goes out over heaven and earth and every creature in them. It is declared that all things befalling us come from God's fatherly hand, and that this includes both the light and shadow of our earthly life. Again, we are told of the benefit of this confession, of the strength it imparts in distress and adversity, and of the thankfulness it elicits in prosperity. The inclusiveness of the confession makes life appear unassailable. All creatures lie in His hand, unable to move or stir against His will.[1]

In the light of such expressions, we may ask whether the confessions are not too anthropocentric. The question has relevance, for the accusation of anthropocentricism has played a considerable role in the controversy over the Providence doctrine. Does not this emphasis on man — on his safety and security — present a case for the proponents of the projection-theory? Do not the confessions, by their manner of speaking, give support to the disciples of Marx and Schopenhauer? Does this faith, after all, have no other basis than our own wishes and needs? In short, do not the confessions only illustrate our lust for security in time and eternity?

True, the cosmic perspective is not altogether missing in the confessions. God's presence with and almighty power over the whole cosmos is confessed. But the accent falls remarkably strong on man, on his comfort and his safety. When it is asked, "What profits us this confession?" the answer is: "That we may be thankful in prosperity and patient in adversity." Does not everything, then, revolve around our own life and our own salvation? Does not the confession of God's Providence concentrate too much on the assurance that we, comforted by our belief, may go serenely on our way?

---

1. Heidelberg Catechism, Questions 26, 28.

The answer to all these questions must be simply that the confessions are not anthropocentric. It is true that the full light does fall on man as he is given his place in the Providence of God. There is, admittedly, an emphasis on the comfort of this doctrine for the believer in his threatened existence. The Heidelberg Catechism, in fact, begins with "our only comfort in life and death." Nevertheless, the confession is not anthropocentric in the sense that it thereby becomes less theocentric, any more than Paul is anthropocentric when he says that the love of God has appeared to man (Titus 3:4), or that Christ is come into the world to save sinners. There is a distinction between anthropocentric and soteriological. The Church's confession is soteriological, but not thereby anthropocentric. The Belgic Confession says, indeed, that God preserves and rules all things "to serve man," but it then goes on to say, "to the end that man may serve his God" (Article 12).

The Scriptures, too, place man in the center of the care and salvation of the Lord. But the knowledge of this salvation is so strangely deep that the saved man, comforted and secure, turns away from the consideration of his own good fortune to the praise of the Lord. Man-oriented salvation is inseparably connected with man's worship. After speaking of Christ's coming to save sinners, Paul is inspired to a hymn of praise: "Now unto the King eternal, immortal, invisible, the only God, be honor and glory for ever and ever. Amen" (I Tim. 1:15, 17). If the word anthropocentric were not so disreputable, and if it did not suggest God being *used* as a means to save man, it would be quite legitimate to use it. Man as "center" of God's providential love does not clash with the *Soli Deo Gloria,* and steals nothing from the glory of Him who is called, not the "center," but the *Alpha* and *Omega.*

* * *

THE KNOWLEDGE OF PROVIDENCE 35

The Providence of God is presented in the confessions in connection with the believer and his gift of salvation.[2] This relation between salvation and Providence is so close that it must have definite significance for our question as to our knowledge of Providence. This question has often arisen in the history of doctrine and is relevant now: Is the confession of God's Providence soteriologically defined? Or has it universal reference? Is knowledge of it limited to believers, or is it a general understanding about the order of nature and history?

Can we perhaps say that our salvation is included in Providence, but only as a special case, as an exceptional application of the general Providence which we confess? Is the confession of a special Providence not a deduction from the idea of general Providence? Can we not, then, define Providence in general terms without the specific soteriological coloring of the confessions? Is there not a Providence by itself, apart from the idea of redemption? Is a soteriologically defined Providence confession not, in fact, an abridgment and a narrowing of general Providence?

There must be a special reason why the confessions speak about Providence in such close connection with man's salvation, and why they do not reason abstractly over a general Providence. There must have been good reason why Providence was placed in the context of the practice of godliness and the life of faith. This soteriological emphasis has a bearing on the problem of our knowledge of Providence.

The problem is whether a knowledge of God's Providence is possible outside of the Christian faith. We touch here also upon a question of natural theology. The relevance of the question is increased by the relentless attack that the dia-

---

2. There are, naturally, variations of accent in the different confessions. In the second Helvetic Confession there is a strong emphasis on the *power* of God over all things, with little reference to the comfort of the believer. In the Westminster Shorter Catechism we read only: "God's works of Providence are His most Holy, wise, and powerful, preserving and governing all His creatures and all their actions."

lectical theology has leveled against all forms of natural theology. Coincidentally, the problem also appears in the renewed controversy with Roman Catholic thought, the bastion of all natural theology. According to Catholic theology, a kind of general knowledge of God's Providence is possible outside of faith, which knowledge needs only to be completed and enriched by the contents of special revelation. In Catholic confessions, then, the knowledge of Providence is not first of all soteriologically conditioned, but is natural and general.

The controversy has become particularly acute in recent years through Barth's emphatic criticism of natural theology and through his unresolved debate with Emil Brunner. To Barth all natural knowledge of theology is in flagrant opposition to the character of revelation, which is ever: revelation of God *in* Jesus Christ. Other than through this revelation there is no knowledge of God, neither of God as creator nor of God in Providence. Outside of Christ, God is unknowable. There is no other way for man to approach Him; there is no other way through which He approaches man. For several years now Barth has thundered against the Catholic division in man's knowledge of God. We have not to do with an "earthly fore-court theology or a Christian world-and-life view, but with a Word of God, thus with the approach and way of knowledge epitomized in the confession: I believe."[3]

Neither does Barth understand Providence as a general relation between God and His creatures, but as the rule of God, "the theater and instrument of His righteous acts, the mirror and echo of His living Word, the analogy of the kingdom of heaven .... Providence is nothing other than God's free grace, and God's free grace in Christ is Providence."[4] There is, thus, only one way to knowledge of Providence: the way of Christian faith. Barth's view becomes more lucid when he comments on the credal confession of God the Al-

---
3. Barth, *Die Christliche Lehre nach dem Heidelberg Katechismus*, 1948, p. 3.
4. Ibid, p. 56.

mighty. God, he says, is not "might in itself." Such a "might in itself," such an unqualified power or sovereignty means chaos. "We could not," he says, "better describe and define the devil than by trying to think this idea of a self-based, free, sovereign ability."[5] Might in itself is the revolution of nihilism, against which God says *No!* God's power is founded in justice, in His justice as Father of His Son, as Father who in Himself is Love. His might is the might of free love in Jesus Christ. It is neither formless nor characterless, but absolutely defined in Jesus Christ. This ability has nothing in common with an arbitrary omnipotence, an abstract *potentia absoluta*. It is the actual Divine might revealed in Christ.

Barth continues to say that we must not separate the "God Almighty" of the creed from the "God the Father." God's almightiness is not a formal power, but a concrete ability, and, precisely in that it is not a general *potentia*, is it a *Divine* omnipotence. The Almighty God is known only in the revelation of Christ. And it is only in Christ that the almighty power of Divine Providence is revealed. Providence, then, along with the creation doctrine, is a uniquely Christian confession.

We may strongly object to Barth's manner of identifying Providence with God's free grace. We may reject the way in which his idea of our *knowledge* of Providence also defines and limits its *nature*. But we must recognize that, as Barth insists, the confession presents not a natural theology, but the way of faith.

* * *

The problem of natural theology introduces the familiar dogmatic distinction between "mixed articles" and "pure articles" of faith. In this traditional distinction the knowledge

---
5. Barth, *Dogmatik im Grundriss*, 1947, p. 54 and pp. 46ff. Cf. *Kirchliche Dogmatik*, (1932-) II, 1, pp. 588ff.

problem becomes acute even in Reformed theology. It raises such questions as, Is the Christian faith the only way to any knowledge of God? Or can we know something of God; for instance, His Providence, through natural means? If the answer to this last question is yes, then we admit a pre-Christian knowledge of God, that is, we acknowledge that a true, though incomplete, knowledge of God is possible apart from faith in Christ. That there is a general knowledge of God in distinction from faith-knowledge, and that there are two pathways to a knowledge of Providence, has always held a not unrespected place in the history of Christian thought. Providence has been said to be one of the "mixed articles"; that is, one of the articles of the Christian confession which can be known by natural reason as well as through special Revelation. An example of a "pure article" of faith would be the Trinity, which is known only through faith in special Revelation.

We may take Bavinck as our starting point for the discussion of this question. Bavinck, after reviewing the Scriptural data, discusses the "witness of all peoples," and comes to the conclusion that "the doctrine of God's Providence is one of the 'mixed articles,' made known to all men through God's Revelation in nature."[6] Does Bavinck, as a Reformed theologian, mean the same thing as do the Scholastics in their distinction between truths discoverable by human reason and those known only from special Revelation?

Roman Catholic thought has through the years consistently maintained this distinction — a distinction closely related to its doctrine of the image of God. The doctrine logically follows from Rome's idea of the ability of human reason, and from its rejection of the Reformed conception of total depravity. Catholicism, in what is the classic presentation of the "mixed articles," teaches consciously and logically the possibility and reality of a natural theology. According to

---

6. Bavinck, *Gereformeerde Dogmatiek*, 4th edition, 1928, II, p. 553.

THE KNOWLEDGE OF PROVIDENCE

Rome, the two sources of knowledge — reason and faith — correspond to the two modes of revelation — natural and supernatural. In the nineteenth century the Roman Catholic Church condemned all who say that man with his natural reason is unable to know the Creator through the created world. There are, indeed, truths, such as the doctrine of the Trinity, which can be known only by way of supernatural, special revelation. These belong to the mysteries of faith and are in the fullest sense of the word "pure articles." But Providence, says Rome, is a "mixed article."

The question arises whether the idea of "mixed articles" is not specifically Roman Catholic, with no legitimate place in Reformed thinking. If so, why did Bavinck refer to Providence as a "mixed article," and what was his real intent? Pursuing his thought further, we find that he adds several qualifications to this idea. For instance, he says that the idea of Providence in pagan philosophy and theology was not the same as in Christianity. For the pagans Providence was more theoretical than actual, more of a philosophical abstraction than a religious doctrine: it failed to touch man in his distress and death. It continually oscillated between chance and fate. Over against his characterization of the non-Christian Providence concept, Bavinck posed the Christian faith as a wellspring of hope and comfort, trust and courage, humility and confidence. In this further elucidation, we touch the heart of the problem. Bavinck is searching for a clear formulation of the Christian Providence doctrine. This faith, he says, relies not only on God's revelation in nature, but far more on His covenant and promises. Bavinck adds that the Christian faith is not a cosmological theory, but a *pure confession of faith.*

What justification is there, then, for speaking of Providence as a "mixed article"? Bavinck underscores the soteriological aspect of the Providence doctrine heavily enough to conclude: "Belief in Providence is, thus, an article of the

Christian faith." The believer views the whole world, as well as his own life, from the standpoint of the forgiving grace of God. The distinction between "mixed articles" and "pure articles" which was used, he adds, already by Tertullian, Irenaeus, Augustine, and Damascene can best be understood in this sense, "that the believer perceives in nature and history the hand of God, of the God whom he first learned to know as Father in Christ."[7] Bavinck nods toward Rome as he says that some hold the natural reason qualified to know certain Divine truths, and that the Reformers rightfully rejected this view. Certainly, they taught God's revelation in nature, but insisted on the other hand that man's eyes were so blinded by sin that he could not truly perceive or understand this revelation.

Reformed theologians used the term "natural theology," says Bavinck, but had in mind a description "of what, according to Scripture, the Christian can know of God through His creation."[8] It is clear now that Bavinck does not underwrite a rational knowledge of God. Rather, he insists on a faith-knowledge rooted in Scripture. Protestant theology, Bavinck knew, had in large measure gone the way of rationalism. Natural theology had become a description of what the non-Christian could, through his own reason, know about God. The end of this for Protestant thought was that faith gave place to rationalism. Having no place in his thought for an independent natural theology, Bavinck was totally opposed to this trend. Providence, too, was a doctrine to which human reason independent of the revelation of God in Christ could not attain. The confession of the Church stands as a thing apart from the non-believing, reasoned concept of Providence, be it called Providence, destiny, fate, or chance.

The phrase "mixed articles" gives the impression of a theological fore-court, of an area common to all human

---

7. Bavinck, *De algemeene genade*, 1894, p. 17.
8. Bavinck, *Geref. Dogm.* II, pp. 46, 50. See Bavinck, *The Doctrine of God*, pp. 41-80. Eerdmans, 1951.

thought, non-Christian and Christian alike. There are no restricted areas in this court, no discrimination, no antithesis. The distinction appears only when we approach certain mysteries of faith which are out of reach of human reason and are disclosed only by special revelation. When Bavinck rejects the distinction so stated, we may conclude that, though he uses the term "mixed articles," he basically rejects its customary significance. He was right. The coordination of two sources of knowledge implicit in the idea of the "mixed articles" carries with it a denial of Paul's contention that the natural and unbelieving mind holds all the truth of God in unrighteousness (Rom. 1:18). Paul's statement holds for Providence no less than for creation. A pre- or non-Christian concept of Providence is not an integral part of the full Christian concept, but a mutilation of its truth. Bavinck himself intimated this in his divorce of a so-called general knowledge of Providence from the Christian confession of it. Why, then, we may again ask, did he continue to speak of a "mixed article" in reference to Providence? The only explanation we can offer is that he did so, not from a misunderstanding of the uniqueness of the Christian Providence doctrine, but from a desire to forestall a rejection of the equally Christian doctrine of general revelation. He was not among those who considered Providence as an article of natural theology, to which the believer could then *add* the other articles unique to Christian theology. "In the cross," writes Bavinck, the Christian "has seen the special Providence of God. He has, in forgiving and regenerating grace, experienced Providence in his heart. From this new, positive experience in his own life, he looks out over his entire existence and over the whole world, and sees there the leading of God's fatherly hand."[9] Bavinck did say that belief in Providence was not identical with saving faith, but nevertheless he refused to sacrifice the unique Christian character of

---

9. *Ibid.,* II, p. 554.

the Providence doctrine. "It stands with the revelation in Christ."

Though their ideas on general revelation reveal very different approaches, both Bavinck and Barth deny the validity of a fore-court theology. Bavinck, like Barth after him, appreciated keenly the noetic problem of our knowledge of God, and, though from another motif, maintained with him that every non-Christian concept, regardless of formal similarity to it, is basically other than the Christian doctrine of Providence. Words like *leading, ruling,* or *destiny* do not necessarily carry the Christian content of Providence. We are not concerned with a general guidance of "a god," a Higher Being, or prime-mover. Providence is the all-inclusive rule of the God who says, ". . . besides me there is no God." (Isa. 45:5).

* * *

In Abraham Kuyper we encounter a construction similar to that which we found in Bavinck. We observe him, too, wrestling with the distinction between the "mixed and pure articles." He saw two dangers inherent in the consideration of our knowledge of God's Providence. The first danger is that Providence should be construed as a "specifically Christian doctrine," to the negation of a more general understanding. The second danger is that Providence be equated with the universal God-concept to the forfeiture of its unique Christian character. The significance of Reformed theology in this respect, said Kuyper, was that it gives due prominence to the truth in both these extremes without committing itself to either of them. It first relates the confession of God's Providence directly to the redemption in Christ. Then, in the doctrine of common grace, it allows room for a universal God concept. Though this line of thought seems to expose a dualistic strain, Kuyper explicitly repudiates epistemological dualism. The Scriptures, Kuyper would say, do not support the idea that man first discovers certain things about God

THE KNOWLEDGE OF PROVIDENCE 43

and Providence by means of the created world and then receives, as an addition, a revelation about Christ.

Neither is there ground for such a dualism in man's faith. There is not first a common belief in a universal Providence and then a second, a Christian belief. Such a juxtaposition of two complementary faiths is, according to Kuyper, Roman Catholic, not Protestant teaching. Kuyper refers to question 21 of the Heidelberg Catechism in which the entire doctrine of creation, like that of redemption, is oriented around Christ. This, he says, is the real genius of the Catechism. The Belgic Confession, though not so explicitly as the Heidelberg Catechism, also relates the confession of Providence to Christ. In article 13, creation is related to Christ, and Providence is viewed soteriologically in connection with sin. Kuyper himself concludes: "The Reformed confession and church is, among all Christian confessions and churches, the only one which definitely does not place Providence alongside of the way of salvation, but defines them both as one unit."[10] It is difficult, in the light of what he says here, to understand Kuyper's fears of Providence being construed as specifically Christian. The more so, since he insisted that the unbelieving heart proposes, over against the Christian doctrine of Providence, only fate or chance. Thus, even according to Kuyper, only the Christian can believe in Providence. He emphasizes this noetic-soteriological character of the Providence doctrine so strongly that he says: "If, in suffering you have ever been heartened, comforted, or soothed by the luster of God's Providence, the ray of light fell on your heart by pure grace."[11]

The danger he sees in viewing Providence as an exclusively Christian doctrine is evidently not present in this instance. Indeed, as Kuyper realized, the danger does not and cannot lie here. We gather that what Kuyper feared was a one-sided denial that there is even a vague God-concept still resident

---
10. A. Kuyper, *E Voto*, 1892, I, p. 217.
11. *Ibid.*, p. 218.

in natural man, an effect of general revelation. It was in the interest of refuting this denial that he hesitated to call Providence a specifically Christian doctrine. But we fail to see in this a valid reason why the confession of God's Providence should not manifest a specifically Christian character. Regardless of what he thought about the non-Christian's possession of a vague God-concept, Kuyper knew, better than most, that outside of true Christian faith there is no real nor true knowledge of God, nor of His Providence. This vague, general concept, according to Kuyper himself, is always caricatured into fate, chance, or "Nature" when Christian faith is absent. Thus, when he comments on the Heidelberg Catechism, he says nothing of "mixed articles." This is not simply because here he happens to be commenting exclusively on the Christian faith. It is rather that his own *positive* expositions foreclose on the validity of any "mixed articles." In Kuyper, then, we actually read only of a specifically Christian idea of Providence. The knowledge of this Providence comes from faith's encounter with God's fatherly care. When Kuyper does speak of "mixed articles," he, like Bavinck, does so only to maintain God's general revelation.

In the *Vatican Council* the teaching of the "mixed articles" is not at all an incongruous element. It coheres perfectly with the Roman Catholic view of human reason. When, however, the idea of "mixed articles" is obtruded into Reformed theology, it is circumscribed with so many qualifications — as in Kuyper and Bavinck — that it soon loses its original meaning. The Reformed teaching of the *corruptio naturae* must, indeed, lead to a denial of any "mixed articles." If one wishes to consistently maintain the idea of "mixed articles" he forfeits all right of objection to the Catholic doctrine of the ability of natural human reason. Neither Kuyper nor Bavinck, fortunately, attempt such consistency. When they confess God's Providence, they do not identify it with the general knowledge of Providence arrived at by the natural reason. The

THE KNOWLEDGE OF PROVIDENCE 45

only conclusion is that in the doctrine of Providence we have a specific Christian confession exclusively possible through a true faith in Jesus Christ.

* * *

Given the exclusively Christian character of Providence, the various and many perversions of the doctrine appear in sharp contrast to it. Consider, for example, the many non-Christian conceptions of destiny or chance. Even from Germany's Hitler we heard an unctuous invocation of "providence." He, of course, used the word providence as a propaganda device to justify and recommend himself as a gift of "special providence," as a Divinely appointed leader.[12] But even his speech betrayed him: the word destiny (*Schicksal*) was just as prominent in his speeches as the word providence (*Vorsehung*). This grotesque perversion of Providence called in to bolster the Third Reich impressed us anew with the dangerous potentialities in a consistent maintenance of the doctrine of "mixed articles."

The relation between belief in fate, fortune, *Schicksal,* or *Vorsehung* and the Christian faith is not one of relative depth or breadth. There is a radical break, an absolute difference between them. While the terms used may seem identical, the gulf between the contents is as wide as the heavens.[13] There is no common background to the various ideas of Providence. Each arises from its own basic God-concept. History illustrates the results of a confession of Providence without Christ, whether in the form of a religiously clothed national

---

12. Cf. Goebbels' comment in his diary on the abortive attempt to annihilate Hitler in 1944. He speaks of the logic of history, of the gracious protection that destiny provided for Hitler. Words such as service, mission, historical calling are common with Goebbels.

13. Cf. Calvin, *Institutes,* I, xvi, 1, "Though they subscribe to the assertion of Paul, that in God we live, and move, and have our being (Acts 17: 28), yet they are very far from a serious sense of his favour, celebrated by the apostle; because they have no apprehension of the special care of God, from which alone his paternal favour is known."

socialism[14] or in the conclusions of a consistent natural theology. Phantoms of gods and idols and deified creatures appear on the stage of human existence. It may be a vague conjecture or a reasoned conclusion, a final or first cause, a prime-mover or ultimate principle, a mysterious X, a sphinx, or a "Guidance" which embraces men with protecting arms. Whatever it may be, it is confusion without Christ, a groping in the darkness. One may still talk of the comfort derived from a non-Christian idea of Providence, but in any such concept there is no real thankfulness in prosperity and, certainly, no real patience in adversity. This Providence is an imposter, acceptable in prosperity; but, in times of terror, when she withdraws her friendly arms of protection, she fails to inspire either confidence or faith. For this reason, the soteriological orientation of the Providence doctrine in the confessions is decisive. It is decisive, not as an anthropocentric abridgment of God's truth, but because the atonement through the cross of Christ points the way to "the only comfort in life and death," yes, the comfort of Providence. The words of Christ, "No man cometh to the Father but by me," apply as well for coming to a knowledge of the Father's Providence.

When we speak of the soteriological emphasis of this confession, we do not mean it in Barth's sense that only the revelation of Christ in the years 1-30 A. D. is true revelation. To speak thus of revelation is to subject the Scripture to one's own criterion and renders unavoidable a Christo-monistic theology. Nevertheless, we insist as emphatically as Barth that no one can believe in the Providence of God without knowing the way to God through Jesus Christ. Paul underscores this thought in Romans 8 in his hymn to God's Providence.

---

14. In a propaganda brochure issued by the Netherlands' Nazi party we read that the prime source of the strength of national socialism is "our trust in God." Mussert in his introduction to the pamphlet declared that in Nazism "a Higher Power holds before our people an opportunity of salvation from our distress."

Nothing forms an absolute menace any longer: neither oppression nor fear; persecution, hunger, nor sword; life nor death; present nor future. But this faith is no general, vague notion of Providence. It has a concrete focus: "If God is for us, who is against us? He that spared not his own Son, but delivered him up for us all, how shall he not also with him freely give us all things?" (Rom. 8:31, 32). All dangers are relativized, contained by this love: the love of God in Christ Jesus our Lord. There is no purer expression than this of the depth of man's faith in God's Providence.

This is the Providence of which the confessions speak. They are defined by this salvation. Only as "disciples of Christ" shall we learn what He teaches in His Word. We read of God's incomprehensible power and goodness, of a human knowledge that leads on to prayer in humility and to respect for the righteous judgment of God. This is the comfort, that we stand at the disposal of a merciful heavenly Father to whom we can with confidence abandon ourselves. It is a specifically Christian confession, a confession at once of atonement and Providence. The Reformed baptismal formula witnesses strikingly to it: "For when we are baptized in the Name of the Father, God the Father witnesses and seals unto us that He makes an eternal covenant of grace with us, and adopts us for His children and heirs, and therefore will provide us with every good thing and avert all evil or turn it to our profit."

Viewed without the perspective gained through reconciliation, all the wonders of nature and history are frozen and petrified. They are molded into idols which obstruct the rays of comfort that stream from beyond them. The world is left in confinement, enclosed by man's natural reason, and productive in turn only of desperate loneliness. The question of "mixed articles" becomes, then, much more than a theoretical problem for the entertainment of professional theologians. On the contrary, the more the world is harassed by terror, the more actual is the crisis of all natural theology. And in this crisis man stands comfortless before the taunting question of whether in such a world his own existence has any meaning or hope.

In Germany, just a year before its collapse, men still tried to comfort themselves with talk of the wendings of fate and of signs of the times. The death of Roosevelt in 1945 was to Goebbels an indication that the Third Reich would yet be favored by Providence. Since then, with destiny's lamp no longer alight and with human life disintegrated, only nihilism remains, and man, in resignation or pride, disposes as he pleases of what is left of his own life.

Perhaps, now, clearer than before, we understand that Christ has the key to Divine Providence. In Him we can withstand the taunt that we constructed the idea of Providence out of our own lusts for security. This criticism — arising basically from the critic's own inward insecurity — can be put to shame only in the irrefutable testimony of Christ-in-us. We cannot prove by argumentation that only our faith in Providence is legitimate as against the general guidance of a Universal World-will. The continual warning to Israel and the Church was not an idle word: "And it shall be as when a hungry man dreameth, and, behold, he eateth; but he awaketh, and his soul is empty" (Isa. 29:8). Isaiah's prophecy is not only relevant to a psychological theory, but is a threat to all who try to assail the Mount of Zion. The alternate possibility, the way of fellowship with Zion, is also implicit in Isaiah's words. It is in this possibility that the security of faith possessed by the old Israelites appears: "Nevertheless I am continually with thee: Thou hast holden my right hand. Thou wilt guide me with thy counsel, And afterward receive me to glory. Whom have I in heaven but thee? And there is none upon earth that I desire besides thee. My flesh and my heart faileth; But God is the strength of my heart and my portion for ever" (Ps. 73:23-26).

This Old Testament hymn comes to life again in the security of the New Testament believers, who also know of a refuge in distress and temptation. This is why it is imperative to understand in the light of the Scriptures what the knowledge of Providence means. If we are to know God's Providence, and if our knowledge is to stand against the attacks of the scientific-, projection-, and catastrophic-motifs, then the decision must fall here, with the Scriptures. There will always be a conflict, not only between the orthodox and the modern Christologies, but between the orthodox and modern confessions of the Providence of God.

If, in previous eras, Christians were not always alert to the dangers of natural theology and its Providence concept, we are now able to see the perils more clearly. The issue appears to us in the refined form of the Roman Catholic natural theology, in the secularized idea of destiny or a "Higher Power," and in the providence idea of modernism. He who confuses the boundaries between any or all of these and the Christian Providence doctrine, dims the light of the cross. He emasculates the imperative of a faith decision. He removes the spectacles of faith through which alone the true meaning of God's hand and the works of His hand can be seen. He may still speak of the hand and work of God, and may use many phrases from the Church's confessions. But, speaking apart from the context of the cross and reconciliation, he must intend another reality than that of which the Church speaks and another "god" than He whom the Church confesses. For the Church's Providence doctrine is wholly other than any human God-concept. It is the confession of the real and gracious Providence of Him who said to Israel at the portals of the promised land: "Hear, O Israel: Jehovah our God is one Jehovah" (Deut. 6:4).

CHAPTER III

Providence as Sustenance

IT IS impossible to study the history of the Providence doctrine without soon meeting the distinction between Providence as sustenance and Providence as government. We confront it in the confessions as well as in dogmatic discussion. It must be remembered, however, that no separation is intended by this distinction. We address ourselves in this chapter to Providence as sustenance, but we wish to avoid abstracting this Divine act from that of the government of the cosmos. The customary intent of this honored distinction is to indicate a two-fold aspect of God's Providence. This is true of the Heidelberg Catechism when it, in Lord's Day 10, describes Providence as the almighty and omnipresent power of God by which He upholds and governs all things. By government we generally mean to emphasize the purpose or end to which God leads all things. In sustenance we underscore their maintenance or preservation. The burden of the confession at this point is that all things, having once proceeded from God's creative hand, are still utterly dependent upon His omnipresent power. The confession sees all things as being indebted for their existence to the preserving act of God; let God cease to act and the universe would cease to exist. With this concept of sustenance the confession at once opposes every claimant to absoluteness in this world—gods and idols, and any who would autonomously and sovereignly pretend to a self-sufficient existence. There is no self-containment in this world, no nature or substance which can exist apart from God through inherent power of being. The confession of Providence as sustenance dethrones all creaturely self-sufficiency, all assumptive independence.

We mentioned the word substance, a word that has occasioned many heated debates in Christian thought. It is immediately evident that when substance refers to that which exists in itself or is self-sustaining it is thereby estranged from the confession of Providence. H. Dooyeweerd has in recent years renewed the attack against the metaphysical notion of substance, meaning thus to warn against all theories "finding an ultimate in the thing in itself."[1] We need only a slight acquaintance with the history of human thought to appreciate the omnipresence of the danger to which Dooyeweerd would alert us. But even with a theoretical recognition of the dependency of all creaturely reality, it is possible in practice surreptitiously to make the creature self-existent. At bottom all deifying of the creature is the consequence of substance theories which invest the creature with self-existence. The incomprehensible act of sustaining renders idle all talk of outright independence. Sustenance — undiscernible, but disclosed by God through revelation: "For of him, and through him, and unto him, are all things" (Rom. 11:36). All things are created through the *Logos* — Who is before all things — and all things together consist in Him (Col. 1:17). The Son upholds all things by the word of His power (Heb. 1:3). Not the slightest thing occurs outside of God's will (Matt. 10:29). The Old Testament is also clear as to this total dependence. "Thou art Jehovah, even thou alone; thou hast made heaven, the heaven of heavens, with all their host, the earth and all things that are thereon, the seas and all that is in them, and thou preservest them all . . ." (Neh. 9:6). "Thou openest thy hand, and satisfiest the desire of every living thing" (Ps. 145:16). "He counteth the number of the

---

1. H. Dooyeweerd, *Wijsbegeerte der Wetsidee,* 1937, III. p. 48. Again p. 52, "As for the idea of substance, my objection is naturally not to the term itself, but to the possible danger that through it new speculative motifs will again find entrance into Calvinistic philosophy."

stars . . ." (Ps. 147:4). "He calleth them all by name; by the greatness of his might, and for that he is strong in power, not one is lacking" (Is. 40:26). Not only the great and dramatic events of this world are related to God's might; all things without exception *are* in His hand. This majestic work of sustaining is no more comprehensible to us than the work of creating. Recall the words of Elihu: "God thundereth marvellously with his voice; Great things doeth he, which we cannot comprehend" (Job 37:5; cf. vs. 15). Sometimes we read of God's command, of His mandate, or of His voice, but we always are presented one act of God which surpasses all our thoughts.

The Scriptures express this in multiformity. Our eyes are lifted to the establishment of God. He has shut up the sea with doors, when it broke out as if it had issued out of the womb, then He brought forth bars and doors, and said: "Hitherto shalt thou come, but no further; And here shall thy proud waves be stayed" (Job 38:8-11). He commands the morning, and causes the dayspring to know its place (Job 38:12). We see Him working everywhere in creation. Nature is never a self-sufficient magnitude. "Who hath cleft a channel for the waterflood, Or a way for the lightning of the thunder?" (Job 38:25). He gives rain to the earth (Job 5:10), and says to the snow, "Fall thou on the earth" (Job 37:6). His Divine breath forms the ice, so that the lakes are like molten metal (Job 37:10). Elihu calls Job to a consideration of all these wonders of God. God is the Almighty whom we cannot probe, excelling in power and plenteous in righteousness (Job 37:23).

We find in the so-called nature Psalms similar glimpses of the continuous Divine working in nature. Here, too, the glory of God's might is sung. The heavens declare the glory of God and the firmament showeth the works of His hands (Ps. 19:1). He has set up a tabernacle for the sun (Ps. 19:4), makes the clouds His chariot, the winds His messengers (Ps.

104:3), and the flaming fire His servant (Ps. 104:4). Not only has He once placed the earth on her foundations that it should never be removed (Ps. 104:5), but even now sends the streams into the valleys (Ps. 104:10), waters the hills from His chambers so that the earth is filled with the fruit of His works (Ps. 104:13). The trees of the Lord are full of sap (Ps. 104:16). He arranges the seasons for sun and moon. He makes the darkness and it is night (Ps. 104:20), and the young lions seek their meat from God (Ps. 104:21).

As the Psalm closes, the author turns to worship: "O Jehovah, how manifold are thy works! In wisdom hast thou made them all: The earth is full of thy riches" (Ps. 104:24). All creatures wait "for thee . . . Thou openest thy hand, they are satisfied with good (Ps. 104:27, 28) . . . Thou takest away their breath, they die, And return to their dust" (Ps. 104:29). Each day manifests anew His exalted and inextinguishable might. Nothing is self-contained. The whole world lies tractable to His Divine sustenance in immediate relation to Him. Man is fascinated by His works. His wonders in the sea and the storm (Ps. 104:25, 26). God stills the storm, and the waves of the sea are still (Ps. 107:29). The holy presence of God is everywhere.

The rainbow is His sign in the clouds which He spreads as a mantle over the earth. Season follows season. All things go onward. But these are not matters to be assumed from the existence of things. They come as gifts from His hand: ". . . I will not again curse the ground any more for man's sake . . ." (Gen. 8:21). Again, "While the earth remaineth, seedtime and harvest, and cold and heat, and summer and winter, and day and night shall not cease" (Gen. 8:22).

The revelation of God's works in the world proposes to us His unfathomable greatness. The clouds gather; man must ask, ". . . can any understand the spreading of the clouds?" (Job 36:29). God's might is sung, yet, "Lo, these are but the outskirts of his ways: And how small a whisper do we hear of him! But the thunder of his power who can understand?" (Job 26:14). The land is His. He visits it and greatly enriches it (Ps. 65:9), and crowns the year with His goodness (Ps. 65:11). Yes, He fills heaven and earth (Jer. 23:24). There is no hiding from Him as though He would not see (Amos 9:3).

The so-called nature Psalms, then, are not dedicated to the glory of nature. Neither do they point a way to God through nature in itself. In them the majestic might of Israel's God is sung (Cf. Ps. 74:12-17, and especially Psalms 19, 33, 89, 104, and 148). Speak of the dynamic Biblical world-and-life concept, if you will; but understand by this *dunamis*, then, the power of God. Understand by it the Divine might within the existence of things in their progressive development. See in it His laws and orders. For all creatures and their existence lie in His hand.

* * *

The confessions distinguish sharply between the Divine acts of sustaining and creation. Bavinck speaks in the spirit of the confessions when he says that creation *passes over* into sustenance. It is, he says, as when man stops work, and rests. This is not to say that sustenance is a less mighty or less Divine act than is creation. The sustenance of the world bespeaks the majesty and incomprehensibility of God's working no less than does creation. Calvin rightly ascribes the continued existence of the world, just as much as its origin, to the presence of Divine might.

Nevertheless, the Church does not hesitate to distinguish between these acts of God. Recall how the Scriptures speak of God resting after He had finished the work of creation: "And on the seventh day God finished his work which he had made; and he rested on the seventh day from all his work which he had made" (Gen. 2:2). This resting of God is obviously viewed in close relation to the perfecting of creation. This relation between resting and finished work is underscored again in the decalogue where the passing of the work week into the day of rest is based upon God's working and thereupon resting; ". . . for in six days Jehovah made heaven and earth, the sea, and all that in them is, and rested the seventh day: wherefore Jehovah blessed the sabbath day, and hallowed it." (Ex. 20:11). Again, in Exodus 31:17 we read that the sabbath is a sign between the Lord and His people: ". . . for in six days Jehovah made heaven and earth, and on the seventh day he rested, and was refreshed." In these and other witnesses believers have correctly read the unique, once-for-all, perfected character of the work of creation.

The phrase "and was refreshed" — a purely anthropomorphic expression — suggests the transition, just as our human "taking refreshment" implies a pause from work and beginning of rest (Cf. Ex. 23:12). This "and was refreshed" connotes, does it not, the unique, done-with character of God's created work? Thus, we can agree with Barth when he says, "He rests, that is, He looks up from and stands away from His completed creation work."[2]

But this resting of God implies much more than a mere transition from creating to sustaining. The Scriptures bring the resting of God into the same context as the salvation of the Lord. The Bible reminds us that we are not dealing with a certain form of cosmogeny, with a cosmological theory. This seventh day — this day of God's rest — is blessed and sanctified by God and thus given in grace to the world — given *for* man, as Christ has taught us (Mark 2:27). The day of rest, then, has a rich significance for all mankind, for Israel first, but now for all. It illustrates pre-eminently the close relationship existing between creation and redemption. Barth in particular has thus read the first chapter of Genesis

---

2. Barth, *Kirchliche Dogmatik*, (1932-) III, 1, p. 242.

and seen the eschatological perspective in the resting of God after creation. God, according to Barth, does not merely look back on the completed work of creation, but looks as well into the future. Thus the resting of God bears upon the purpose of the world's history, upon "the coming of God for man and for the whole world, which coming was prepared in the history of Israel and culminating in an event, and thus bears upon Jesus Christ, as the goal of creation, explained and justified in view of God's rest on that seventh day of creation."[3] The history of Israel and the coming of Christ unto redemption are pre-figured in the resting of God of Genesis 2. The creation sabbath, says Barth emphatically, belongs to creation. In this sabbath God shows Himself to be not only Creator of the world, but the living, abiding, Lord of creation. "In the world created with the inclusion of this Divine rest of the seventh day, the kingdom of grace is no foreign element; its history is part of creation order . . . ."[4] The sabbath can be interpreted only through Christ. The "creation saga," says Barth, speaks prophetically of Him. The "coming kingdom of grace is rooted in the resting on the seventh day." This consistent Christological interpretation of the creation story is deeply involved in Barth's entire concept of the relation between creation and redemption. Just as the approval of God — the "and it was good" — on creation signifies for Barth that God's creation is "the appropriate place, the appropriate implement, because man in the midst of this created world is the appropriate object of the Divine work, which has its beginning, its means, and its end in Jesus Christ," so the sabbath is full of Christological content and significance.[5]

Our first comment on Barth's exegesis is that the Scriptures do indeed indicate a bond between the sabbath of Gen-

---

3. *Ibid.*, p. 251.
4. *Ibid.*, p. 254.
5. *Ibid.*, p. 423.

esis 2 and God's later work of salvation in Jesus Christ. Scripture teaches quite plainly that the fall did not force God to change His plans. He does not appear as disappointed at the failure of His experiment, and then obliged to design an entirely new plan. On the contrary, the Scriptures reveal the unbreakable unity of the work of God in creation and redemption. This unity is clear already in the fourth commandment of the decalogue, and not less in Hebrews 4, where the writer exhorts to enter into the believer's rest in the same context as he speaks of the sabbath of creation. It is here also that we read that God's work was prepared from the foundation of the world (Heb. 4:3).

The continuous line runs from the resting of God after His work of creation through history to the rest into which believers shall enter, to the rest that yet remains for the people of God (Heb. 4:3, 9). God shares with man what He takes for Himself. In Genesis 2 the rest of *God* comes primarily to view, but the Scriptures elsewhere reveal that the Genesis 2 passage is closely related to the rest that remains for the *people* of God. Genesis 2 must be the starting point for observation of the later passages. God arranged for the future rest of His people from their works even "as God did from his" (Heb. 4:10). The parallel or analysis suggested by the word *as* is clear if we pre-suppose the resting of God in Genesis 2. If the sabbath has eschatological significance and if it was from the beginning a sign pointing to the rest that remains for God's people, then the historical report that God rested on the seventh day is determinative for all that follows. The sabbath is "given to the earth after the relation between the earth and entire universe was established in peace and found to be very good."[6] For this reason, the maintenance of the sabbath after the fall is of unusual significance. There is a very intimate relation between the creation sabbath and

---

6. K. Schilder, *Wat Is de Hemel?* 1935, p. 310; cf. p. 269.

the abiding sabbath as a token of the coming salvation of the Lord (Cf. Ezek. 20:12).

Thus, it is not at this point that we can raise objections to Barth. The bond that he emphasizes has long been recognized and acknowledged. As Schilder writes, "the whole cosmos, the entire universe, with the earth under judgment — theater and workshop of the covenant — was, as He said, determined in His eyes in the bond of peace, before He, the Lord, purposed to celebrate His sabbath with the covenant child of the earth. The cosmic peace was, thus from the beginning, servant to the covenant joy of Jehovah with His elect race."[7] The manner in which Barth allegorizes Genesis 1 and 2 does violence to the text and robs paradise of its historical reality. But this need not tempt us to deny the profound relationship which Barth has seen. Barth correctly asserts that God's works were perfected from the foundation of the world.

The foreboding possibility suggested by Psalm 95, "That they should not enter into my rest" (Ps. 95:11; cf. Heb. 4:3) — the possible exclusion — does not negate the rest of God nor the rest yet to come, which is the purpose and end of His holy activity. We are not offered here an abstract philosophy of history. We are given an urgent exhortation not to harden our hearts, but rather to enter into His rest, the shadow of which is seen in the rest to which Joshua of old led God's people (Heb. 4:8). There is perspective in this exhortation, the perspective of promise. "His rest is not His own self-seeking, tightly grasped prerogative, but is intended as a blessing for man."[8] *The* sabbath is yet to come, the rest from all work, the analogy of the Divine sabbath. "There remaineth therefore a sabbath rest for the people of God" (Heb. 4:9).

---

7. *Ibid.*, p. 312.
8. Zahn, *Hebräerbrief*, 1913, p. 102.

PROVIDENCE AS SUSTENANCE

Keeping this relationship before us, we shall never be able to contemplate the world, the finished work of creation, as a formal or neutral cosmological witness to the fact that God *still* holds the world intact. We do not have here a mechanical coordination between God and the world. The sustaining of the world is not an isolated act with no real meaning of its own other than, that by it, the world still stands. It is a mistake to look on sustaining as merely furnishing the material for the more purposeful ruling of God. The sabbath of Genesis, Exodus, and Hebrews shows us how inseparably sustaining and ruling are bound up in one act of God's providential might. In its own right, sustenance displays God's teleological activity reaching out into the perfect peace of His eternal Kingdom. With this, the sustenance doctrine is relieved of the abstract character of a theory about the mere continuation of the world's existence.

This sustenance doctrine, then, does not present us with the material for an independent natural theology, which pretends to explain the enigma of the continuation of the world. For everything that God has revealed to us concerning the sustenance — the continuation or prolongation — of the world is organically connected with the salvation that He has brought. He who searches, outside this salvation, into the inscrutables of the origin, continuation, and future of the natural world will never understand the Church's confession of God's upholding all things. In the eschatological atmosphere of the last book of the Bible, this is the word of adoration: "Worthy art thou, our Lord and our God, to receive the glory and the honor and the power: for thou didst create all things, and because of thy will they were, and were created" (Rev. 4:11).

* * *

We shall proceed further into the significance that all this has for the synthetic view of sustenance and government in the unity of God's Providence. However, it is necessary first to address ourselves to the question of whether God's sustaining of the world may be considered a continuous creation. Sometimes the expression *continuous creation* is used to indicate the greatness of the act of sustaining beside and along with the act of creation. If only for this reason, we should be cautious in our judgment of those who use the expression. For, as is evident, there is a great deal of difference in how the term *continuous creation* is understood. Compare, for example, the use of the term by such men as Karl Heim with its use by Reformed theologians.

Heim applies the idea of creation *out of nothing* universally and literally: "We may say with justice that the universe, as it now appears, is created each instant out of nothing, just as in the first day of creation."[9] Here is a consistent expression of the continuous creation idea. We may be sitting at a table that has stood for fifty years, says Heim, and not be certain that it shall be standing at the next instant. The continuation is never certain. It remains a mere "possibility." The future lies in "pure possibility," in the nothingness of the not-yet. The concrete world, for Heim, is perpetually occurring out of the nothingness of pure possibility. Heim's intent in using the concepts "nothingness" and "possibility" may be to suggest the absolute dependence of all things on God for their moment-by-moment existence. There is, however, a remarkable contrast between the Scriptural concept of the world's dependence upon God and the thoughts of Heim on this point. The Church, too, as we shall see, has always reserved the term *creation out of nothing* for God's primal act of creation. In Heim's conception, since creation out of nothing is a continuously re-occurring act, the world constantly falls back into nothingness between the moments of creation. If we were to take Heim seriously we would have to conceive of the world as perpetually falling out of

---

9. K. Heim, *Glaube und Denken*, 1931, p. 230.

existence into nothingness and being called back into existence again by a fresh Divine act of creation. This is the only valid consequence of viewing sustenance as a continuous creation.

The Church has always reserved the term *creation out of nothing* for God's primal act, and has insisted that since creation there can be no more nothingness. She confesses that nothing in the universe exists for an instant independent of God's power. But she speaks also of a creaturely reality that, through His sustaining act, possesses both stability and continuity.

There is often in the idea of continuous creation a tendency to dissolve the world in atomistic and incessantly repeated "acts" of God, a tendency toward a peculiar Divine dynamism that devours creaturely existence and continuity. It has been argued that our own consciousness denies Heim's type of continuous creation, that we are conscious only of continuity. This common sense argument, though true, is not decisive, since the theory has regard to atoms of moments unperceived by human consciousness. We must turn to the positive statements of Scripture in which we read of a creation out of nothing "in the beginning," of the "foundation" of the world, because of which "nothingness" lies forever behind us. Through Divine sustenance the possibility of a nothingness into which the world could fall, be it for an atom of an instant, is absolutely excluded.

In the light of this, then, we must reject the thought of a continuous creation out of nothing, though this should not keep us from asking whether a continuous creation may be spoken of in a better and more correct sense. It is true that consistent ideas of continuous creation usually fail to appreciate the significance of the phrase "in the beginning" of Genesis 1. It is also true, however, that even Reformed theologians, while maintaining the full value of Genesis 1, have spoken of continuous creation. Though the term is found in both Lutheran and Reformed theologians already before Schleiermacher, we may perhaps best represent the argument by referring to Bavinck and Kuyper.

Bavinck uses the term more or less incidentally. He calls Providence a *creatio continua,* a work just as great, mighty, and omnipresent as creation. Creation and Providence form, really, one act of God, the difference between them being only a thought distinction. "Creation and sustenance are, thus, not to be distinguished objectively and materially as works of God, in God's essence, but only in thought."[10] Yet, says Bavinck, something occurs in creation that does not occur in sustenance. That unique something is the becoming of the world out of nothing. "If Providence were a momentarily renewed creation, the creatures would have to be produced each moment anew out of nothingness." Bavinck rejects this consistent application of continuous creation, and when he does, nevertheless, use the term, it is with the intention of honoring sustenance as a work of God no less great than creation. Sustenance is, thus, not a continuous calling of the world out of nothingness. It presupposes a once-for-all creation. The real distinction between sustenance and creation, Bavinck admits finally, is a mystery. Each is a calling, though of a different nature. Creation calls out of nothing into existence; sustenance calls to continued existing.

Kuyper discusses the idea of continuous creation more amply.[11] There is, he says, something at once similar and dissimilar in creation and Providence. As for the similarity, "We must definitely insist that providence is a *creatio continuata,* to be understood in the sense that from the hour of original creation until now, God, the Lord, has done the same thing as in the moment of creation: He has given all things power of existence through His power." For support he

---

10. References to Bavinck in this paragraph are from *Gereformeerde Dogmatiek,* II, pp. 566-568. Tr., *The Doctrine of God,* Eerdmans, 1951.
11. References to Kuyper in this paragraph are from "Locus de Providentia" in *Dictaten Dogmatiek,* (no date), pp. 28-42.

points to the Heidelberg Catechism which speaks of God's all pervasive power. In this he already reveals an antipathy to Heim's type of continuous creation. He goes on to say that continuous creation is not at all "an atomistic perpetuation of separate creative acts, but an organic binding of the work of Providence with that of original creation." The cosmos "possesses continuity." It is not "created, then destroyed, and again created." Thus sustenance is also dissimilar to creation. "Creation refers to what comes into existence; Providence to what, already existing, is continuously upheld by God's power." If we wish to know whether a man thinks straight on creation, says Kuyper, we need only ask him what he thinks regarding Providence.

Thus, though Reformed theologians use the term continuous creation in order to emphasize the greatness and divinity of the work of sustaining, they, nevertheless, reject the idea in the sense of renewed acts of creation out of nothing. We may ask, then, whether there is good sense in using the term. Heim consistently intends by it a perpetual creation out of nothing. If we were consistent in our use of the term, we would end in agreement with him. Certainly the greatness of the sustaining by God of the universe can be emphasized without the use of this dubious expression.

In connection with this, it is interesting that the confessions use the term *new creation* to describe regeneration. Naturally this is not meant as a scientific definition, but to mark the sovereign, Divine character of salvation. This work of God is "not inferior in efficacy to creation or the resurrection from the dead."[12] In this analogy there is something in the way of a creation out of nothing: regeneration, has nothing to do with the work of man, it is not of flesh and blood, but is a gracious act of God. Why do the Canons of Dort use such a strong expression as *new creation?* The Canons of Dort, it will be recalled, were drafted in protest against

---

12. Canons of Dort, III and IV, art. 12.

a refusal to appreciate the exclusively Divine character of grace. Thus the term is used to honor the work of God. It also reflects the magnificent manner in which the Scriptures speak of this renewing, this awakening from the dead. Romans 4:17, for example, in connection with salvation speaks of God as He ". . . who giveth life to the dead, and calleth the things that are not, as though they were." The use of the term *new creation* is in the Canons of Dort antithetically defined and religiously significant. There is no creation of a new substance, no created *donum superadditum*. Since the canons mean to accent the priority of grace in the saving work of God, analogical reference to creation is quite valid and helpful. It is different here in soteriology than in the sustenance doctrine. In the sustenance doctrine the *difference* between sustenance and creation is underscored. In soteriology the similarity between the new birth and creation is emphasized. We may better reserve the term *creation out of nothing* for the original creation and follow the example of the Heidelberg Catechism which describes sustenance simply as the power of God which upholds all things.

Bavinck did not share Hodge's suspicion that the older theologians destroyed the distinction between creation and Providence by their talk of continuous creation. In this Bavinck was right. There was generally no speculation about "non-being" or "nothingness" in the old theology. Nor was there an excessive actualism that forfeited stability and continuity to dynamism. But Hodge, it must be said, had a good eye for the dangers involved. When Hodge writes that "preservation is not a continued creation,"[13] he is really underscoring the continuity in the created world and is warning about the dangers of pantheism — dangers against which Kuyper also warned even though he used the dangerous term. There is no good reason to maintain this expression. It is enough, instead, to direct our attention to Him, who in ma-

---

13. Hodge, *Systematic Theology*, 1873, I, p. 577.

jesty and goodness does not abandon the work of His hands. Thereby, the good intentions of those who have retained the term may be fully recognized while the misunderstandings caused by the use of the term may be avoided. We may even respect Luther's *intent* when he said, ". . . we are created out of nothing by the goodness of God, and out of nothing continually recalled." Luther means to accent the greatness of God's power, of His calling to continued existence. But he who would fully appreciate this constant flow of the power of God must at the same time always recognize the once-for-all-ness of God's creative work. Our confession does this when it speaks of the good God, who "after He had created all things did not abandon them."[14]

The Scriptures speak with similar accent. "Of old didst thou lay the foundation of the earth" (Ps. 102:25). But the power of God is now no less necessary to creaturely existence than in the beginning, the time "of old." The unity of God's work must be acknowledged and, at the same time, the Scriptural distinction between beginning and continuation maintained. It is often noted that the Hebrew has no word for the sustenance of the world, and that sustaining and creating are both indicated by *bara*. This does not weaken the distinction between them, but does underscore the Scriptural testimony to the unity of God's word, and the implied dependency of all creation. "I form the light and create darkness" (Is. 45:7). To see the work of God in nature and history — this is to understand that God is as magnificent in His work today as in the first day of creation. The word *bara* indicates "Divine origination"; not only the Divine origination of creation out of nothing but also the Divine origination of each moment. Thus, we have the grandeur of the Divine work of sustaining, without losing the continuity of created reality within perpetually repetitive creative acts.

---

14. Belgic Confession, art. 13.

On the contrary, the Scripture always emphasizes the stability of creation. God Himself looks back upon His creative work: "I have made the earth, and created man upon it: I, even my hands, have stretched out the heavens; and all their host have I commanded" (Is. 45:12). He spreads the heavens as a curtain (Is. 40:22). He laid the foundation of the earth (Is. 51:13). Unlike its passing generations, the "earth abideth for ever" (Eccles. 1:4). The world and its fulness are founded by Him (Ps. 89:11). The mountains are set fast by God's power (Ps. 65:6). "Canst thou with him spread out the sky, which is strong as a molten mirror?" (Job 37:18). The world also "is established, that it cannot be moved" (Ps. 93:1).

There is coherence and continuity, but these are maintained only through the perpetual attendance of God. There was once a call out of nothing; now there is a call to continuation. "Yea, my hand hath laid the foundation of the earth, and my right hand hath spread out the heavens: when I call unto them, they stand up together" (Is. 48:13). He called them in creation. In His sustenance He calls them still.

The New Testament proceeds in the same spirit as the Old in regard to the beginning of creation. More than once we read the phrase: "from the beginning of the creation" (Cf. Mark 10:6; Heb. 1:10; II Pet. 3:4; Matt. 19:4, 8). There is a laying of the world's foundation, indicating that the creation began before the world had its existence, and that the world was not formed from previously existent matter.

The Scriptures compel us to make the distinction between creation and sustenance. We do not suggest that the relation between the distinct acts of creation and sustenance within one work of Divine power is conceivable. To ask that it be humanly conceivable is to ask the forbidden. At this point we reach what Bavinck, for lack of words, called the "mystery." We make the distinction and say that it is nevertheless one work, and then stop at the limits of revelation. The Bible leads us to think in terms of the *historical relation* between creation and continuation — both being the revelation of the power of God. This wards off any speculation that would do injustice either to *the beginning* or to *the continuing*. To think within the limits of Biblical formulation is to avoid dissolving *the beginning* in a timeless idea of creation, and to avoid making the created world an independent substantive.

* * *

Divine sustenance is not simply a conservation or preservation. There are many things which men "sustain" in order to keep them as they are or were. We understand how roads, parks, buildings, and such are maintained to keep them from falling into decay and we are inclined to apply such a notion of maintenance to the idea of God's sustenance of the world. But the sustaining of the world by God's omnipresent power is not a mere keeping of things in proper condition: God does more in sustaining than hold the world intact. Sustaining is a moving, unfolding, unlocking process, revealing continually a galaxy of diversity. It was Kuyper who was most vocal in protest against the shallow conception of Providence "simply as maintenance." He was of the opinion that few points of doctrine were so superficially handled as Providence. "Imagine," said Kuyper, "that creation were a lifeless metal or granite structure! One can conceive of a granite mountain ridge, or of metal, gold, or silver structures preserved from decay. But then there would be only a dead structure lying in eternal stillness, and Providence would mean only that creation had been preserved in existence."[15] Kuyper insists that God is the fountain of life and that creation lives. For this reason Providence can be no mere preservation. If nature were constant, remaining identical with what it was, there would need be only a "preservation from disintegration." But God sustains a world that is continually changing and pro-

---

15. Kuyper, "Locus de Providentia" in *Dictaten Dogmatiek*, p. 59.

gressively developing. Sustenance is directed toward an end. It is not related to Divine government merely as that which preserves the stuff to be governed. It is also purposeful. Sustaining means that God's hand is in all that is and grows and develops according to His purpose. Sustenance has to do with the entire process in which all things move toward God's arranged end. For this reason, again, God's sustenance and ruling cannot be viewed as two separate deeds. It is, in fact, impossible to think of God's sustaining without at once bringing the rule of God into the picture. When the Church and her theology nevertheless continue to use the words separately, they mean to say that God in ruling the world leads it to its designed end, and that *in* this He continues to sustain the world; hence, sustaining and governing together form the one work of Providence. Thus all things are carried forward on their charted course, and creaturely reality unfolds amidst continual change. The wonder of creaturely reality is that change is not undefined, that the structural pattern of the created world is always preserved, and that there are laws and ordinances to which life in the midst of change remains subject. The distinction, then, is valid so long as ruling is not abstracted from the present existence of the world, nor sustenance from its final purpose. The distinction is real, but no more than is the unity of both within the one work of Providence.

If sustaining is not a mere "maintenance," nor a neutral entity alongside of government, what is the *nature* of the continuation of creaturely reality? What is the sense behind this prolongation? The question gains point if one takes the fall seriously, and it finally comes to this: Who is the God who wills to sustain the world in spite of the fall of man? This is no speculative problem born out of a theologian's curiosity. In the Scriptures, sustenance is related to the purpose that God has proposed. There is no "sustenance in itself." It is always bound to the great work of God, Creator, Reconciler, and Redeemer, as He leads and governs the world. This frees the Biblical idea of sustenance from all suspicion of being an abstract cosmology.

This becomes clear eminently in the covenant with Noah. Here, uniquely, is the problem of why God prolongs this world. God Himself specifies His intention to continue the world in spite of the flood crisis. "I will not again curse the ground any more for man's sake . . . neither will I again smite any more everything living, as I have done. While the earth remaineth, seedtime and harvest, and cold and heat, summer and winter, and day and night shall not cease" (Gen. 8:21, 22). The special significance of this word is the more apparent since the Scripture previously had said that God, because of His mounting anger, regretted that He had created man on the earth; "I will destroy man whom I have created from the face of the ground; both man, and beast, and creeping things, and birds of the heavens; for it repenteth me that I have made them" (Gen. 6:7). The threatened judgment appears to put the continuation of human life in serious jeopardy. But then the light breaks through the darkness of this crisis: "Noah found favor in the eyes of Jehovah" (Gen. 6:8). The family of Noah is preserved, and, after the flood, God institutes His everlasting covenant with Noah, his seed, and every living creature of the earth (Gen. 9:10, 12, 16). The living, gracious God commits Himself to the earth again after the judgment of His holiness had sentenced creaturely reality to extinction.

There is a break, a first and a second history. But there is also a continuity made possible by grace. It was not the moral excellency of Noah by which he was able to survive the first history. Noah's faith was directed to God's grace. And grace made continuity possible. It is evident, then, that we have in the second history no tentative, still neutral and unformed, prolongation of the world. It is positive from its inception and stands in inseparable relation to God's disposition toward the world and to His grace and mercy. We do not meet the problem of prolongation for the first time in the Noahic covenant. We encounter it in the preserving of the world and in the Divine promise of redemption immediately after the fall. But the prolongation appears particularly problematic in God's sparing of the world after the crisis of the judgment and anger of God in the flood. It need not surprise us that intense discussion as to the disposition of God toward the world has arisen in connection with the story of Noah. Here the problem of common grace and the Noahic covenant begins. Since sustenance signifies more than a mere holding in existence and has to do with the sustaining God, it is necessary to engage ourselves further with the important question of the mind of God as revealed in His sustaining of the world.

* * *

When the Noahic covenant was first introduced in connection with the question of common grace, hardly anyone suggested that it ought to be dissociated from the covenant of grace. A common conviction existed that this promise to Noah was related to the grace of God in Jesus Christ. Now, however, this covenant has become a point of marked dispute occasioned by a denial that any element of grace is involved in the prolongation of the world as such. It is now said by some that the continuation of history forms only an undefined neutral basis for the working of God; the history of the world forms the substratum for the realization of God's eternal counsel, but is in itself not indicative of any gracious attitude toward humanity.

This view has, in the Netherlands, been worked out by Klaas Schilder, who directs his criticism mainly against the classic expression of common grace given by Abraham Kuyper. It may help us to get at the heart of the problem, then, by noting Kuyper's idea of common grace. Kuyper insisted that common grace must be seen in the light of the longsuffering or forbearance of God, the attribute pre-eminently honored in the common grace doctrine.

Kuyper sees the Noahic covenant as the historical point of departure for the doctrine of common grace. "From Noah to the Maranatha proceeds the uninterrupted continuation, harmony, and order of created existence." In the Noahic covenant "God has performed an act of preserving grace reaching out through the entirety of human existence."[16] True, the beginning of common grace goes back beyond Noah's time to that immediately following the fall. Adam did not die upon committing the first sin. He lived, in fact, nine long centuries. This continuing of life, after its fall under judgment is "a most powerful work of common grace, affecting all humanity, to say nothing of us as individuals."[17]

Schilder, on the other hand, sees no grace in this continuation of life, nor in the cultural development of the world. "This continuation and development manifest no grace. Neither do they manifest condemnation or judgment." They are the *"sina qua non* of grace and judgment, their substratum."[18] A history of many centuries is interpolated between the fall and the final judgment. But this is not to realize the work of salvation within history. It is rather to fulfill Christ's twofold significance as Savior-Redeemer and Savior-Judge. All history, in this sense, is Christologically defined by the double end: blessing and judgment. Only in these eternally conceived ends does history have meaning. The world and its history exist to furnish a substratum for the achievement of these ends. Sustenance is not in itself related either primarily or specifically to salvation. It gives only a basis on which life can mature in two direction: salavtion and damnation. Thus, in respect to the reprobate, the sustaining of the world

---

16. Kuyper, *Gemeene Gratie*, 1931, I, p. 94.
17. *Ibid.*, p. 95.
18. K. Schilder, *Christus en cultuur*, 1948, p. 63.

is not gracious. It only provides the possibility for their damnation.

There is a logical consistency to this view. It is a logic which deduces from the decree and final purpose of God, rather than from the word of God to man in his historical matrix. It involves Schilder in a schematization of the content of Scripture. This forces him to neglect the fact that Scripture does not direct our thoughts primarily to the separate and ultimate ends of two diverging lines in history. The central message of Scripture is the salvation of God which has come into the world and its history. God's redemption of a lost world forms the focus point in revelation, and thus rules out a view of history as an equilibrium between blessing and curse.

Sustenance must then be viewed as still unqualified, a neutral substratum which is neither good nor bad, neither a blessing nor a curse. Schilder writes: "Consider, if God willed to punish only as many persons as He, in fact, shall punish eternally, would not these persons still have to be born? Thus, God has had to prolong time to attain a hell with just so many objects of wrath as there shall be."[19] In this way Schilder reasons in an abstract-hypothetical fashion about those things which are outside the bounds of Divine revelation. Such reasoning is certain to do injustice to Biblical revelation. The God that is here proposed is not the God who revealed Himself in Jesus Christ. Schilder concludes, by way of abstract logic, the *necessity* of the continuation of history. It is clear, then, that a conflict had to come over the mercy or longsuffering of God in respect to the extension of time. If it is of necessity, then it is not of grace. Schilder argues, against Kuyper, that God allows the generations to continue, not out of one, but out of all His attributes. The Scriptures, however, often associate a certain work with one of God's attributes without injustice to the unity of all His perfections.

---

19. Schilder, *Ibid.*, p. 63.

God's love is revealed in the sending of His Son (John 3:16); His justice in the redemption of Zion (Is. 32:17). Kuyper's accent on the longsuffering of God can, then, hardly be rejected on the basis of this argument. He has, in fact, recognized a fundamental theme in the Scriptures, where the motif of longsuffering and patience of God is often accented. Consider, for example, what the New Testament says about Noah's ark: "... when the longsuffering of God waited in the days of Noah, while the ark was a preparing ..." (I Pet. 3:20). The flood — God's judgment on consummate sin — came at a defined time; before the ark was ready life went on, with the possibility of further development. During this time, by means of Noah's preparations, a constant call to conversion went out and an invitation to salvation was given. Peter suggests a waiting period of some length, a period of longsuffering, and of patient holding back of judgment, a period filled with the holy presence of God *in* the call to repentance.

God's forbearance! This is what the days of restraint reveal. His heart beat fast as the ark was being readied. We cannot reason from God's decree nor from the later arrival of the flood in judgment to a denial of the longsuffering that is revealed in these days of invitation. The concrete speech of Scripture, when listened to, forbids such abstraction. The message of Divine longsuffering is implicit in the actual extension of the time of opportunity. No logical scheme must ever be allowed to cut short the actual speech of Scripture, not even a scheme deduced from the eternal decree of God.

Schilder spurns the term longsuffering as an anthropomorphism. Man, says Schilder, may describe God's extension of time before judgment as longsuffering, but God cannot view it so. The Scriptures, however, which come to us as a revelation from God, often bear an anthropomorphic character. All our speaking of God must, in fact, be anthropomorphic. We need not, on that account, devaluate Scripture's ascription of longsuffering to God. To do so consistently would be to rob Scripture of much of its own vocabulary.

To illustrate what happens to the actual words of Scripture when a timeless scheme is the norm of interpretation, consider Schilder's exegesis of Romans 2:4: "Or despisest thou the riches of his goodness and forbearance and longsuffering, not knowing that the goodness of God leadeth thee to repentance?" Schilder understands Paul as saying that the forbearance and longsuffering seemingly suggested in this text mean only that the real and proper disposition of God to the sinner is not as yet revealed. God's "apparent" longsuffering, then, is at bottom only concealed wrath, a mere forestalling of doom. It is only, says Schilder, "that God does not yet manifest His wrath." That the wrath has not yet blazed forth entirely in consuming fire does not at all indicate a gracious attitude in God. It proves only that God loves created life, His creative work. God deals, then, not with real persons, but with abstract creatureliness. God's love can have human nature abstracted from the concrete man for its object. "He loves His creature always: He loves it *in* Satan or, be it, *in* the anti-Christ," says Schilder.[20]

We may apply to Schilder's system his own protest against the Arminians and the Jesuits: "Working with imaginary magnitudes and ledgers may be fitting to mathematical-abstract thought, but certainly is not appropriate to living reality." What an unsophisticated Bible reader hears revelation say about the longsuffering of God is silenced by abstract reasoning. The historical process of revelation shows God as longsuffering, working, calling, waiting, inviting, and warning. This revelation of God's grace is frozen by such an abstraction as creatureliness. The bearing of all this on the sustenance doctrine is by now clear. Since the Biblical idea

---

20. Cf. C. Van Til's criticism of this abstraction. *Common Grace*, 1947, p. 73. "We cannot intelligently speak of God's love of creatureliness in the devil. God once upon a time loved the devil. But that was before the devil was the devil."

of sustenance is not merely another cosmological theory, but has reference to the God who sustains, the question is bound to arise as to God's relation and disposition to the world as He sustains it.

The synod of the Christian Reformed Church in 1924 resolved that God was favorably disposed to mankind in general, as well as to the elect. At that time, Herman Hoeksema, reasoning from supralapsarianism, denied this favorable attitude in God as well as that there could be a serious invitation of salvation to all men.[21] There is, he said, only pure wrath in God's relationship to the non-elect. There can be neither a favorable disposition toward nor any kind of grace offered to the objects of God's wrath.

Both Hoeksema and Schilder fail to do justice to the concrete testimony of Scripture. In Matthew 5:45, for instance, we are called to love our enemies so that we may be children of our Father in heaven who, without distinction among men, causes his sun to rise and the rain to fall on both the evil and the good. This favor of God to the wicked is turned by Schilder into a disguise of the real disposition of God. Luke 6:35 reveals, Schilder admits, a certain kindness to sinners, but we have no right, he insists, to conclude a favorable disposition from "the simple fact of decent provision." Nor does Hoeksema see in either of these texts a gracious attitude toward the sinner, since, as he says, "all the Scriptures witness that God does not love, but hates His enemies, and purposes to destroy them — except those whom He chose in Jesus Christ." God is "kind to the unthankful and evil," but, "He is not kind to the reprobate unthankful and evil."[22] One must, adds Schilder in turn, never conclude from the gifts the Giver's disposition.

The exegesis of neither Schilder nor Hoeksema has gone unchallenged. C. Van Til reminds Schilder that though it

---

21. For Hoeksema's views, viz. *The Protestant Reformed Church in America*, 1936, and *The Wonder of Grace*, 1944.
22. Hoeksema, *The Protestant Reformed Church in America*, p. 317.

may be true that we cannot reason from the facts to God's disposition, these passages specifically tell us "that God's attitude is revealed in the facts."[23] John Murray, too, says that it is impossible to separate the gifts of God from His disposition. "There can be no escape from the conclusion that goodness and beneficence, kindness and mercy are here attributed to God in His relation even to the ungodly."[24]

We cannot gloss over the speech of God in time in order to deduce conclusions from the decree of election and reprobation. To do so is a devaluation of the historical revelation. Van Til justly criticizes Hoeksema for neglecting the element of time, the earlier and the later in history. To neglect the historical aspect must also, by implication, involve the conclusion that God's wrath can never, in time, rest upon the believer, just as His favor can never rest upon the reprobate. Van Til remarks, Biblically, that the elect fell with Adam and thus became, as sinners, objects of God's wrath. If not, then Christ need not have come in time to reconcile them to God. Systematic deduction from the eternal decree of God allows for two eternal perspectives: wrath-reprobation and love-election. It rules out Divine favor in history for the non-elect, and wrath for the elect. There are no decisions in history; all is lifted up into eternity. History is reduced to two straight lines. All contours in the terrain of history are leveled. God's attitude is sealed in His eternal decree, and this decree has no room for longsuffering. In the resultant tension and contradiction between the hidden, decretive will and the revealed will of God, the revealed will is shorn of real significance.

We need not, however, be forced to minimize the particularity of grace nor the reality of God's wrath if we take the concrete revelation seriously. There is a close relationship, historically, between the longsuffering and the wrath of God.

---

23. Van Til, *Common Grace*, 1947, p. 32.
24. J. Murray, "Common Grace," in *Westminster Theological Journal*, Nov. 1942.

The link between them is man's despising of God's forbearance and common gifts. Recall the words of the Preacher: "Because sentence against an evil work is not executed speedily, therefore the heart of the sons of men is fully set in them to do evil. Though a sinner do evil a hundred times, and prolong his days . . ." (Eccles. 8:11, 12). The Scriptures, thus, denounce any rash conclusion which the sinner may draw from the prolongation of human existence. In the longsuffering of God, in His extension of history and human life, we can hear the gracious call of the sustaining God. The link between forbearance and wrath is man's continued sin.

The wicked may grow as the grass, and the workers of iniquity flourish (Ps. 92:7), "But thou, O Jehovah, art on high for evermore. For, lo, thine enemies, O Jehovah, For, lo, thine enemies shall perish; All the workers of iniquity shall be scattered" (Ps. 92:8, 9). These verses, like other similar ones, do full justice to the forbearance of God. His longsuffering stands in indissoluble connection with His word, His call to repentance. Thus, the continuation of the world is full of longsuffering, and, therefore, full of deepest seriousness. The teaching of common grace must never take the edge off this earnestness. Every outbreak of sin implies the existence of common grace. But this does not weaken the confession of the corruption of human nature. Kuyper viewed common grace not as a power that renewed the heart, but as a force that held sin in restraint. "Thus, God, through His Providence, bridles the corruption of nature so that it does not issue immediately in death. But He does not purify that nature inwardly."

Hoeksema will honor nothing in the natural world as being the influence of the grace of God. Civil righteousness, the practice of virtue, and external order exist because the sinner recognizes the utility of the Divinely established laws, means, and relations, and uses them. This use has nothing to do with a gracious work of God. Hoeksema observes that the confession speaks only of a small remnant of natural light through which man retains some knowledge of God and is able to distinguish somewhat between good and evil. But he offers no explanation of this natural light. He fails, furthermore, to show how it is possible, given an unlimited and unchecked penetration of radical corruption into the human heart, that man still has the ability to distinguish between right and wrong, or how it is possible for right and wrong to exist side by side, the one tolerating the other.

Our problem here is a perennial one. After we have confessed the perversity of human nature, we find it difficult to rhyme the concept of *total* depravity with general experience. Do integrity and nobility live side by side with total human perversity? Hoeksema seeks the solution in the organic development of the race and in the growth of sin in proportion to the development of civilization and culture. Sin has not yet reached its consummation, yet it is always absolute. He explains this by saying that "not every man commits all sin. Each individual is but a branch in the organism of the human race, and he bears that particular fruit of the root-sin of Adam which is in harmony with his place in the organism."[25] But this does not solve the problem of evil in all its varied proportions and gradations. Nor does it explain the practice of outward virtue. Moreover, the Scriptures and history tell us that man commits sins that are *contrary* to nature, that is, sins that are inconsistent with the "organic development of the race." Consider how Paul speaks of man's being full of *all* unrighteousness against God and his neighbor, and how he not only does these unnatural things himself, but takes pleasure in others that do them (Cf. Rom. 1:29-32). Here we have no neat proportion between man's sin and the race's organic growth and development. This is simply the wrath of God revealed from heaven against unrighteousness, the

---

25. Hoeksema, *The Heidelberg Catechism*, 1943, p. 206.

wrath in which God gives man over to these sins (Rom. 1:18, 24, 28).

The idea of the human race as an organism appears at first sight to explain the variations and gradations of sin, but it is not the Scriptural explanation. Its weakness is most evident when Hoeksema describes the development of sin. "It is confined by the gifts and talents, times and circumstances, character and disposition of the individual person. Not every person commits every sin; sin comes to full development and manifestation in the race as a whole; each person sins in his place and according to the measure of his powers and means. It is connected with all sorts of contradictory motives in the deceitful heart of sinful man, while the motives themselves remain ever sinful. Fear of punishment, shame, desire for honor, and many other motives contend with other lusts, thus holding man back from the acts of sin that would otherwise be committed. Yet, this fear, shame, and desire for honor, are just as sinful as the immediate impulse toward a definite sinful act."[26] The weak point in this argument — even from Hoeksema's standpoint — is that while naming fear and shame as defining factors, he fails to explain how even these can come from an absolutely corrupt man. Hoeksema views the working of man and God dualistically, as alongside of and over against each other. Thus, he cannot bring into full account the fact that God rules and directs not only the external development of things, but works in the deepest thoughts and motives of every man.

The restraining work of God does not lessen the guilt and responsibility of man. Neither does it moderate the total corruption of man's heart. Nevertheless, in His creating and sustaining of history God's forbearance reveals itself. Hoeksema's entire argument rests on a misunderstanding of the nature of the activity of God *in* the activity of man. His

---
26. Hoeksema, *Drie scheuren in het fundament der Gereformeerde waarheid*, 1927, p. 61.

protest against the idea that common grace restrains human depravity imports a dualism into the activity of God: between God's work in the organic development of the race and God's work in the concrete man. With such a dualism as an alternative, one can appreciate how Kuyper, precisely on the basis of the radical perversion of the human heart, could come to his view of common grace and its relation to the forbearance of God. He who fails to recognize this relationship must come to a construction of sustenance as a mere neutral maintenance of the world. And this would affect our knowledge of the sustaining God. Only as He is seen, as He reveals Himself to be the longsuffering God in the redemption of the world in Christ, can we understand and confess Providence as sustenance.

* * *

The story of Jonah is pertinent here. Recall how Jonah objected to the forbearance and patience of God. Nineveh was ripe for the judgment of God; but Jonah, sent as preacher of this judgment, did not believe that God would come to Nineveh as the strict Judge. Having no confidence in God's proclamation of judgment, he deserts his commission. Later, he gives his reason for fleeing: "Therefore I hasted to flee unto Tarshish; for I knew that thou art a gracious God, and merciful, slow to anger, and abundant in lovingkindness, and repentest thee of the evil" (Jonah 4:2). Jonah protested against the longsuffering of God! His protesting sentiment, however, was opposed by the emotional stirrings in God's heart. Judgment was preached to Nineveh, and the day of judgment was set. But when the forty-first day dawned, the sun still shone, and the hearts of the people were made glad after their reflection and repentance. God saw their works of conversion and He regretted the evil that He had promised, and He did not do it (Jonah 3:10). Jonah would rather have given the city of a million inhabitants over to fire and destruction, but God would not. He taught Jonah by means of the miracle tree, the tree that Jonah neither planted nor nourished, but which grew and gave Jonah comfort, and then died and moved Jonah to anger. God applied the lesson: ". . . and should not I have regard for Nineveh, that great city, wherein are more than sixscore thousand persons that cannot discern between their right hand and their left hand?" (Jonah 4:11). Cornill, the contemporary expositor of the book of Jonah, says that he has read the book of Jonah more than a hundred times and still cannot read it through with dry eyes. No wonder. Here are the depths of Divine longsuffering. And it is real. We must not destroy it by disparaging it as mere "anthropomorphism."

The Scriptures testify with extraordinary clarity to the time of God's longsuffering and patience, time filled with the message of His grace. It is no neutral period. It is the time of salvation; its history is full of God's promising, His gracious warning, and His serious calling. This longsuffering can be misunderstood and misused as a frivolous game in which man sinfully exploits the prolongation of life that God in mercy gives. If Nineveh does not understand the new light of the forty-first day or the following days and turns back to its wickedness, the judgment will yet be executed. Nahum prophesies: "Jehovah is slow to anger, and great in power, and will by no means clear the guilty: Jehovah hath his way in the whirlwind and in the storm, and the clouds are the dust of his feet" (Nahum 1:3). "Who can stand before his indignation?" (Nahum 1:6). "Woe to the bloody city! it is all full of lies and rapine . . ." (Nahum 3:1). This does not mean that the lifting of the judgment after Jonah's preaching is a mere "postponement" of the judgment. Nor can Psalm 92:8 apply in this connection to show that the temporary continuation of the Ninevites was only so that they could be destroyed in eternity. The reason for the later judgment lies in the *newly erupted sin* when God's longsuffering was grievously misused.

History rolls on, and, with the Gospel, God is in history. "Go ye therefore, and make disciples of all the nations." How clear it is that the Providence of God as sustenance is no flat dogmatic theory. It is actual in the passing of each night into day. When the scoffers of Peter's time pointed in ridicule to the quiet and unbroken progression of the world since the day of creation, Peter gave the explanation for the continuing of history (Cf. II Pet. 3:4). There is no talk of delay or slackness of the promises. There is only revelation of God's longsuffering.

We cannot make a logical scheme of the speech of Scripture. No one can comprehend God in His holy wrath and grace, in His ruling and sustaining, in His tolerating and sparing. But let no one in the face of these incomprehensible realities sacrifice God's longsuffering to His wrath, or His wrath to His longsuffering. We need only to fix our attention on what the Scriptures reveal of salvation, of the earlier wrath and the later grace, and on what they teach us of the continuation of the world amidst the preaching of the decision for or against salvation.

We do not deal with wrath and grace as two balanced determinants in history, but as a message that comes to the world so that mercy may turn away anger, and that wrath be not accumulated unto the day of judgment. We confess Providence as sustenance. We can confess it purely only in true faith in the sustaining God. He who knows God in His grace and forbearance with the world knows that the confession of sustenance is not a theological refinement, but a call to preach.

CHAPTER IV

Providence as Government

WE HAVE remarked that sustenance and government should not be isolated from each other, but must be seen as two aspects of the one almighty and omnipresent act of God. In thinking of Providence as government, we accent the purpose that God proposes and achieves in His holy activity. The sustaining of the world, as we have noted, is also related to His purpose for the future. The only difference is that in the government of God we deal with the purposefulness more explicitly.

This rule has neither spatial nor temporal boundaries. It proceeds from generation to generation. No less than the doctrine of sustenance, God's government reveals His grandeur and incomprehensibility. Earthly analogies are common to us; we know governments, kings, and other authorities. But it is not possible to fathom the rule of God. Who can trace the paths where His foot treads? "For my thoughts are not your thoughts, neither are your ways my ways, saith Jehovah" (Is. 55:8). His ways are beyond those estranged from Him; but neither can those who know His fellowship comprehend Him. Inspired Israel sings in Psalm 77 of God's ways, His ways in the sanctuary: "Who is a great god like unto God?" (Ps. 77:13).

Recalling the miracle of the exodus excites delight and inspires reverence in Israel. "Thy way was in the sea, And thy paths in the great waters, And thy footsteps were not known" (Ps. 77:19). The unfathomableness of God's works, however, forms no obstacle to Israel's trust in His salvation.

Psalm 77 ends with the writer, while impressed by the unsearchableness of God's activity, contemplating His salvation: "Thou leddest thy people like a flock, By the hand of Moses and Aaron" (Ps. 77:20). The enigmatic methods of God's government do not inhibit worship. Paul concludes his chapter on the mystery of God's work in the fall and rejection of Israel and the accepting of the Gentiles by exclaiming: "For who hath known the mind of the Lord? or who hath been his counsellor? O the depth of the riches both of the wisdom and the knowledge of God! how unsearchable are his judgments, and his ways past tracing out!" (Rom. 11:33, 34).

* * *

As God's rule is incomprehensible, so is it invincible. His throne is not moved. He breaks through all resistance, and makes the universe servant to the coming of His kingdom. "Thy throne is established of old: Thou art from everlasting. The floods have lifted up, O Jehovah, The floods have lifted up their voice; The floods lift up their waves. Above the voices of many waters, The mighty breakers of the sea, Jehovah on high is mighty" (Ps. 93:2-4).

The invincibility of God's purposeful ruling cannot be measured with human standards, nor exhausted by analogies of human might and power. But that the rule of God is invincible is certain. He is invincible in a Divine way; his method is strange to human techniques. He is the Lord of Hosts, but His conquest is best revealed in the shame and forsakenness of the cross of His Son. He conquers, but He stoops to darkness and distress. Yet, one day the Divine victory shall rise as a sun to everlasting morning.

The rule of God is the gladness of His people: "Say among the nations, Jehovah reigneth" (Ps. 96:10). He rules from age to age: He is the King of Eternity (I Tim. 6:15). The Scriptures do not teach this in systematic outline. They reveal it in the dynamic movement of history, in God's leading, guiding, and compelling of races and individuals. It is the living God of history who bends and breaks His challengers, who makes an end to wars and directs the wars of the Lord, and who as the Holy One is active in all the world, spanning the length and breadth of it. In no phase of the world's history is the rule of God in danger. "Jehovah will reign for ever, Thy God, O Zion, unto all generations" (Ps. 146:10). This rule is no abstract, immobile potency. It is the acting of the God of Israel in Israel's history. Nothing is too wonderful for Israel's God, the Almighty of Jacob. In the face of His invincible power — in which the people share through faith — all threats from hostile powers are neutralized. He is always the All Highest; He who dwells in His refuge abides in the shadow of the Almighty (Ps. 91:1). "A thousand shall fall at thy side, And ten thousand at thy right hand; But it shall not come nigh thee" (Ps. 91:7).

He, in grace, is the Protector of Israel, His mountains are about Jerusalem (Ps. 125:2). He slumbers not nor sleeps, and guards the goings and comings of His people forever (Ps. 121:8). "He is my refuge and my fortress" (Ps. 91:2). The future is His future; the so-called powers of fate lie in His hands: "My times are in thy hand" (Ps. 31:15). "And which of you by being anxious can add one cubit unto the measure of his life?" (Matt. 6:27). There is no sphere in which dread need possess the believer's existence. For the spheres that He spans are wider than those that encircle man. The believer is never the victim of the powers of nature or fate. Chance is eliminated. "He humbled thee and suffered thee to hunger . . ." (Deut. 8:3). In the judgment of their sin, too, Israel rediscovers the presence of God, when he has consumed their days "in vanity, And their years in terror" (Ps. 78:33). He destroyed their vines and their cattle with hail (Ps. 78:47, 48), and "spared not their soul from death" (Ps. 78:50).

Israel's relation to Him is not like that of the heathen to a nature-god, static and unchanging. He is the God of salvation and judgment. His acts are judgments when the people forget His favors (Ps. 78:11) and fail to remember that their whole existence rests upon His election. He cleaves the rocks in the wilderness and causes water to run down like rivers (Ps. 78:15, 16). And in the distress of judgment Israel rediscovers God.

God's purposes are in all His activity. When He seems most distant, even concealed, He is often near in judgment. But in the judgment He never loses sight of His purpose. He compels Israel to ask again for His comforting presence (Is. 63:15 ff.). God sells Israel to Jabin of Canaan as judgment on her sins, but in turn brings Jabin to account (Judges 4:23). When Israel again honors His holy name, He again draws near in blessing: feeds her people with manna, leads them against their enemies, guides them with the cloud and the fire. The people learn the limitlessness of His rule; they learn that all life from conception to death lies open to Him as a book. Israel offers a paean to His greatness: "For thou didst form my inward parts: Thou didst cover me in my mother's womb. I will give thanks unto thee; for I am fearfully and wonderfully made: Wonderful are thy works; And that my soul knoweth right well. My frame was not hidden from thee, When I was made in secret, And curiously wrought in the lowest parts of the earth. Thine eyes did see mine unformed substance; And in thy book they were all written, Even the days that were ordained for me, When as yet there was none of them" (Ps. 139:13-16). Then, having recognized God's knowledge of the beginning, Israel looks to the future: "Lead me in the way everlasting" (Ps. 139:24).

Past, present, future. In unshaken certainty, Israel is led through life in His hands. He imparts strength and courage to go on.

Earthly and human factors play their part, but the problem of first and second causes is not experienced as a real difficulty in the light of the overshadowing power of God. "Remem-

PROVIDENCE AS GOVERNMENT 87

ber, I beseech thee, that thou hast fashioned me as clay . . . . Hast thou not poured me out as milk, And curdled me like cheese? Thou hast clothed me with skin and flesh, And knit me together with bones and sinews" (Job 10:9-11). Thou! Thou! It sounds all the time — through birth, nature, and history.

In modern times "enlightened" human thought grants nature independence from God. Thunder and lightning, rain and clouds, conception and birth, historical events and their consequences — these are tracked down to their natural causes and endowed by human thought with their own immanent force. They form an independent power, which the Divine activity seems able only to limit and curtail.

Not so with Israel in her fear of God.

Israel, too, knows of conception and birth, of streams that go to the sea, and of the cycle of nature. But this knowledge does not stifle her "Thou, O Lord." In her knowledge, she still looks to the living God, the Unchangeable. This is no primitive religious naivete that later is sloughed off with increase of intelligence. "The voice of Jehovah cleaveth the flames of fire. The voice of Jehovah shaketh the wilderness; . . . the voice of Jehovah maketh the hinds to calve" (Ps. 29:7-9). This is Israel's understanding of natural events. For Israel's eyes are trained on Him.

The might of the Lord is not seen as a consuming energy that rules out all human activity. But neither does His use of human means limit the scope of His activity. "I was cast upon thee from the womb; Thou art my God since my mother bare me. Be not far from me; for trouble is near; For there is none to help" (Ps. 22:10, 11). This direct relation to God embraces the whole span of life. He is Israel's expectation even from her youth (Ps. 71:17). Scripture stands, thus, in polar opposition to every form of deism which isolates God from the affairs of the world. His immanent leading spans all the ways of man and reaches into the intents of the heart: "A man's heart deviseth his way; But Jehovah directeth his steps" (Prov. 16:9). The heart of the king is in the hand of the Lord as the watercourses. He leads it wherever He pleases (Prov. 21:1). The poet, moved by the marvels of His activity, writes: "There is no wisdom nor understanding Nor counsel against Jehovah" (Prov. 21:30).

Now He impresses us with His guidance of the great, then with His leading of the small; now with the universal, then with the particular. It has been suggested that the notion of God's rule over individuals was a later phenomenon in Israel's religious history. Eichrodt, for instance, says, "Gradually, as the people gained faith in Providence, the destiny of the individual was included in its scope."[1] But Eichrodt himself would agree that personal trust in God's guidance is revealed very early. Joseph in Egypt already expresses it: "And as for you, ye meant evil against me; but God meant it for good, to save much people alive" (Gen. 50:20). God includes the people in His view, but Joseph knows that God also encircles his individual life. This is the way with Abraham and Sarah, with the marriage of Isaac, and with the life of Jacob. All facets of life are embraced in God's rule.

The plurality of life is brought under one perspective. It is not that there is a confusion of countless atomistic events in all of which God's activity is manifest. There is a pivot, a centrum, which unifies the diversity of His activity. The unity includes the progress of events from His promise at the time of the fall to the completion of the formation of His holy people. It is not surprising that Israel, when reflecting about God's activity, always looks back to the old days. The intervention of God in the exodus always remains a searing reminder of her dependence on God. In the history following the exodus it is made clear that the Lord has interfered in the life of Pharaoh and stretched His arms out against the Egyptians (Exod. 9:5). Moses and the children of Israel

---

1. W. Eichrodt, *Theologie des Alten Testaments*, II, 1933, p. 91.

sing of the intervening hand of God: "Who is like unto thee, O Jehovah, among the gods? Who is like thee, glorious in holiness, Fearful in praises, doing wonders?" (Exod. 15:11). His right hand brings the decision (Exod. 15:12). It is directed against Pharaoh, but means leading and redemption for His people (Exod. 15:13). The entire 15th chapter is a song to His wrath (Exod. 15:7), His gentle leading (Exod. 15:13), the strength of His arms (Exod. 15:16). "Jehovah shall reign for ever and ever" (Exod. 15:18).

God's works must be seen as His immanent activity — works not confined to Israel, though defined by His purpose for and in her. These acts of God are reviewed for Israel through the generations. Israel's entire history is controlled by Jehovah, just as her formation was conceived by Him. "When Old Testament piety is reminded of the power of God, it thinks of God's deed at the Red Sea, the act that completed the exodus."[2] If Israel is estranged from God's gracious leading, the prophets remind her of the power and grace of God. "For I brought thee up out of the land of Egypt, and redeemed thee out of the house of bondage; and I sent before thee Moses, Aaron, and Miriam" (Mic. 6:4). It was His path in the sea. He led the people (Ps. 77: 19, 20). "I am Jehovah, your Holy One, the Creator of Israel, your King. Thus saith Jehovah, who maketh a way in the sea, and a path in the mighty waters; who bringeth forth the chariot and horse, the army and the mighty man . . ." (Is. 43:15-17).

Not only the exodus manifests the ruling of God. Israel is reminded of the consul of Balak, and of how Balaam the son of Beor answered him (Mic. 6:5). Israel sings of God's paths and works in the desert: His sending of manna (Ps. 105:40), His cleaving of the rock (Ps. 105:41). They remember His judgments when they tempted Him (Ps. 106:14), His wrath at their images (Ps. 106:29). These are not incidental acts, but cohesive elements in His continu-

---

2. Kittel, *Theologische Wörterbuch zum N. T.*, Vol. II, 1940, p. 293.

ous guidance. Israel is expected to know that her God is He who rules all things. He, the Holy One of Israel, is Redeemer God of the whole earth (Is. 54:5). The Old Testament is not the history of the Eastern peoples. They do, however, stand in the shadow of Israel's election, through which, as was promised, all the peoples of the earth were to be blessed. God goes *through* Israel to the lost world. His grace and judgment is directed to the future, His salvation for the world.

* * *

To explain away this purposeful activity of God evolutionistically or subjectively is to miss the deepest secret of Israel's history. The secret is buried in the sovereign rule of God that leads to His full salvation and to the redemption of the world. Though the rule of God goes uncomprehended by us, His paths are lighted up in various ways by the Scriptures. We see him working in the historical matrix of human counsels, plans, and deeds. Stauffer has quite rightly spoken of the trend often observed in Divine government as "a law of deflection." "The more the adversary opposes, so much the richer becomes the revelation of the infinite superiority of God."[3] This is because God's rule is executed and manifested in and through human activity. There are not two powers working apart from and parallel to each other, the Divine and the human, each limiting the other. Yet, we see men performing extraordinarily important roles in sacred history.

Joseph's brothers devise and execute their plans; aroused by jealousy they gradually commit themselves irrevocably to their chosen course. The plan to kill Joseph is frustrated, but the historical reason even for this falls within the orbit of human devices. Reuben comes between. Thus the story of Joseph is a tale of human initiative from his sale to the Midianites to his arrival in Egypt. It is first in Genesis 39 that a new element enters the story: we are told, "And Je-

---

3. E. Stauffer, *Theologie des Neuen Testaments*, 1948, p. 186.

hovah was with Joseph." Then the "deflection" takes place as the plot of the brothers runs itself out. The activity of God is revealed, not as a *deus ex machina,* but *in* the action of the brothers. Their evil plan achieves historical realization, but the historical events are products of the Divine activity. God's good intents follow the mischievous path of the brothers or, rather, the brothers unwittingly follow the path that God has blazed. They work in His service. The purpose of God lights up the horizon of evil, jealous, malicious activity. The dispute in Jacob's house turns into an important link in the way of God with His people. Joseph, with his background of experiences in Egypt, understands something of this, and later explains it to his brothers — for their consolation.

God's hand *in* history!

This does not mean that the work of God is always evident in the interlacing of Divine and human activity. We cannot set Divine action under any one common denominator. He does not, for instance, always allow human plans to be consummated. He often frustrates their execution by an interference from outside. He thwarts Pharaoh in his fury against Israel. There is an intervention from without history as well as a "deflection" from within, a thwarting as well as a bending. God can allow the heathen aggressor to reach his goal, using the pagan triumph as a judgment on and humbling of His people. But, on the other hand, He can also resist Sennacherib's attack on Jerusalem and thwart all his plans. He can hear Hezekiah's prayer in a concrete situation and open His eyes to the danger (Is. 37:17). He can hear the reproach of Rabshakeh. "Therefore thus saith Jehovah concerning the king of Assyria, He shall not come unto this city, nor shoot an arrow there, neither shall he come before it with shield, nor cast up a mound against it . . . For I will defend this city . . ." (Is. 37:33, 35). "And the angel of Jehovah went forth, and smote in the camp of the Assyrians a hundred and fourscore and five thousand" (Is. 37:36).

Yet it is striking to observe how often the purpose of God is reached without radical intervention. On the surface there may be nothing to see except human activity creating and defining history on a horizontal level. But in revelation the final sense of the historical events is unveiled. We could illustrate this historical activity from scores of Biblical examples. We shall mention only a few.

In Judges we read of a conflict between the citizens of Shechem and Abimilech. The dispute arises from the treachery of the men of Shechem, which treachery seems to be the determining factor in the story. The conflict actually executes a judgment on both Abimilech and the Shechemites. God sends an evil spirit between Abimilech and the citizens of Shechem so that the crime committed by Abimilech against the seventy sons of Jerubbaal is turned on both Abimelech and the Shechemites who had aided him (Judg. 9:24). God's activity is *in* the conflict. "The uprising of the Shechemites was not undertaken to expiate a crime of which they themselves were also guilty. They did not know themselves what they were doing. They were instruments of God."[4]

Or, observe Saul's battle against Amalek. A purely horizontal perspective cannot explain this war, but revelation shows that it executes judgment against the Amalekites for what they did against Israel in the then almost forgotten days right after the exodus (I Sam. 15:2). Saul's attack on the Amalekites is not inconsistent with his sparing of the Canaanites, since they, unlike the Amalekites, were friendly to the Israelites in their migration (I Sam. 15:6). God's leading spans the centuries, and in His leading the action of man is taken up as instrument in His service. Man's activity falls, as the smaller of two concentric circles, completely within the greater circle of God's purpose.

The nature of God's activity is seen uniquely in the establishment of the monarchy in Israel. Here, too, there is an

---

4. Kittel, *Theologische Wörterbuch zum N. T.*, IV, 1942, p. 711.

interweaving of Divine and human acts. The installation of the monarchy is closely related to Israel's sin of rejecting, in principle, the Lordship of God. God Himself describes their action thus, sees it as evil, and commands Samuel to warn the people before announcing the decision to give them their king. Human disloyalty to God, then, seems to have created the monarchy. We can imagine similar developments in other nations. But in the setting up and historical development of Israel's monarchy the free and overruling activity of God is revealed. Through the disloyal rejection of His Lordship and the establishment of the monarchy comes the messianic future.

We encounter similar lines in the rupture of the kingdom, born out of sin, but revelatory, nonetheless, of God's activity. The split is the fruit of Rehoboam's sin. Yet, God says, "This thing is of me" (I Kings 12:24). This becomes clearer when the rendering of I Kings 12 is viewed against the background of I Kings 11:29ff., where Jeroboam and Ahijah meet alone in the field, and where Jeroboam hears that the Lord has said: "Behold, I will rend the kingdom out of the hand of Solomon, and will give ten tribes to thee" (I Kings 11:31). God works in Rehoboam's sin so that Rehoboam actualizes the word that He has spoken through Ahijah. God's wisdom triumphs in Rehoboam's foolishness. In every "deflection" it becomes clear that God's activity is not limited by man's sin. He is conqueror even *in* man's sin. This is the light that shines through Israel's entire history.

God's "thinking it for good" makes His enemies accessories to the salvation of His people. We see this also in the threatened judgments which gather as dark thunder clouds over the people. The exile, for example, is as mere human activity historically unaccountable. Jeremiah in his vision sees the historical factors leading to the fall of his people as a nation: a seething cauldron with its face toward the north (Jer. 1:13). From the north shall come evil against the inhabitants of the land. This, it would seem, is still human activity exclusively. But another perspective lies in the threat: "For, lo, I will call all the families of the kingdoms of the north, saith Jehovah; and they shall come, and . . . I will utter my judgments against them touching all their wickedness, in that they have forsaken me . . ." (Jer. 1:15, 16). Once again, the revelation of the judgment of God *in* history.

The activity of God is revealed again in the return from the exile, even though the human, historical factors seem to predominate in the event. Cyrus, the Prince of Persia, arises on the horizon but, on his way to greatness, becomes another instrument of God. He becomes the liberator of God's people. Another exodus! There is always perspective in God's activity, always a pivot on which everything turns, a purpose to which everything is servant. From this center the lines of God's rule are drawn around the foreigner Cyrus. He is aroused to march from the east against Babylon. Nations are sacrificed to this heathen so that nothing may hinder his triumphal march. "Who hath wrought and done it, calling the generations from the beginning? I, Jehovah, the first, and with the last, I am he" (Is. 41:4). Of Cyrus, He says, "He is my shepherd, and shall perform all my pleasure, even saying of Jerusalem, She shall be built; and of the temple, Thy foundation shall be laid" (Is. 44:28). Cyrus is the annointed, the messiah of the Lord (Is. 45:1). For the sake of His people, God enlists Cyrus though he did not know Him (Is. 45:4). The affair with Cyrus is summarized thus: "I am Jehovah, and there is none else; besides me there is no God . . . I form the light, and create darkness; I am Jehovah, that doeth all these things" (Is. 45:5, 7). Cyrus liberates God's people, builds God's city, and lets His people go, "not for ransom nor for gifts," so that, in and through Cyrus, the Divine rule is raised above doubt.

And, as with Babylon and Cyrus, so is it with Assur. Assur is the rod with which God disciplines His people. In his deceit, the fire of judgment flames. God rouses Assur to lead the Assyrians to attack (Is. 10:5-13). That these events are prearranged comes out more clearly in that, at the same time, a double woe is spoken over Assur. The Assyrian Assur, servant to God's purposes, oppresses Jerusalem; but then God saves Jerusalem by oppressing Assur. When Assur boasts over his achievements, Isaiah says to him, "Shall the axe boast itself against him that heweth therewith? shall the saw magnify itself against him that wieldeth it?" (Is. 10:15).

* * *

We encounter similar relationships in the New Testament. When Stauffer spoke of the "law of deflection," he mentioned the suffering of Christ as well as the history of Joseph. The interweaving of Divine and human action can, indeed, be observed in the life of Jesus Christ, not only in His suffering, but beginning already at His birth. The story of the nativity begins in Luke 2 with human activity. The general order for the registration of the people comes from the man Caesar. The path of Joseph and Mary, too, falls within the circle of human sovereignty, and, as consequence of this human act, they find themselves in Bethlehem. The course of human events climaxes at the city spoken of in Micah's messianic prophecy. Again, there is a deflecting toward God's proposed purpose. (On the other hand, it is true that the more immediate method is used in the intervention in Herod's plans by means of a dream revelation to Joseph.)

The interlacing of Divine and human activity is revealed pre-eminently in the history of Christ's suffering. Satan and men act out their part. The disciples of Jesus play their role, too, through their denial, disloyalty, and desertion. Their action brings Christ into total loneliness, and in this loneliness God executes His judgment. Christ experiences Divine abandonment in the crucible created by human enterprise — in the opposition against Him and the delivering of Him to the death of the cross. God acts *in* men's acts: in Pilate's sentence, in Judas's betrayal, yea, in everything that men do with Christ. God's activity embraces all these and leads them along His mysterious way.

The New Testament sees human actions as being nonetheless fully responsible. Christ was nailed to the cross by unrighteous, responsible men. You, says Peter, have killed the Prince of life (Acts 3:15). You, and Herod, and Pilate, you were in league with the Romans and the Jews against God's holy child Jesus, *but* — "to do whatsoever thy (God's) hand and thy counsel foreordained to come to pass" (Acts 4:28). From our perspective it becomes evident that the tramping of human paths paves the way of God, that all these things work together toward the achievement of God's purpose. He is delivered up by the determinate counsel and foreknowledge of God (Acts 2:23). There is no accident on Christ's journey into suffering. It is a Divine must, as Christ Himself says to the Emmaus travelers: "Behooved it not the Christ to suffer these things, and to enter into his glory?" (Luke 24:26).

The relation between Divine and human activity is illuminated also in the role played by Caiaphas (John 11:47-53). In the confusion and indecision of the high priests and pharisees, Caiaphas hits upon a suggestive idea, a broad hint at a solution: "Ye know nothing at all, nor do ye take account that it is expedient for you that one man should die for the people, and that the whole nation perish not" (John 11:49, 50). This is the stimulus to reorganization of the opposition forces. From this day on they deliberate as to how they shall kill him. Caiaphas's suggestion is the turning point in Christ's path of suffering; but God acts in this human act too. John makes this explicit by way of a two-verse parenthesis (John 11:51, 52). Caiaphas does not speak merely out of his free thoughts as a man, but officially as high priest and prophet. In Caiaphas's extremist opposition to Jesus, God's revelation of the meaning of Christ's suffering and death becomes more clear. He unintentionally gives a definition of substitutionary suffering. This is not a matter of Caiaphas's cunning or guileful ingenuity, but a revelation of the profound congruity between God's and man's actions. Schilder remarks pointedly, "When Caiaphas formulated his answer thus, *one must die for all,* he ended the last sacrifice-hungry priestly discourse with the same conclusion, the same aphorism that was written before all time in the Book of God as the principle and ultimate rationale of the covenant of peace: *one for all, one for all.*"[5]

* * *

In all this we can observe the overruling power of God. He is the Holy One, the Incomparable who fulfills His purposes in the actions of the sinners of all generations. To place God and man in one line as comparable powers is to fail to understand this activity of God. He who listens to the preaching of Scripture knows that God works thus for good. God is no blind force or foreign "will" who plays His incomprehensible game to confound us. He who does these things is the God of salvation, the God of Abraham, Isaac, and Jacob. And who has withstood His will? God does not give the initiative for His work over to the Devil, though He allows sinners to serve Him. In the light of revelation, God's own initiative is disclosed in its invincibility, mysteriously disclosed even in the acts of His enemies.

Paul — to conclude this array of examples — observes with profound respect this activity of God in the transition of salvation from Israel to the Gentiles. Israel's unbelief bothers him to the extent that he prefers himself rejected if his rejection could save his brothers (Rom. 9:3), but he sees the work of God in Israel's unbelief: ". . . by their fall salvation is come unto the Gentiles, to provoke them to jealousy. Now if their fall is the riches of the world, and their loss the riches of the Gentiles; how much more their fulness?" (Rom. 11:11, 12).

---

5. K. Schilder, *Christus in zijn lijden,* 2nd ed., I, 1949, p. 60.

Every word of Paul's interpretation is teleologically directed. "For if the casting away of them is the reconciling of the world, what shall the receiving of them be, but life from the dead?" (Rom. 11:15). In this way — through Israel's fall and unbelief — the original Divine plan is executed, and the purpose is achieved: the redemption of the world. This is the way of God, which Paul in another place summarizes by saying: God was in Christ reconciling the world unto Himself. Thus the words about the fruitful significance of Israel's fall can be recorded without minimizing its seriousness. And when Paul ends his discussion with: "O the depth of the riches . . ." he is not moved by an inscrutable, arbitrary force that puts the finger over one's lips. It is the fullness of God's love and wisdom that inspires Paul to exultation.

It is said that there are accents in Paul which the Church has hesitated to assume. Where the Church has thus hesitated she has impoverished herself and blurred her outlook on God's activity. Hesitation where Paul was bold has caused the Church often to make only a problem of God's rule and man's responsibility. She thus undermines either the Providence of God or human responsibility. They do not exist together in the Scriptures as something problematic. They both reveal the greatness of Divine activity, in that it does not exclude human activity and responsibility but embraces them and in them manifests God on the way to the accomplishment of His purposes.

God's purpose, while involving *all* His activity, is peculiarly coupled with the mystery of reconciliation, from the standpoint of which faith finds her rest in God's universal rule. How could anyone oppose *this* purpose and this ruling power? He who waits on Him learns to know His loveliness, though it be in the tempest through which His course sometimes leads us.

This God of grace and judgment is, in the revelation of His power, disclosed to faith as the Merciful and Trustworthy. He is the Shepherd of His people: "He will feed his flock like a shepherd, he will gather the lambs in his arm, and carry them in his bosom, and will gently lead those that have their young" (Is. 40:11). Israel's way is not hidden from Him (Is. 40:27). He gives strength to the tired. The richness and abundance of His mercy sustains His people on their way into the future (Is. 63:7). He takes them up and carries them as in the days of old (Is. 63:9).

* * *

In His sovereign rule God brings in His Kingdom and prepares the coming of the Messiah for the redemption of the world. God comes into history; His coming is foretold in the earliest moments of salvation's history as the blessing which is to come for all the generations of the earth (Gen. 12; 26:4; 28:14). God Himself shall bring in the future, and He is Himself surety for the fulfillment of His promises. "The sceptre shall not depart from Judah, Nor the ruler's staff from between his feet until Shiloh come . . ." (Gen. 49:10). The heathen Balaam calls out: "A sceptre shall rise out of Israel" (Num. 24:17). And though at that point in the history of revelation the Messiah was not completely and clearly delineated by this scepter it is in the light of further revelation to be understood only as messianic. The revelation of God's messianic activity is given only in gradual augmentation. It is never impeded by Israel's sin. Contrariwise, their sin often occasions a new step in the revelation. It receives in David its typological epitome. After that, the coming of the messianic King is inseparably bound to the house of David. The prophet says this in plain language to David himself: "When thy days are fulfilled, and thou shalt sleep with thy fathers, I will set up thy seed after thee, that shall proceed out of thy bowels, and I will establish his kingdom. He shall build a house for my name, and I will establish the throne of his kingdom for ever" (II Sam. 7:12, 13). This, in contrast to the kingship of Saul: "but my lovingkindness shall not depart from him, as I took it from Saul, whom I put away before thee. And thy house and thy kingdom shall be made sure for ever before thee: thy throne shall be established for ever" (II Sam. 7:15, 16).

David speaks in his dying words about his certainty regarding the future: "There shall be one that ruleth over men righteously, That ruleth in the fear of God" (II Sam. 23:3).

This special course of the history of revelation and of God's salvation in the world does not abridge the Divine sovereignty over all things and all peoples. On the contrary, the whole world lies within the sphere of God's purposeful activity and, in her universal development, stands beneath His scepter. We do see, nevertheless, the concentration of His redemptive activity in His particular line of sacred revelation — in Israel and, more particularly, in David. We hear that God shall raise up for David a righteous scion, who shall reign as king, caring for justice and righteousness in the land, and who shall be called the Lord our Righteousness (Jer. 23:5). This King from the house of David shall, through redemption, bring His people into service for God (Jer. 30:9), so that "David shall never want a man to sit upon the throne of the house of Israel" (Jer. 33:17). And, just as God's covenant of the seasons will not be forgotten, so God's covenant with David His servant will never be broken. As numerous as are the stars of the night, as countless as the sands of the sea, so many shall be the seed of David (Jer. 33:21, 22). God shall never reject the seed of Jacob and David, for he will cause their captivity to return and have mercy on them (Jer. 33:26). David's house, though fallen, shall always rise again (Amos 9:11).

* * *

Isaiah, too, points to Him who shall wear the government upon his shoulders and to the magnitude of the government, to its peace which shall have no end, and to the throne of David which shall strengthen and confirm His kingdom through eternity. The zeal of the Lord of Hosts shall perform it (Is. 9:5-7). The King shall come with justice and salvation (cf. Zech. 9:9), and, in the King, God's plan of salvation for the world will be fully revealed. His shall not be an imperious force, but a unique ruling authority, singular for that this King shall be at once King and Priest. In Him peace shall prevail between the priesthood and the kingship. This is why salvation and forgiveness both shall come from His kingship. In Isaiah's prophecy we receive light on the question of how God shall rule over the world.

The Messianic expectation has too often been explained apart from the reality of God's promise. The eschatological outlook of Israel is often accounted for on the basis of the foreign influence of other religions, and the kingdom expectation out of purely human and earthly motivations. The source of Israel's eschatology is construed to be the disaster situation in which the people become involved and in which they satisfy their desire for relief by projecting their future glorious redemption. This type of construction stubbornly ignores many pre-exilic texts. Israel's eschatological anticipation does not arise out of a psychological need occasioned by national emergency. It is found in prosperous times as well as in crises. It is a trusting response to the prophetic word regarding the coming King. God Himself shall in the course of history establish His eternal kingdom. Though the eschatological expectation becomes keenest in times of crisis, it is clear that it has its root, not in wish projections, but in the promise of God.

This is perhaps most apparent in the emphatic manner in which Scripture speaks about the remnant. The Bible revelation of God's ominous judgment on the sins of His people always has as its correlative the comforting word about the remnant. The idea of survivors has its origin in the saving activity of God. The light of the remnant promise shines in the darkness of the grimmest judgment. The remnant and the coming kingdom are eschatological correlatives. "And I will make that which was lame a remnant, and that which was cast far off a strong nation: and Jehovah will reign over them in mount Zion from henceforth even for ever" (Mic. 4:7). On the other side of judgment lies the mercy of God on behalf of the remnant. The possibility of this remnant lies outside Israel's sin. Her sin, viewed alone, gives sense only to totality of judgment. "Except Jehovah of hosts had left unto us a very small remnant, we should have been as Sodom, we should have been like unto Gomorrah" (Is. 1:9). The remnant, plucked as a brand from the burning, stands as a monument of God's miraculous grace. God acts in judgment and grace — and through the grimness of judgment it is revealed that His deliverance is Divine deliverance, mighty and holy, giving mercy from generation to generation (Luke 1).

The prophecy of Daniel also adds illumination to the coming of the kingdom, God's definitive work with this world. Here the coming kingdom is preached to Israel in calamity as a reminder that God is still working. Daniel sees in his visions the glory and invincibility of God's rule, especially in relation to and in contrast to the kingdoms of this world. Nebuchadnezzar's dream, too, reveals the events of the future (Dan. 2:29). He sees a huge and brilliant image, and then a stone — hewn by no human hands — that hits and shatters the image (Dan. 2:34 ff.). Daniel, explaining the dream, points out first that the God of heaven has given Nebuchadnezzar his kingdom and made him ruler over men, but that another kingdom should come after Nebuchadnezzar's kingdom and those of others have been destroyed. Against this kingdom, all others are impotent. It is the kingdom of God, in which He, through the Messiah, shall reign forever in invincible might.

* * *

This is enough to indicate that the entire Old Testament is full of prophetic expectation of the kingdom of God. The gist is that God Himself shall establish His kingdom in justice and mercy.

There can exist no doubt as to whether the New Testament contains, in the revelation of the kingdom in Jesus Christ, the inceptive fulfillment of this prophecy and anticipation. Jesus is the King who, through redemption, puts His claim on all things. He is the Son of David (Matt. 22:42, et. al.), and is in this sense King entirely in His own right. (Cf. prophecy of Zechariah.) His kingdom is not of this world, which is to say, it does not arise from this world's power but is, nevertheless, an actual kingdom to be established on this earth. John the Baptist, as forerunner of Christ, proclaimed the approach of the kingdom. Christ's power comes out in the victory over the demons, as expressed by Christ Himself: "But if I by the Spirit of God cast out demons, then is the kingdom of God come unto you" (Matt. 12:28). This is a revelation of the authority of God. In Christ, the kingdom becomes actual in the present world of time and history.

The coming of the kingdom is sometimes called a "break through," an invasion. This gives something of the picture. Powers are unthroned; "possessed" territories liberated. Christ was tempted in the wilderness to take possession of the kingdoms of this earth and thus forsake His true calling, and, in His loyalty to His calling, the kingdom begins to reveal itself. The strong become weak before Him (Matt. 8:28-34). The decisive difference is in Christ's revelation as a fundamental reconstruction of the times, as the breakthrough of Divine salvation, as the overthrow of the rulers of this world. In the might revealed in Christ the disciples whom he called were conscripted and given this commission: ". . . heal the sick that are therein, and say unto them, The kingdom of God is come nigh unto you" (Luke 10:9). And when the seventy return exuberant that the devils were subject to them, Christ said: "I beheld Satan fall as lightning from heaven" (Luke

10:18). Then they received power, that is to say, authority, to tread on snakes and scorpions, and over all the power of the enemy.

* * *

The entire New Testament witnesses irrefutably to the kingship of Christ, and from this witness we can learn something as to its nature. It is no rule of terror and brute power. Men derided Him in His suffering because of the strange nature of His kingdom. It remained in its true nature hidden to those who watched Him on His way to death. "Art thou a king then?" asked Pilate (John 18:37). In His affirmation, Jesus gave a hint to the nature of His kingship: "To this end have I been born, and to this end am I come into the world, that I should bear witness unto the truth" (John 18:37). But it remains a riddle to Pilate the sceptic. "What is truth?" he asks (John 18:38). For the Jews, too, His royal pretensions were an offense. They testify against Him that He claimed to be Christ, the King (Luke 23:2). And in His kingship He is jeered: "Hail, King of the Jews!" (Matt. 27:29). They can only sceptically inquire and shamefully mock as they measure His strange kingship according to earthly patterns and fail to see the revelation of royalty within His utter humiliation, as the prophecy of Zechariah is fulfilled in this King without troops, in His transition from suffering to glory. But he who can see the light of revelation falling upon this poverty, sympathetically understands the prayer of the murderer who turns to the middle cross and discovers there a King.

What does this kingship mean, this kingship which was "today" fulfilled in their ears (Luke 4:21)? What means this victory in the midst of death? What does this kingship mean as Christ rises from the dead and ascends to heaven, there to sit at the right hand of God? What means this kingdom of

God's beloved Son in which we too have been made citizens (Col. 1:13)? Is it relevant to God's Providence? Or is its place, dogmatically, in the study of christology when we discuss His kingly office? Is there a sharp distinction between the kingship of Christ — His lordship and authority over all things (Matt. 28:18) — and the royal rule of God over all things? Or is there such a profound congruity between them that we must discuss the kingship of Christ in our reflection here upon the government of God?

This question sets us immediately in the midst of many discussions which now again occupy the center of theological interest. We refer to the discussions about *theo*cracy and *christo*cracy, and about the kingdom of Christ and the kingdoms of this world. The relationship between Christ's kingdom and the kingdom of God is too important for us to avoid. The Heidelberg Catechism has a statement that has immediate relevance to these discussions. The article "sitting at the right hand of God" is explained in the 19th Lord's Day thus: "Because Christ ascended into heaven for this end, that he might there appear as Head of his Church, by whom the Father governs all things." The Catechism does not merely state generally that the Father rules all things. His ruling is indicated as a ruling through Christ. What must, then, be understood by the Father's ruling through Christ?

This question is currently raised in the discussion of the so-called christological basis of the state. We are not concerned here with a particular theory of the state, but we cannot avoid the question altogether since it touches on the nature of God's ruling. The Heidelberg Catechism, too, in saying that God rules all things through Christ, urges us to further reflection.

That the relation between God's government and the kingship of Christ is of such interest is easily understandable considering the manner in which the New Testament speaks of the power of Christ. Paul talks in Ephesians 1:22, 23 about the overwhelmingly great power of God, according to the working of the strength of His might which He has wrought in Christ to awaken Him from the dead and to set Him on His own right hand. Jesus is now set above all governments and powers and authorities. God has put all things under his feet and has given him to His body, the Church, as Head of all that is. Christ, then, is given to His Church as Authority over all. Other passages, too, attract our attention in the same way. Christ's own words, for example: "All authority hath been given unto me in heaven and on earth" (Matt. 28:18). Again, "the Lamb shall overcome them, for he is Lord of lords, and King of kings" (Rev. 17:14). And *this* name is "written on His robe and on His thigh." We read in Psalm 2 that God has annointed the Messiah as King over Zion, and hence urges: "be wise, O ye kings: Be instructed, ye judges of the earth. Serve Jehovah with fear, And rejoice with trembling. Kiss the son, lest he be angry, and ye perish in the way . . ." (Ps. 2:10-12). These references suggest that the kingdom of Christ rises out of His redemptive work. Has He not received His authority through His cross and resurrection? Has He not been promoted to the highest place; and has He not received a Name above all names? Has He not disarmed the governments and powers of the world, publicly triumphing over them? Reading these Scriptural passages one may perhaps wonder how it is possible that there could be such intense debate around them.

In answer we may say that the problem does not arise as to whether or not there is a kingdom of Christ; this is denied in the discussion by no one. The problem lies in the relationship between this, Christ's kingdom, and the kingdom of God, and also in the relationship of both to the governments of this world. We may phrase the question thus: Does earthly government stand in a special relationship to Christ through the fact of His resurrection and His receiving of power over all things? Or does human government exist through the grace of the triune God, quite apart from Christ's resurrection and ascension?

This is where a rather profound difference of opinion currently arises. Generally, it is in circles where Barth's theology has been most influential that the christological basis of the state has found most support. Barth posed the question when he wrote in 1938 that the current interest in the relation between the kingdom of Christ and the kingdom of God begins where the Reformation confessions leave off. The reformers confessed the validity and authority of governments as emphatically as they confessed the justification of the sinner, but the relation between the two never became too clear. Government, in the mind of the reformers, lay in the sphere of general Providence. It was established because of sin. Calvin, it is true, when discussing government brought in Psalm 2 and spoke about the "Christian state." But Barth asks, "Christian in what respect? What has Christ to do with government, we ask, and are left with the question essentially unanswered, as though a special rule of a general, to an extent anonymous, Providence has the last word here."[6] Our fathers reveal, according to Barth, an hiatus basic in the matter of the christological basis of state and government. Did they base political power *in* the power of Christ, or did they indicate another basis for it ? And did they, Barth asks, perhaps speak of God, but not of the Father of Jesus Christ?

* * *

This is not a question in which the dialectical theologians have exclusive interest. The problem of whether governments rule as subject to God the Father or as subject to Christ as crowned by the Father has been subject to debate in non-dialectical Reformed circles. We may best understand the modern discussions by first reviewing the contribution of Kuyper[7],

---
6. Barth, *Rechtfertigung und Recht*, 1938, p. 5.
7. For the discussion of Kuyper's views presented here, cf. *Dictaten Dogmatiek*, Locus V, pp. 186, 209 and *Gemeene Gratie*, III, pp. 124, 278-280.

who pioneered in the problem of christocracy or the problem of whether earthly governments rule by the grace of Christ rather than by the grace of God — a problem which he called "extremely difficult and complex." Kuyper was afraid that men would view the rule of Christ as a competitor to the rule of God. To avoid this he made a distinction between the essential rule and the temporary rule of grace (*regnum essentiale* and *regnum oeconomiam*). The essential rule is grounded in original creation, in the exercise of the sovereignty of God as Creator. This kingdom is permanent, and to it belong the governors of the world. They are immediate instruments through which God exercises His sovereignty on earth. The governments of the world, then, belong to what Kuyper calls the essential rule of God, the creation order. They do not belong to the temporary rule of grace. The rule of grace — also called the special rule — has only a mediating character, having as its purpose the reconstruction of the essential rule which has been temporarily disrupted by sin. This mediating kingdom shall some day disappear, leaving the essential rule forever remaining, after the fashion of I Cor. 15.

The point of contact between these two kingdoms, according to Kuyper, lies in the person of the Mediator, who is King in the rule of grace and, at the same time, second person of the Trinity. This personal connection between the two kingdoms is suggested in the Scriptures by the expression "sitting at the right hand of God." Kuyper sees a sort of duality between the essential and the special rules. He misses this duality in the Heidelberg Catechism which says, ambiguously, according to Kuyper, only that it is Christ "through whom the Father rules all things." There is, says Kuyper, a *special* relation between Christ and earthly governments, *besides* that relation which exists in virtue of Christ's being a member of the Trinity and thereby sharer in the essential rule of God over governments. This *special* relation is subservient to the essential, but it is nevertheless real in itself.

PROVIDENCE AS GOVERNMENT

Governments rule by the grace of God and possess their origin, not in Jesus Christ the Mediator, but in the triune God. The Scriptures say that Christ has power over all things, but this would be unthinkable, Kuyper says, "if He were not at the same time, as Second Person of the Trinity, the Mediator of creation." Kuyper is opposed to construing the matter "as though the Father, having given all things over to His Son — let it be said with respect — retired into the background for the time, abdicating as God and becoming temporarily unemployed." For this reason he opposes the so-called christocracy and points to the confessions which, when dealing with Providence, do not discuss the rule of Christ, but "the work of God exclusively."

This protest against what Kuyper calls the abdication of God is quite justified. It is not as though, after Jesus' ascension "the Providential rule of God Triune is suspended temporarily and given over to the Mediator . . ." The majesty of the Mediator is never shoved into the place belonging to the majesty of the Divine Being. Besides, recalls Kuyper, when Christ was questioned about God's Providence, He always pointed to the Father, not to Himself.

All this, though true, does not solve the problem; and Kuyper had no illusions that it did. He writes: "Still, we would not conceal the fact that with this we have not yet reached a clear insight into the relationship with which we are here concerned." In the rejection of the abdication idea, Kuyper creates the opportunity of giving the really quite unambiguous word of the Heidelberg Catechism in Lord's Day 19 its full say. For in the light of the Scriptures, there can be no exercise of power by Christ which is, though for an instant, abstracted from the government of God. The Scriptures, too, should be allowed to speak about the unique significance of the glorification of Christ. *In* the ruling of Christ we encounter "God *in* Christ." There is no dilemma here between Christ's and God's rule. It is not, as is sometimes said, that

God's rule is something abstract, while Christ's kingship is historical. God rules *in* Christ. Though rejecting any sort of abdication theory which views God as retiring in the face of Christ's ascension to the throne, Kuyper was nevertheless profoundly impressed by the universality of Christ's kingly authority, and without reservation named Him as King over all things. Christ rules, but this does not mean that God has abdicated. In this connection, Kuyper points to the modification in the Divine government that took place with Christ's ascension: God's rule then receiving a mediating character through Christ's sitting at His right hand. In this way Kuyper intended to do justice to the historical aspect of God's ruling. A change occurred only in the *mode* of God's rule. After Christ ascended, the same activity that was formerly immediate became mediate through Him who sits on God's right hand.

At this point, Kuyper's view links up with the discussions of the present day, which, in great measure, are concerned with the kingship of Christ, and particularly with the christological basis of the state.

* * *

What is really meant by the christological foundation of the state? Brunner calls the idea of a derivation of the institutions of law and state from the rule of Christ fantastic and impossible. On the other hand, he fully recognizes that state and church both stand under the lordship of Christ.[8] Cullmann interprets Brunner's statement as allowing for a christological basis for the state. He then goes on to say that when the New Testament speaks of Christ's rule over all things, it means a rule that is distinct from His rule over the Church.[9]

According to this view, the universal kingship became effective with Christ's ascension, while its basis was secured in

---

8. Cf. E. Brunner, *Gerechtigkeit*, 1943, p. 321.
9. O. Cullmann, *Königsherrschaft Christi und Kirche in N. T.*, 1941, pp. 7, 8, 11ff.

His death and resurrection. It had an historical beginning, then, and will have an historical end — with Christ's return. Christ's kingdom is "redemptive-historical." Angels and authorities, together with all other things, are now subject to Him, as to the King of kings and Lord of lords. He is Lord of all creation, and, thus, of the state. For this reason, says Cullmann, we may speak in the state's christological basis. But the question still remains as to the real import of this aspect of Christ's rule. For, in Cullmann's view, the kingdom of Christ is not only distinguished from the Church, but both are distinguished from the kingdom of God. The kingdom of God is future, while that of Christ is historically present.

The rule of God, then, seems separated from the rule of Christ. But certainly the Scriptural speech is never this absolute in its distinctions. It sometimes even combines the rules, for example, as the "kingdom of Christ and God" (Eph. 5:5). The kingdom of Jesus Christ is at the same time the kingdom of God.

We would be doing injustice to the New Testament by abstracting the authority of Christ from the government of God. An anthithesis between theocracy and christocracy is the fruit only of speculative thinking. The New Testament sees the ascension as historically unique, but at the same time it shows us that *God* rules the world in Christ. This rule *in* Christ is a particular mode of the Divine government. Our inability to plummet God's method of ruling should not lead us to close our eyes to the irrefutable givens of Scripture; the mystery of the Divine rule in Christ is inseparable from the mystery of the Word become flesh and, like it, shall never be fathomed by us. This is why we may not lightly yield to the notion of a christological basis of the state, which can lead only to attenuation of the trinitarian activity of our God. We can, quite responsibly, say with the Belgic Confession (Art. 36) that God has established governments and that, after the ascension, the more specific relations between Christ, the second person of the Trinity, and governments come to the fore. Barth is incorrect when he says that a hiatus exists in the evangelical confession in regard to government. Nor does such a hiatus exist in Calvin, who speaks of the second Psalm, a Messianic Psalm, in this connection and still does not give the state a so-called christological basis. There is no polarity in his scriptural and historical thought, as there is in that of Barth.

He who consistently maintains the christological basis of human government faces the question of what the basis of the state was before Christ's death and resurrection. The answer, typified in Cullmann, is that even then it was "established in subjection to Jesus Christ." But then he weakens his argument of the historically unique significance of the ascension. And he, in turn, fails to do justice to the scriptural significance of Christ's being placed at God's right hand. We must not and cannot divorce *this* hand of God from the hand with which He rules the world and all things in it. The placing of all powers beneath Christ — the fruit of His suffering and death — limits neither the working of God nor His authority, while it does allow for the unique significance of the ascension in the progression of the one work of the triune God. The scriptures speak quite emphatically about this. Christ has received dominion over all things (Matt.28:18) and a name above every name, that at His Name every knee should bow and every tongue confess that He is Lord, to the glory of God the Father (Phil. 2:10-11). This position of strength is revealed always in a universal and unbounded perspective.

These words must not be emasculated by saying that they mean only that nothing, neither governments nor "powers," can prevail against Christ and His kingdom. The Heidelberg Catechism in Lord's Day 19 speaks concisely of God's ruling through Christ, while the Belgic Confession in Article 36 says that God rules through governments. The discussion should, then, center about the *nature* of God's rule through Christ. It is here that we observe the interdependence of the so-called christological foundation of the state and a distinct view of the connection between government and angelic "powers." This is seen in Barth and Cullmann, among others, and, since it controls their concept of Christ's authority, we should discuss it a bit further.

* * *

The new exegesis of the "powers" of the New Testament[10] proposes that the New Testament reveals a double attitude toward the state. First, there is the positive attitude revealed in Romans 13:1-7. The question is asked how Paul, in view of the total situation, comes by this "remarkably positive statement" regarding the state. It must be remembered, we are told, that Paul sees a connection between government and angelic powers, so that when he speaks of government, the idea of angels always lurks in the background. This notion is derived from the fact that Paul uses the same names, *exousia* and *arche*, for both angelic powers and earthly governments. Paul, it is said, really has angelic powers in mind in Romans 13, and this is the explanation of his respect for the state. He sees something sacred in the angelic powers that stand behind government and he says that it is to them that we must subject ourselves. The angels, after all, are God's creatures, "God's extended arm." They have their origin in God and are His servants.

But this is only one aspect. We cannot limit ourselves to the positive attitude of Romans 13, Barth says, lest we transform the living dynamic of Biblical thought to dead staticism. There is, in the second place, also a marked aloofness, a distance, indeed a critical attitude, in the New Testament over against the state. We begin to grasp this second line of

---

10. Cf. Barth, *Rechtfertigung und Recht*, 1938; Cullmann, *Christus und die Zeit*, 1946, p. 169ff.; also, W. Aalders, *Cultuur en Sacrament*, 1948, p. 63f. For a criticism of this exegesis, see G. Kittle, *Christus and Imperator*, 1939, p. 48f.

thought when we recall that angels can fall. They are, it is true, created in Christ and have Him as their head, but they can also, as angelic powers, become God's enemies. As fallen demons, they can possess governments. The government of Romans 13 can become the government of Revelation 13 — the beast out of the abyss. Thus, because of the nature of these powers, their relationship to the state must be dialectical, and this is revealed in the dialectic of New Testament thought: ordained of God — possibility of fall. In government we may be dealing with fallen angels. They are, through Christ's victory, rendered impotent in principle, but they still, nonetheless, exert their influence and must be withstood.

Barth formerly, in an extraordinary exegesis, interpreted Romans 13 negatively. In his commentary on Romans (date 1922) he explained this chapter as being a prohibition of all revolution, since revolution merely exchanges one form of existence for another and does not bring existence itself under judgment. Since then he has modified his interpretation to that which we have presented above. He says that when the New Testament Church thinks about the state she has before her eyes "the image of . . . active angelic powers." In this way he supposes to explain the "apparent opposition to the state that we find in the New Testament."

A relevant question is: concretely, how can we bring the connection between angelic powers and government into bearing on the kingdom of Christ?

According to Barth, Christ has in His resurrection triumphed over all powers. The state, which originally belonged to Christ, can be demonized, but even when it is under the sway of demons, it has not fully escaped from the rule of Christ. Every rebellion can end only in "the form of unwilling service to the kingdom of Christ." Emancipation or escape from this original arrangement is impossible during the time between Christ's resurrection and His return. The empirical state-power becomes the executive agent of the angelic powers. But the angelic powers must not be construed exclusively as evil. The Gnostics looked on them so and for that reason their great antagonist, Ireneaus, opposed the interpretation of *powers* in Scripture as being angelic powers. If angelic powers were evil powers and nothing else, Paul would not have called us to be in subjection to them. There is no such ultimate dualism in the New Testament. Having been subjected to Christ, these powers have lost their evil character, according to Barth, and now stand under His authority, though this holds only so long as they "remain under Him and do not seek emancipation from their status of servitude." Even now they have a certain limited freedom, and it is within this freedom that they can manifest a tendency toward self-emancipation. In this possibility of breaking away lies the possibility of the demonization of the state. Hence, Barth argues, the Church may not always view the state as under Divine rule. It is a question as to how, in Barth's view, the state can still elicit respect as a positive institution of God. The powers are placed in the service of the kingdom of Christ and are thus deserving of respect. But, on the other hand, it is admitted that they can from time to time escape from their servitude and reveal their demonic character. In its origin the state is not Divine; it receives its respected functions only since it is bound under the kingly authority of Christ. One can, then, hold to a christological founding of the state and still be kept from a truly positive respect for government — at least from such respect for government that we find in the Old Testament: "By me kings reign, And princes decree justice. By me princes rule, And nobles, even all the judges of the earth" (Prov. 8:15, 16). Barth and the other dialectical theologians can see in such a verse only an "earmarking" for future subjection to Jesus Christ, who in the time of the Old Testament had not achieved His present royal position. Only after being bound do the demonic powers receive authority in Christ's kingdom.

* * *

It need not surprise us that this exegesis of Romans 13 has been attacked from many sides. It is clearly not in harmony with the positive statements of Scripture. What is the real meaning of *powers* in this chapter? Out of the approximately ninety times that *power* (*exousia*) appears in the Scripture, it refers in at least eighty of these to the power that someone actually possesses. In this, the constructive element of the angelic power theory becomes clear. The powers to whom "every soul" (Rom. 13:1) must be subject are obviously human governmental powers, which possess their authority as a result of their being instituted by God. We find this not only in Paul, but also in Peter when he writes: "Be subject to every ordinance of man for the Lord's sake: whether to the king, as supreme; or unto governors, as sent by him for vengeance on evil-doers and for praise to them that do well" (I Pet. 2:13, 14). There is a positive respect for government in this passage, in which authorities are concretely specified just as in vs. 17 of the same chapter, in which Peter exhorts us to honor the king (cf. also I Tim. 2:1 ff. and Titus 3:1).

That Peter calls them human institutions does not mean that they carry any less Divine authority. We must, in fact, subject ourselves to them for the Lord's sake, though they remain, nevertheless, purely human institutions, real and concrete powers on the human level; there, visible and demonstrable. The word human indicates the matrix in which the institution operates. It does not denote its origin. The fault of the Barthian exegesis is that it brings the angelic powers into an *essential* connection with government, and sees the grounds for our subjection to government not in its institution by God, but in the conquest of the evil angelic powers by Christ and their servitude in His rule. Actually, according to this concept, the demonized state is the only state, and the state accordingly merits precious little respect. Positive respect is directed to the overpowering by Christ's kingdom, but not to the state itself.

We certainly do not mean to deny that earthly government as a human institution cannot come into league with fallen angels. Scripture, indeed, does speak of this possibility and directs our attention therewith to the background of national life. Consider the human-angels of the Old Testament, of which we read, for example, in Daniel 10:13: "But the prince of the kingdom of Persia withstood me one and twenty days; but, lo, Michael, one of the chief princes, came to help me . . ." This "prince" is generally construed to mean a spiritual power who stood antithetically opposed to Michael and, through him, to the people of God. There are evidently definite evil spirits who exercise influence on the activity of peoples. It is certain that these spiritual disruptive and corruptive influences also go out to earthly powers and governments. We recall also Isaiah 24:21, in this connection, where we read of Jehovah's judgment over "the host of the high ones on high, and the kings of the earth upon the earth." Over against these evil spirits and their influence stands Michael, who "standeth for the children of thy people" (Dan. 12:1). Thus, a close relationship between governments and demons is possible. Kuyper suggested this, too, when he wrote that the influence of fallen angels reaches out over all of life, and not least over governments.

The aims of this kingdom of darkness are the thwarting of God's purpose and the disruption of God's order on earth. God's preservation of life and order with an eye to His kingdom in Jesus Christ is certainly high on the fallen angels' list of targets. The longsuffering revealed in the disposition that God makes of earthly governments is seized as an opportunity to frustrate the use to which God would put government. These demonic powers still have time and power. Revelation 13 can stand along with Romans 13 in the same New Testament. This is not because there is an original and essential relation between demons and governments, but because government is sovereignly instituted by God, inherently analogous to the kingdom of God, and, because of this, an object of Satanic opposition. Satan's opposition to and seduction of government forms a new invasive element in governmental life as instituted by God. It involves a possibility of fall, if government forsakes her Divine calling to service or oversteps the limits of her authority. The new exegesis of angelic powers arises from an awareness of the dangers of the demonized state which tyrannizes life rather than serves it. But this exegesis cannot really stimulate resistance to the totalitarian state. It can only weaken the concept of the positive Divine institution of earthly rule and order. It fails to see where the dangers really lie. The dangers lie in the despising and violating of Divine sovereignty which expresses itself in governmental authority.

This suggests, in turn, that obedience to government also has its limits. These limits become evident whenever the Divine authority that rests on human shoulders is misused. (This danger exists not only for government, but also for other bearers of authority, such as parents. Parental authority can also be demonized. Parents can misunderstand their calling and forget that theirs is a given and responsible authority.) The government can throw off its responsibility and became a power without service, a tyranny denying its own boundaries, boundaries to which Paul so clearly points in Romans 13 (cf. vs. 4). This defiance is certainly inspired by demonic influence, but, on the human level, it in itself progresses to an exaggerated tension with and opposition to the economy of God.

This Divine economy, since Christ's ascension to the right hand of God, is subject to the power of Jesus Christ, the glorified Lord. Through Him, the Father rules all things. His ascension, then, is of decisive historical significance. Though the establishment of the state is not christological but trinitarian, the victory of Christ becomes a crisis for the state — and an intensification of the call to service. The kingdom of God has come with decision, and in this decision and the authority of Christ implied in it, all attempts by the "powers" to gain autonomy are revealed as senseless. Nothing can triumph over this kingdom; neither the presumptive powers of the earth, who refuse to acknowledge their limitations, nor the powers "of the air" — powers concentrated in one power, in the power that fell as lightning from heaven when the kingdom of heaven triumphantly approached (Luke 10:18). The decision still falls in government decisions for or against service to God.

This is not to say that only a Christian government is a valid government. When the cause of the Christian state is pleaded, it is not meant that only Christian government constitutes true government, nor that the Church should involve herself in government, but simply that, in the light of the Gospel, the state should be understood as servant, and that it should recognize and operate within its Divinely imposed limits. In the service of justice, which is continually menaced by human sin and by demons, the state makes the path of the kingdom of Christ through the world a path through an ordered world. The state is not to be despised as being of trifling and external significance in the rule of God. To despise the state is to despise the Noahic covenant, is to underestimate the cross which restores and reestablishes God's justice and law in the redemption of the world.

A shyness to accept this bond between Christ and government has often been prompted by a fear that that which ought to be kept distinct may be confused and that Christ's kingdom would devaluate the laws and punishments of the state. This fear is, indeed, historically understandable for men have not seldom, out of conviction of Divinely forgiven sin, protested against earthly judgment, punishment, and armed might. Men arguing the law of love have given themselves to chaos and lawlessness, passivity and nihilism. These excesses resulted from a misunderstanding of love, from the fallacious idea that only the love of God, and not His justice, could be associated with the kingdom of Christ. His kingdom, however, is rooted in the cross, and allows for no tension between love and justice. In the cross love and justice have been inseparably united (Rom. 3:25). This is why Christ's kingdom can extend over all of life, government included, and why, through Him, the Father can rule all things. There is a Divinely ordained place on earth, then, for government; it is meant to serve the kingdom of Christ in the specific function which it has received by Divine commission. Government takes up its service, its liturgy (Rom. 13:6: *leitourgia*) and in it becomes something comparable to the angels in their liturgical (Heb. 1:14: *leitourgika*) service.

The liturgy of government is — true enough — offered on this earth; it serves in an area of danger, danger of apostasy and demonization. The greater, then, is its responsibility now that the kingdom of Christ has been established and the One Name rules all things. If it is true that the term "liturgy" connotes something of ceremony for Paul, then it becomes even more evident that the government is not glorified and given "sacred" untouchableness, but that the respect owed to government derives from the service it is meant to perform and from the fact that "God through Christ is the recipient of its services."

* * *

It is clear that the laws and the service of government cannot operate in a dialectical or antinomian tension with the kingdom of Christ. However, these laws and this service stand in danger of sin and demons. The government cannot through apostasy become an independent power with independent sig-

PROVIDENCE AS GOVERNMENT 121

nificance, free from the royal lordship of Christ (Rom. 8:38, 39), though, within this lordship, government, in apostasy, can severely distress life and, thus, the Church as well. However, even in apostacy, the powers are bound to serve the kingdom of Christ and will finally be stripped of their evil influence (I Cor. 15:24). The "prince of the powers of the air" still works "in the sons of disobedience" (Eph. 2:2) but every time he trespasses his limits he only underscores the limitlessness of Christ's kingdom. Whenever the image of the state found in Revelation 13 becomes actualized, the believers shall know that this power is no worthy rival of the power of Christ but has already been defeated by Him. The reality of the evil powers avails nothing against Him. The perseverance of the saints is, nevertheless, still necessary (Rev. 13:10) — the saints, who keep the commands of God through faith in Jesus (Rev. 14:12). (It is noteworthy that the perseverance of the saints appears in Revelation 13 — the chapter of the beast.)

Meanwhile, believers are called upon to pray for "kings and all that are in high place" (I Tim. 2:2). Paul indicates by his repetition of synonyms how important he considers this duty: "supplications, prayers, intercessions, thanksgivings." We are to pray and supplicate before the face of God for His blessing on earthly government in her service in the world "that we may lead a tranquil and quiet life in all godliness and gravity." We are to ask God that He, through government, will bless our lives and spread His justice through the world so that life may have opportunity to expand in service to Him. The course of the kingdom of God is not in our hands; He charts the course. The Heidelberg Catechism is relevant to this when it says: in prosperity, thankfulness and in adversity, patience. Faith in God's rule through Christ may be tried when we are faced by the powers of the world and when we hear many, who had laughed at the idea of real demons, again talking seriously about the demonization of life. Only the light of the Gospel can dispel this confusion and hold our eyes open for Christ's kingdom.

* * *

When the new idea of government and angelic-power relationship was first discussed, the Providence of God was also brought into consideration. It has been said, for example, that the Providence doctrine cannot be understood apart from the angelic powers or demons. Without accepting the new exegesis, we must agree that dogmatics runs the danger of considering the confession of God's ruling too abstractly. Faith in what the Scriptures say about angels and demons was attacked at its root long before the crisis of the Providence doctrine of this century. Biblical acceptance of the influence of angels and demons was considered as a concession to or conditioning by the unenlightenment of the times. In our informed era, we were told, such supernatural nonsense must be sifted out of the New Testament. The elimination of demonization played a role in the "genial providence" notion of the eighteenth century, and the theology of the nineteenth century also assumed that this part of the New Testament could be disregarded. Kuyper, in the nineteenth century, said that a rejection of evil spirits and the Devil ends with a denial of the existence of angels in any form. And we observe that, outside of theological circles, to the present day angels do not receive the recognition that they do in the New Testament. If they are not consciously denied, they are relegated to a vague sentimental recollection of their appearances in sacred history or to the hymn singers in the field of Ephratha on Christmas eve. In fact, the Church by and large today is probably more conscious of demons than of angels.

Modern theology, however, prompted by the tensions in and devilishness of the modern state, is again earnestly discussing angels. The danger of this sudden revival of interest in angelology is that the nature and function of angels shall be defined by the cultural phenomena of a certain time. This is certainly at present the case. As previously first demons and then angels were rejected, so now, via the demons, angels have returned to the attention of theology. The tension of the times has led to an unacceptable notion of the relationship of angels to government, but this should not hold us back from further reflection on God's ruling through Christ to Whom all angelic powers are subject. And since demonization is currently on the agenda of dogmatic study, it is not impossible that, precisely in this time, Scripture may be listened to more attentively than before as it speaks about the angels of God. The tension of the times can lead to new insights.

Currently the problem of demonization is posed in connection with the terror of the totalitarian state and with the dehumanization to which our century, in spite of its background of development, has been witness. This could lead us to a better appreciation of what the Scriptures teach us about angels, their service (Heb. 1:14), their worship (Is. 6; Luke 2:14), and their joys (Luke 15:7, 10). The understanding of the service of angels must involve, in addition to seeing it as an example of the fulfillment of the will of God, an appreciation of their work under God's rule in Christ whose kingdom they are permitted to serve. Should not the teaching about the relation between the service of the angels and our salvation keep us from attenuating our thinking on this subject? And should not the scriptural teaching about angels have existential significance now that the problem of the state is unprecedentedly acute, and when study of demonology marks the demise of the last remnant of nineteenth century theology?

It may be that the offence of the words of Scripture is still too strong. It may be that subjective bias still prejudges the idea of angels. But it may also be that with demonology in the center of theological interest the "depopulated heaven" may be felt to be an impoverishment. Within the convulsed life of the peoples, threatened by the dangers always implicit in the service of the government, the Church must become concrete in praying for the salutary service of angels. Angels are not in the center of the stage where there is room only for the Lord Himself, but they do service in the wings; and this service is directly connected with the main performance — the coming of the kingdom. Our doctrine of angels must never become anything like Roman Catholic mariology. But neither must we ever think, as did the nineteenth century theologians, that no angels or demons stand between us and God.

He who sees the kingdom of Christ revealed, according to the Scriptures, in the irresistibleness of His justice and love, may well be praying earnestly in the near future, not *to* the angels, but *for* their service. The angels *serve* in the kingdom that has come, comes, and is yet to come. There is no place here for speculation. The Church must be warned away from all abstract thought in her Providence doctrine. This may now mean that we realistically anticipate the service of the angels in the kingdom of Christ.

CHAPTER V

A Third Aspect?

COOPERATION, or, as it is otherwise called, concurrence, usually receives a place in dogmatics between the other two aspects of Providence, sustenance and government. The idea of concurrence has occasioned a good many debates in the history of dogmatics: some wishing to expell it from dogmatics as a "foreign body," others honoring it as a valuable insight into God's Providence. What is intended by this idea of concurrence? If we understand this we shall be better able to evaluate the differences of opinion surrounding it.

Bavinck uses the term concurrence as expressing "the manner in which God exercises His Providence in the world."[1] We can speak of the cooperation of God, says Bavinck, since it is apparent that each creature within God's Providence possesses and maintains his own being and nature, his own life and life-pattern. The entire creature is dependent on God, but receives, through the working of God, the possibility for its own creaturely activity. "God, nevertheless, maintains things in such a state, and works in them in such a way, that they themselves cooperate as second causes."[2] The Providence of God, Bavinck insists, does not negate, but rather honors and develops that which God created. Bavinck then accepts the doctrine of concurrence and second causes, an idea which, he says, can find a proper place neither in pantheism nor deism. In pantheism the second causes are identified with God, while in deism the second cause is divorced from the first cause, that is, God.

---
1. H. Bavinck, *Gereformeerde Dogmatiek*, II, p. 569.
2. *Ibid.*, p. 570.

It appears, then, that the term concurrence has to do with the relation between Divine and human activity. It is this relation which the doctrine of concurrence is intended to illuminate. The question to which we must then address ourselves is this: Is there sufficient reason to consider Providence as concurrence (or cooperation) in addition to Providence as sustenance and government?

* * *

This problem has perennially arisen, understandably, since it involves the question of whether total human dependence upon God leaves room for significant creaturely activity and full human responsibility. Bavinck formulates the problem by saying that the second causes are absolutely subordinate to God as first cause, but nevertheless remain, in this subordination, genuine and actual causes. What does this mean?

The relation between God's work and man's work is a problem that is not peculiar to the Providence doctrine. It appears also — and then most acutely — in the doctrine of salvation. There it is the problem of the connection between God's grace and our faith, between grace and freedom, and between grace and works. The Church's struggle with pelagianism, semi-pelagianism, and other forms of synergism were defined by this question. The Scriptures themselves awaken our attention to the relationship, as Paul says: "Work out your own salvation with fear and trembling; for it is God who worketh in you both to will and to work, for his good pleasure" (Phil. 2:12, 13). Paul cuts straight through the apparent dualism (though not the duality) between God's work and ours. He indicates a unique connection, which is expressed particularly in the word *for*. Our activity finds its persistent motivation in the fact of God's working *in* us.

The idea of concurrence is not limited specifically to soteriology, however, but is employed in a more general sense which

A THIRD ASPECT?

includes all creatures. We deal not only with a warning and command: Work! for God works!, but with an objectively existent relation, so to speak, between God's work and all creaturely activity. It is this relationship that man has tried to understand and explain with the help of the doctrine of concurrence. It was meant to show that God's activity did not exclude or annul human enterprise, but that, conversely, human activity became the more significant as the activity of God revealed itself more fully and richly. One can say — to use an expression common to the theological debate — that the Divine activity is all inclusive, but not all exclusive. There would seem to be little that is problematical in these views, since the Scripture nowhere suggests that God's work is limited by human activity or that God's activity negates human enterprise. Yet much debate has been waged around the idea of concurrence. And it will reward us to go into the question, since implicated in it is a believing understanding of the nature of Divine work and our activity and responsibility.

The teaching of concurrence has been opposed for various reasons. Some see it as made necessary only by the traditional, scholastic Church teaching of sustenance, which applied only to the substance of things, leaving their activity unexplained. Hence, the idea of concurrence. "Reject the scholastic distinction between activity and substance," it is said, "and the teaching of concurrence will be resolved into that of sustenance."[3] Paul Althaus's criticism is of a different nature. He rejects concurrence, as he rejects the idea of "permissive will," because "with it, the rule of God and man are, in an impossible manner, finally identified in our thought."[4] Althaus suspects that the concurrence doctrine is an attempt to fathom the mystery of God's activity in its re-

---
3. Horst Stephan, *Glaubenslehre*, 1928, pp. 104ff. Cf. also Schleiermacher, *Der Christliche Glaube*, 1884, I, pp. 218ff.
4. P. Althaus, *Die Christliche Wahrheit*, 1948, Vol. II, p. 109.

lation to ours. We do not have the courage, he says, to let Scripture speak, so we seek a logical synthesis.

We find a similar objection, though from another quarter, in Charles Hodge. Hodge is of the judgment that in the concurrence doctrine man tries "to explain the inexplicable," not content with "the simple and certain declaration of the Bible that God does govern all his creatures and all their actions." In concurrence we want to know more than this, we want to know "how this is done." But such knowledge is out of the question, since "the mode of God's action we cannot possibly understand." The result is, in Hodge's mind, that we land in all sorts of metaphysical questions which no one can solve. "What real knowledge does it communicate? All we know and all we need to know is 1) that God does govern all his creatures, and 2) that this is His own infinite purity and excellence."[5]

There is a good element of truth in these criticisms. It is true that we are continually tempted to probe into hidden things. The question is important, therefore, whether we, in the concurrence doctrine, succumb to the temptation to try to "explain the inexplicable," or whether the doctrine actually offers valuable aid to our understanding of Divine Providence.

* * *

An interest in the relation between God's work and ours certainly need not lead to speculation. The Scriptures continually speak of such a relation. And if the concurrence doctrine intends only to underscore the fact that God's work does not blot out human activity, but defines and contains it, then there can be no single Scriptural objection to it. But it would then be difficult to understand why concurrence should be given a place in dogmatics alongside of God's sustenance and government. For if concurrence means nothing more than a rejection of all identification of or dualism between Divine and

---

5. C. Hodge, *Systematic Theology*, II, pp. 604ff.

A THIRD ASPECT?

human activity, it is fully dealt with in the other two elements of Providence. One may ask, then, and not without reason, if all that is relevant to the study of Providence is not limited to the two aspects: sustenance and government?

Reflection on the relation between God's activity and ours was intensified by the rise of deism. In opposition to deism it was said that God continually had to move in his creatures with His almighty and omnipresent power in order to be the real cause of their actions, and to see that the divinely decreed effect was attained. But in the concurrence doctrine worked out at that time, no really new light was shed that had not been observed in former times — by Calvin, for instance. It is indeed a question whether the various views of concurrence were not symptomatic of an obscuration of the original Reformation insight. It has, in fact, been observed that the idea of concurrence as an aspect of Providence was first developed only when the florescence of the Reformation had begun to decline. Over against deism it might have been well simply to have confessed in Biblical fashion Divine sustaining and Divine ruling, both of which are diametrically opposed to all forms of deism. The idea of concurrence adds nothing independent or new to the confession of Providence. He who understands well the Biblical teaching of God's government knows that it is no despotism, compulsion, or sort of overpowering which renders real creaturely activity null or impossible. He knows that it is a Divine ruling *in* and *over* all creaturely enterprise. Our fathers were, with their insight into Providence as they expressed it in their confessions, well armed against deism and pantheism without having the doctrine of concurrence. Does it now serve a purpose to speak of *co*-operation in the relation between God's work and ours? It is hardly avoidable that the idea of cooperation — be it unintended — carries with it the suggestion that God *co*-operates with His creatures. The term as such does not sufficiently avoid the appearance that we begin with human activity and then see God as co-operator or co-runner (*co*ncurrence) with already active man.

Theologians have often seen the unsatisfactoriness of this term and, to avoid misunderstanding, have said that the Divine activity is simultaneous, coincident with human activity. Divine concurrence is, they have insisted, not an activity following upon the activity already initiated by man; not a single act is performed or begun without Divine Providence. Still, human activity forms the point of departure for thinking in terms of concurrence, while God is seen as thereupon cooperative. This makes it hard to purify the concept of concurrence of every off-color element. The intent — to take the middle road between deism and pantheism — is clear, and we honor it, but this intent does not make the doctrine of concurrence any more helpful in presenting the all-embracing activity of God in its unfathomable reality.

There is no poverty of insight in the confessions. The ramparts over which the Church must stand watch, against pantheism and deism, are quite evident in them. That we have found it necessary to posit a third locus, concurrence, alongside sustenance and government certainly is no indication of progress — to say nothing for the moment of the many speculative ideas often occasioned by this doctrine which have only weakened the force of the creeds.

The concurrence doctrine is not intended only as a defence against pantheism and deism. It is also an attempt to elucidate the relationship between the work of God and human *sin*. It was above all the problem of this relationship that the idea of a Divine concurrence in all human activity emphasized. Bavinck, for example, writes that God enters with His omnipotence into every second cause, is present with His essence in the beginning, continuing, and end of every second cause, and, thus, causes both its willing and working according to His good pleasure. We must respond, however, by asking how he wishes us to understand this *in respect to sin*. His

A THIRD ASPECT? 131

words fittingly indicate the reality of man's act of faith within the work of God, but what about man's sinful acts? This is the question that faces us in the concurrence doctrine: how are we to conceive of Divine cooperation in sin? Does cooperation include sin, or is it only in good works that we may speak of God's cooperation?

We read in Philippians 2:12 that God works both the willing and the doing. This has to do with His act, which the believer recognizes in profound thankfulness and because of which he bestirs himself toward attainment of salvation. Not the ability to will alone, but the willing and doing themselves are accomplished by God. But now, if Philippians 2 is quoted to illustrate the concurrence doctrine, does it also illustrate the connection between God's working and man's sinful willing and doing? This question receives extensive treatment in every consideration of the idea of cooperation and is generally prefaced by the confession that God cannot be the author of sin. But how can this premise — to which Calvin attached such great importance — be made to function in the concurrence doctrine? That is the crucial question which we always run up against.

We can illustrate the difficulty by observing how Bavinck handles the problem.[6] He emphasizes that there is no division of labor between God and man. As for the effect of an act: "the product is in the same sense wholly a product of the first and wholly a product of the second cause." And sinful acts? Is sin wholly a product of the first as well as the second cause? To escape this dilemma the old distinction between form and matter is generally used. Bavinck formulates it thus: "Man speaks, acts, believes, and it is God alone who lends the sinner all the life and energy that he needs to commit a sin; yet, the subject and author of the sin is man, and not God." This construction gives the impression that man receives the ability or power and then, on his own, misuses it. The gift has

---
6. H. Bavinck, *Gereformeerde Dogmatiek*, II, pp. 575ff.

nothing to do with its use or misuse; it is, in itself as given, unqualified. God, according to Bavinck, lends ability, and, thereupon, man uses this ability in the wrong direction. But this still does not place the critical question of concurrence and sin before us. Bavinck goes further by way of analogy: "Wood burns, and it is God alone who makes it burn. Formally, however, the burning must be ascribed, not to God, but only to the wood as subject." The phrase "makes it burn" is a much stronger and more exact expression than the phrase "lending of ability" which Bavinck first used. But substitute, now, "makes him sin" for "makes it burn," and it becomes clear, first, how difficult our problem is, and, secondly, how little the form-matter scheme helps to solve it. Bavinck himself speaks of an "influx" of God's omnipotence into every second cause. It is quite true that, as Bavinck says, the sinner receives all his ability from God and then misuses it. But this does not really explain concurrence; at most, it only takes the sharp edge off the problem. Bavinck himself knew this, as his analogy of the burning wood shows.

Kuyper, alert to the fact that concurrence was more than a lending of ability, spoke of the so-called influx of God's omnipotence. This means, according to Kuyper, that God not only provides the ability so that through it the sinner can work, "but that He Himself is the 'Worker' in everything." It follows from God's omnipresence that "He can never be unemployed and, further, that He cannot merely deposit a supply of power."[7] The influx is not a mere provision of ability, but an active, personal operation. This, according to Kuyper, brings out the specific Reformed character of the confession of Providence. There is a Divine energy in all things: "the energy, by which sin is committed, is a power of God."[8] This seems to suggest that God cooperates in sin. Kuyper answers this possible objection by saying that the ethical quality which

---

7. A. Kuyper, *Dictaten Dogmatiek*, Locus III, p. 66.
8. *Ibid.*, p. 191.

A THIRD ASPECT? 133

defines an act as sin "is not created by God, but by the moral creature in that he wills with sinful disposition and sinful intent."[9] This is about as sharply as the problem of concurrence can be formulated, but it still does not clarify the relation between God's activity and man's sin. It only reminds us again that we shall never fathom the Divine over-ruling, certainly not in regard to the sinful activity of man.

This inscrutability need not shock us nor fill us with a panic which might haunt our entire lives. The problem is resolved, though not rationally, in confession of guilt and in faith. There is a solution, but it is the solution of faith, which knows its own responsibility — as it knows the unapproachable holiness of God. He who does not listen in faith to God's voice is left with an insoluble dilemma. God's revelation does not crucify our thinking; it only judges our proud and sinful thinking. To persist in unconverted thinking is, in the end, to shove our own guilt and responsibility aside. No distinction between the formal and material sides of sinful activity can be of help here. To use this distinction is to pay continual toll to the pressure toward logical synthesis. How could we expect to grasp the awful majesty of God with a form-matter scheme?

Now and then one finds an intuitive discernment. For example, consider the formulation of Berkhof. He begins his discussion of concurrence by rejecting certain incorrect constructions: 1) that it consists merely in a general communication of power, without determining the specific action in any way, and 2) that divine concurrence is only partial: God doing a part of the work and man a part. On the contrary, says Berkhof: "The fact is that the same deed is in its entirety both a deed of God and a deed of the creature. It is a deed of God in so far as it is determined from moment to moment by the will of God. And it is a deed of man in so far as God realizes it through the self-activity of the creature. There is inter-penetration here, but no mutual limitation." Indeed,

---
9. *Ibid.*, p. 149.

"the impulse to action and movement proceeds from God . . . . There must be an influx of divine energy before the creature can work."[10] Berkhof uses, as did Bavinck, the form-matter distinction in sinful activity: "the divine concurrence energizes man and determines him efficaciously to the specific act, but it is man who gives the act its *formal* quality and is therefore responsible for its sinful character." But Berkhof does not consider this a solution: "the problem of God's relation to sin remains a mystery."[11] He is quite right in this. The distinction between form and matter sheds no new light; it merely restates the problem.

The distinction is, however, often offered in dogmatic studies as a solution. Actually, the terms themselves have little significance for this problem. Let us note Heppe's use of the distinction. "*It is clear* that God is hereby not the author of sin as long as in the sinful act, in and for itself, the material element (the physical action) and the formal element (the sinful disposition adopted in it) are correctly distinguished. Man is literally driven by God to the act in and by itself, that is to say, God gives him the physical basis for his sinful attitude. However, the *sinfulness of the disposition* is so exclusively the fruit of man's own will that, while He does not hinder the awakening of sin in the heart of man, which is altogether just on His part, and intentionally allows the aroused sin to become an act, God is in no sense the efficient cause of sin, though He may be called the negative cause."[12] But the problem remains unsolved by saying that the power of God in all things is a permitting or not-hindering. The point of departure for the influx idea was that all activity both in disposition and act falls under and does not limit this Divine influx of power. That the physical basis for sin is distin-

---

10. L. Berkhof, *Systematic Theology*, 1941, p. 172ff.
11. *Ibid.*, p. 175.
12. H. Heppe, *Reformierte Dogmatik*, 1861, p. 186.

A THIRD ASPECT?

guished from the disposition which drives man to sin offers no further help.

Support for this argument is often sought by a negative qualification of the sinful act, as when it is said that sin lies not in the act as such, but rather in a lack of a positive good activity. Matthew 25:42, 43 is quoted, then, in which Christ rebukes, not so much an act as a lack of action. The argument, however, breaks down as we observe that this reproach is actually part of a broader judgment on the *"workers* of unrighteousness."

We can respect the distinction between the formal and material aspect of sin in so far as its intention is to maintain the holiness of God even in His omnipotent ruling of a sinful world. The way in which the distinction is often used, however, leads repeatedly to a vitiating of the preaching of the Word.

We should be alerted here for every logical systematization. Recall once more the word of Philippians 2:12, which at first sight appears to offer a logical solution to a complex problem. It may seem possible to deduce a *general relationship* from this verse even though it appears in a soteriological context. But the fact of sin immediately raises misgivings about this generalization. The text makes it clear that the relation between the work of God and that of man is such that the believer has only God to thank for the beginning, progression, and completion of his salvation. For true faith this causal relationship is self-evident. May we, however, generalize in the same way as to our *sinful* activity — to satisfy our need for logical consistency? One feels that we have, precisely at this point, arrived at the border of our thinking, and that it is not permitted us to set forth as a logical conclusion: we do the sinful deed, *because* God works in us to will and to do *sinfully*. The believer speaks otherwise and confesses that God is not the author of sin; he confesses his own sin. Rather than seeking to resolve the problem by way of the concurrence doctrine, we must let the Scriptures speak and must respect the boundaries that they set up for our thinking. It is, from this point of view, gratifying to observe the hesitations with which the concurrence doctrine is usually circumscribed. The formidable logical structure is shattered when, for example, Bucan observes that the Divine influx is different in the good act than in the evil act,[13] and also when Turretin admits that concurrence does not offer the solution, but that it belongs to the most difficult questions of dogmatics.[14]

Mastricht said that God is not the author of sin, since it is an a priori that He cannot disobey the law, that He is "higher than all law."[15] Having said this, he has made the relationship between God's work and our sin no more perspicuous. But he does in this way try to consent to the Scriptures and accept implicitly the *absolute holiness of God*. This was the point of departure for the reformers, particularly for Calvin. Calvin accepts as axiomatic that the sinner may never throw the guilt of his evil acts on God. He is convinced that God has Satan and the ungodly so under His power that "He directs their malice to whatever end he pleases."[16] The reformer also opposes the distinction between God's permission and His will, which distinction, he says, is only a subterfuge. If God does all that He wills (Ps. 115:3), then His doing, like His willing, pertains to *all* activities of man. Calvin refers to Job, who, robbed by *Satan* of all he owned, said, "The *Lord* has taken away."

Calvin was particularly concerned with this problem in relation to the complexities of history, to God's acts in the acts

---

13. "Deus non infundit malitiam in voluntates malorum, sicut infundit bonitatem in corda piorum." (Quoted by H. Heppe, *Reformierte Dogmatik*, p. 203.)
14. Turretin: quaestio "ex difficilimis, quae in Theologia occurrant," cf. also "Ex nostris quidam concursum tantum praevium volunt quo ad bona opera gratiae, et in aliis omnibus simultaneum sufficere existimant." (*Institutio Theologiae elencticae*, 1734, I, p. 559.)
15. From H. Heppe, *Reformierte Dogmatik*, p. 202.
16. J. Calvin, *Institutes*, I, 18, 1.

of men — in the acts, for instance, of the Jews, of Pilate, and of Judas in the suffering of Christ. If, says Calvin, Christ was not crucified according to God's will, whence would come our redemption? Even in sin there is a certain impelling influence of God; the evil spirit which drove Saul on is a spirit sent by God. God is incomprehensible, but He lives, at the same time, in unapproachable *light*. Calvin anticipates the objection which inevitably and continually arises: ". . . if God not only uses the agency of the impious, but governs their designs and affections, he is the author of all crimes; and therefore men are undeservedly condemned, if they execute what God has decreed, because they obey his will."[17] But Calvin recognizes here the limits of our thinking and he bows before the holy, Divine activity, which is always wise and good. This recognition must lead to a humble listening to all that the Scriptures teach. We do not find the theological distinction between form and matter in Calvin. He has no need of a perspicuous synthesis; it is enough for him to know the holiness of God and that man is the subject of his own sin. He bows before revelation, which is perspicuous enough for him who will humbly listen to it.

Calvin, therefore, also considers the idea of Divine permission as an obscuration of the Scriptural insight. This need not suggest an absolute rejection of the use of the word. The term permission has played a legitimate role in Reformed theology. But when the word is used in order to bring the relation between Divine and human (sinful) activity into a logical synthesis the Divine activity is limited, since it is then placed on the same level with human activity. Consistently maintained, the concept of permission always introduces a tension that is foreign to Biblical revelation. The word permission suggests that God allows the sinner to decide in freedom against God's command. God is, then, in His Providence, a balcony observer of a contest whose outcome is never

---
17. *Ibid.*, I, 18, 4.

certain. It suffices Him to create a playground and leave the decision to man whether it will be the scene of sin or of obedience. Sin, then, lies ultimately in man's power of decision. and God's action becomes mere reaction to man's decision. Reformed theology, therefore, dismisses the "bare permission" idea as too simple a solution and rightly recalls us to the work of God as it, with particular lucidity, is here and there concretely indicated in the Scriptures, revealed in all sorts of sinful human activity, as well as in Divine hardening and reprobating.

According to Ebrard,[18] Reformed theology teaches that God, in ethical matters, does not determine but allows free reign. In the ethical arena only God's foreknowledge is active, and that passively rather than effectively. Ethics form God's boundary. Actually, however, this sort of boundary imposed on God is precisely what Reformed theology rejects. When Reformed theology does speak of permission it does not intend this sort of self-restriction. The term permission is used, especially in reference to the fall, to indicate the element of freedom, the responsibility, which man was given in paradise. But the idea of permission is always qualified as being active in nature, and as forming no limitation to God's purposeful activity. Divine permission is, in fact, meant by Reformed theology as a work of Divine majesty.

That the word permission is not totally repudiated by Reformed theology can be accounted for by its strong distaste — on Biblical grounds — for determinism and by a desire to express the thought that good and evil do not originate in the same way, as "effects" of one general Divine causality. This is a genuinely Biblical motif. One also finds the idea of permission in the Scriptures: "Who in the generations gone by suffered all the nations to walk in their own ways" (Acts 14:16). But that this "suffered" is no passive permission appears from the fact that God's deed, God's judgment, was *in*

---

18. Ebrard, *Christliche Dogmatik*, I, 1862, pp. 389, 390.

the paths of sin, and that God "gave them up . . . unto uncleanness" (Rom. 1:24-28). He who accepts the idea of permission as a *solution* to the problem of the relation between God's work and man's sin succumbs to the natural desire for logical synthesis. He can thereupon arrive only at a dualistic division of labor between God and man. And this is to pervert the testimony of Scripture.

It is also noteworthy that some theologians of the twentieth century have had an eye for this danger. Althaus, for example, considers the idea of permission as an evident emasculation of Biblical preaching. In the doctrine of permission there is a "deleting of a number of events from the work of God and, thus, a conceiving of the work of God and that of man, not as coinciding, but as parallel in the nature of two finite powers. In truth, man may not abstract anything in history from His doing, not even the sinful acts of men, lest the Deity of God be sacrificed."[19]

Barth, too, discusses the idea of permission at some length. Whenever the distinction between the "efficient" and the "permissive" will of God is made, says Barth, it is "evidently with an eye to the problem of theodicy." According to Barth, there is no terrain that is independent of God. There is no other possibility than to "seek the ground even of this sphere in God's will." Nevertheless, with this in mind, Barth still wishes to speak of a permissive will. There is a will of God "by virtue of which He not only gives the creature his existence and reality, his proper independence and freedom, and therewith his true creaturely Being, but by virtue of which He, because He wills the creature's free obedience and, thus, his salvation, chooses not to render impossible the creature's misuse of independence and freedom, and therefore chooses not to make it impossible for man to make impossible and destroy his creaturely Being."[20] Thus, God's efficient will

---
19. P. Althaus, *Die Christliche Wahrheit*, II, p. 109.
20. K. Barth, *Kirchliche Dogmatik*, II, 1, p. 670.

is at the same time His permissive will. Says Barth: "None of these propositions may be weakened: neither the character of evil as evil, nor the absolute goodness of the will of the Divine Creator, nor the omnipotence, even over evil, of the Divine Lord's will." Thus, sin is definitely not to be considered out of the reach of God's will. Permission, an *act* in the full sense of the word, is a *necessity*. "A will, which would be so self-seeking (even though it were the Divine holiness and righteousness) that it could only maintain and perpetuate itself, and could not also make concessions would not be a Divine, but a demonic and Satanic will."[21] Barth tries to keep the permissive will from being opposed to the effective will of God. But his identification of the idea of God's permission with the notion of concessions, and his accent on the Divine *necessity* of permission are fruits of speculation. They give a solution which only raises further problems at another point. Besides, the limits of the unsearchability of God's manner of working are trespassed. Nevertheless, Barth is right in his criticism of the idea of permission as a limitation of the work of God. There is, Barth insists, no inoperative, passive will in God.

There is every reason to exercise the greatest care in speaking about God's permitting. To view it as a self-limitation, out of a desire for a logical synthesis, is to give pertinence to Calvin's sharp criticism. When permission is really used to indicate the manner of Divine ruling, by which He grants room *within* His ruling for human freedom and responsibility, then the line of Biblical thinking has not been wholly abandoned. For this freedom, this creaturely freedom, receives a place *in* God's rule of the world. Here the panorama of the fall and the resultant history of sin and perdition unfolds before our eyes. He who does injustice to this freedom does injustice to the Word of God, which already in paradise places man at a crossroad and gives him the choice of which road he will

---

21. *Ibid.*, p. 672.

A THIRD ASPECT?   141

take. But in the light of Scripture, it is decisive that this creaturely freedom poses no threat or limitation to the sovereign and almighty Divine enterprise. This exposes the heart of the problem. When we put emphasis on this it is not that we hope in this way to explain the relation between God's ruling and man's sinning. On the contrary, it is precisely in this incomparability of the sovereign work of God, unlimited by creaturely freedom, that explanation is made impossible, and we are forced to direct ourselves to the Divine revelation which reveals to us the almighty activity of God and, at the same time, teaches human responsibility. In this way, history, as it progresses under God's providential rule, becomes tremendously serious. And anyone who does not take both this Divine ruling and human responsibility seriously can never rightly understand history. He will always assume one or the other of two basically erroneous perspectives: either he will make man the lord of history, creator of events, holding history in his hand or propelling it through the power of his personality — with the "leaders of men" blazing the trail; or he will make history a Divine game in which human beings are pushed about like chessmen, void of responsibility.

* * *

In regard to the sovereignty of the Divine providential activity and the place which man takes in it the question always arises whether this, in fact, must not lead to rigorous determinism — in spite of creaturely freedom. Is it possible to avoid determinism once we accept God's sovereign rule over all things? Do not all historical figures, their creaturely acting, willing, and deciding notwithstanding, become marionettes or, as the Scriptures themselves say, clay in the hands of the potter (Is. 45:9)? Is the absolute dependence of all things on God perhaps a theological bromide, disguising what is actually Divine, whimsical and pitiless sport? This is the persistent, burning question: how can we divorce (to distinguish is not enough) the confession of God's Providence over all things from what one generally considers a heartless determinism? This question is of primary significance for the correct understanding of the Providence doctrine and for preaching the Providence of God in an age badly infected by deterministic influences. It is certainly no theoretical question, but a problem that at once touches the practice of faith. What then is the relationship between faith in Providence and determinism?

* * *

It is undeniable that deterministic motifs have influenced theology and have often cast a shadow on the confession of God's Providence. This is historically explainable from the fact that the Reformation had to stress its opposition to the notion of free will which was then current, and from the fact that determinism also seeks its strength in denying free will. Superficially viewed, this common battle against free will seems to imply an important point of agreement between Reformation thought and determinism. But while monistic determinism seems, when shallowly considered, to reveal certain points of agreement with Reformed teaching, it is in essence nevertheless utterly foreign to the Reformation doctrine of Providence. Only a clear perception of the radical difference between the Providence doctrine and determinism will guard us against much confusion — confusion that can rob the believer of the comfort of his trust in Providence. The real meaning of many words will have to be unmasked. We shall have to be dissatisfied when we hear someone speaking of, and even quoting Scripture about, sovereignty or absolute determinism, or of a "sense of utter dependence" (Schleiermacher). We shall have to ascertain the real content that hides within these ideas.

In the history of human thought, the dilemma is usually construed as: determinism or indeterminism. As is apparent, the dilemma revolves particularly around the problem of the freedom of the will. It is true that not all determinists are fatalists. Fatalism proposes fate or destiny as the determining factor, while theological determinists sometimes speak of determining by Divine sovereignty. But this does not remove the basic structural correspondence between determinism and fatalism. To demonstrate why determinism is unacceptable we may begin with the observation of the deep cleft between determinism and naive consciousness. Most persons live with a non-scientific and, for the most part, an uncritical concept of freedom in which they assume that they "freely" act from moment to moment. Despite all the relationships in which man is involved and which in great measure define his activity, he lives with an ineradicable conviction that he of himself chooses, decides, and acts. There is, thus, observable in all non-scientific thought and action a tendency toward indeterminism, a striving for freedom and autonomy, for the possibility of spontaneous and undetermined choice. Man wants to take and hold life in his own hands, in spite of all objective and at times strong fetters.

These tendencies are apparent not only in naive and pre-scientific thought, but in scientific and philosophical thinking. Here, too, again and again, we observe an animated defence of human freedom. Especially when mechanistic natural science resolved all of life in quantitative relations was there always either silent or vocal protest. As Dooyeweerd strikingly puts it, there was always an insistence on the primacy of personality over against the tyranny of natural science, which, consistently maintained, left no room for the "spirit," nor for real human freedom. This explains why, in an irrationalistic age with its savage antagonism to the total rationalization of human life, the idea of freedom assumes the center of attention, as is true, for example, with Jean Paul Sartre.

Determinism lives in strained relations with all such notions of freedom. Determinists contend that the popular, naive consciousness is mistaken and needs corrective criticism. If one were willing to dig a bit deeper, it is said, he would of necessity arrive at determinism. For, though man apparently chooses freely and with a free will in the various situations which involve him, his free will is itself definitely determined. "I usually will what I wish, but I always will what I must." says the determinist. The idea of freedom is, according to determinism, only an illusion, a misunderstanding of the real human situation, a gross overestimate of one's own independence. The illusion is understandable, but runs aground on fixed, determined reality. Determinism finds its grounds in the idea of an all-embracing, all-governing causality. All things have a definite cause. They never stand on their own, neither can they be lifted above the interdependence of all events. As the formula 2 times 2 equals 4 is unassailable and determined by fixed mathematical laws, so does one unavoidable event follow another, though man is usually quite unaware of the causal relation. We are determined in everything: we are not free, but absolutely fettered. Nothing we choose or do is new; everything is a natural result of previous situations. Atheistic determinism goes no further with these causes than the boundaries of this world.

But there is also a non-atheistic determinism, which traces causality to God, whom it views as the absolute determining first cause who brings about all things in their relationships. Bondage of the will is the immediate implication of the almighty activity of God. The burning question for non-atheistic determinism has always been whether man, being thus determined, can still be held responsible for his acts. Is it not so, that man acts, but acts exactly as he, out of absolute necessity, must? Does not this kind of causality, then, exclude human responsibility, since absolute necessity and human responsibility are mutually exclusive? And do not guilt and punishment become just as invalid and meaningless as responsibility?

A THIRD ASPECT? 145

All determinists, of course, have not gone on to these conclusions. Many, in one way or another, have tried to reserve a place for responsibility, and therewith for guilt and punishment, within life's determined circle. It has been remarked that we can often observe in determinism a sudden relapse into indeterminism. This is nothing but a flight from its own consequences. For he who measures man by causal categories and sees him as defined in every situation by his bondage, as determined by facts and factors that coercively govern each moment of his life, must also relieve this determined man of his responsibility.

One is reminded here, by way of parallel, of the war criminals who defended themselves by saying that they acted according to order: "A command is a command." A concept of absolute determining causality is sympathetic with this kind of talk. If a judge of law were to accept such a theory, he would have to excuse every delinquent from sentence. A criminal is only a non-responsible link in a causal chain. In determinism man is never responsible for a new act in a definite situation and, thus, can never be considered guilty regardless of which act he chooses to perform. Deterministic causality principally and consistently pronounces man morally free by denying him his volitional freedom.

We need not accept determinism-indeterminism as the only alternatives. It is possible that the problem is not altogether fairly formulated in this dilemma. This is why one should take care that he, from aversion to determinism, does not, without further reflection, flee into the arms of indeterminism. This caution is the more necessary since indeterminism, as we meet it in the history of thought, often appears in the garb of an idealistic anthropology which attempts to rescue the free, autonomous personality from the tyranny of natural science. The plea for indeterminism usually implies a plea for the sovereign freedom of the autonomous individual. The sovereign individual of indeterministic philosophical idealism does not tolerate determinism. He will not be ruled. He will himself rule. The battle against determinism rises, thus, out of a desire for sovereign autonomy. Opposition to determinism becomes identical with opposition to all heteronomy, including theonomy! It is thus highly questionable whether, as Brunner says, "the Christian doctrine of freedom is infinitely closer to idealism than to materialistic determinism."[22] Brunner argues that while idealism may misunderstand the freedom of human existence, it still sees freedom as essential to human beings. But that is not the question. For the freedom concept of idealism implies the deification of the sovereign individual, and this deification, besides being itself sin, assumes that freedom under theonomy is impossible. It is, then, certainly incorrect to speak, as Brunner does, of a "primitive affinity" between the idealistic and the Christian concept of freedom.

The alternatives, determinism or indeterminism, are true alternatives only on a horizontal, anthropological level. They pose a dilemma which is resolved in the relationship that man sustains to God. This vertical relationship between God and man alone gives possibility to a correct understanding of the problem of freedom. Both determinism, which destroys free personality, and indeterminism, which declares personality sovereign as well as free, at bottom neglect the religious aspect of the problem. This is recognized by Brunner when he writes: "The false idea of freedom is positively the quintessence of sin."[23] It is the humanistic battle cry of freedom which usually inspires indeterminism in its fierce opposition to determinism. This accounts for the fruitless pendulum swing of human thought between determinism and indeterminism, between "bondage" and "liberty" — an oscillation in which a correct choice is never possible.

---

22. E. Brunner, *Der Mensch im Widerspruch*, 1937, p. 265.
23. *Ibid.*, p. 277.

A THIRD ASPECT?

Determinism, nonetheless, seems to possess a certain level of congruity with the Christian confession of God's providential power over and in all things. Does not the idea of causality, which plays such an important role in determinism, have significant, even decisive place in Christian thought? We refer now to the distinction between first cause (God) and second causes, a distinction with which dogmatics often operates, especially in the Providence doctrine. Could this not be the door through which we may go over into a Christianized determinism? Atheistic determinism refuses to speak of God as first cause, but logically it still needs a first, eternal, cause of some sort. At any rate, do not determinism and Christianity agree on the absence of freedom and the predetermination of all human acts? Is there perhaps a grain of truth in the setting of Christianity alongside of the fatalism of the Turks or Mohammedans who can go into battle with contempt of death, since, according to their teaching of predestination, they cannot precipitate or forestall death anyway? If, one may ask, we were not so frightened by the sound of the word, would determinism still be held as such a great error? Was Zwingli, after all, really mistaken with his concept of necessity or was he simply the most consistent representative of the Reformation, daring to express what he saw as the logic of the Reformation God-concept, namely, the absolute necessity of all human activity?

This question could well be considered the most important question of theology. The answer to it must, as we see it, demonstrate that an identification of Christianity and determinism can lead only to immeasurable evil for the Church and theology. The Christian doctrines of predestination and Providence are actually something wholly other than determinism, even though the latter is sometimes brought under the Christian denominator.

Determinism threatened to influence Christian thought even at the time of the Reformation, in the midst of the flowering of a new understanding of the Scriptures. This fact is closely related to the reformers' profound protest against the notion of free will. Brunner remarks somewhere that the reformers were forced to write strongly against the idea of free will in their day, but "had Luther been obliged to reckon with such a determinism as that of today, his *The Bondage of the Will* would never have been written."[24] It need not be denied that certain deterministic tendencies are evident in the dogmatic form that Luther, as well as Zwingli, gave to his protests against free will. Luther, however, did not set determinism over against free will. He attempted to focus the entire problem of freedom on the central, religious relationship of man to God, which relationship is defined, not by the concept of necessity, but by the antithesis between sin and grace. Determinism seeks to solve the anthropological problem by means of the scheme: causes, causing, caused. Luther and Zwingli made use of this determinist design, an element inherited from medieval thought, undoubtedly because of its apparent parallelism to the decreeing, foreordaining, and ruling of God. Zwingli was in acute danger of accepting this apparent analogy as a real identity, but so was Luther, especially in his debate with Erasmus. Luther, in his justified protest against Erasmus' notion of freedom, was not always able to give proper form to what moved deeply within him. This is apparent, for example, when Luther writes: "Nevertheless, natural reason herself is compelled to confess that the living and true God must be such an one as, by His own liberty, to impose necessity on us. For He must be a ridiculous God, or an idol rather, who did not, to a certainty, foreknow the future, or was liable to be deceived in events, when even the Gentiles ascribed to their gods 'fate inevitable.' "[25] This comparison of Providence with the pagan idea of fate must have made it difficult for Erasmus to understand the real religious intent of

---

24. *Ibid.*, p. 260.
25. M. Luther, *Vom unfreien Willen*, F. W. Schmidt edition, p. 177.

Luther's protest. But it is not to say, of course, that Luther is a fatalist in his theology.

Luther's religious intent becomes quite clear when he formulates his protest against the independence and self-rule of man. In this he exclaims, with Paul: "Who can withstand His will?" Luther's deepest intent is to show the almightiness of God. Therefore he says that God's eternal Providence and our own free will stand opposed to each other "as do fire and water." He sets himself in opposition to the arrogance of the human reason which revolts against the all-inclusive Divine activity and against His Divine hardening and reprobating of evil men. "It is this that seems to give the greatest offence to common sense or natural reason . . ." Luther can understand such offence. "And who would not be offended. I myself have been offended more than once, even unto the deepest abyss of desperation; nay, so far, as even to wish that I had never been born a man; that is, before I was brought to know how healthful that desperation was, and how near it was unto grace."[26]

It is Luther's desire to recognize the Divine over-ruling. He refers to Judas' betrayal in connection with God's Providence and there seeks to distinguish between two kinds of necessity: one that implies a blind coercion and another that implies only that something must occur. Luther means only the latter, and with it intends to praise God's rule, His independence and majesty. Judas betrayed Christ with free will and without coercion. And when Luther expresses his conviction in regard to free will, he speaks not about a determining first cause which excludes freedom of the will, but about the wrath of God revealed from heaven against man's suppression of the truth in unrighteousness. Luther's argument against Erasmus is not based on the relationship between first and second causes, but on the fettered, fallen will of man and on the wrath of God. The argument against free will was not a logical

---
26. *Ibid.*, p. 178.

deduction from the all-embracing activity of God. His argument was the speech of Paul in Romans 1. It becomes evident, then, that we do not find ourselves with Luther in an atmosphere of determinism.

This introduces an important difference with Zwingli, who, far more than Luther, reasoned from the idea of God as first cause and prime mover. Zwingli reasoned thus: if God is first cause, then He is also the only cause, and therefore there can be no argument for the freedom of the will. Zwingli, then, concluded this denial of free will from his view of the relation between God and humanity in the abstract. The problem of the freedom of the will was considered apart from man's historical fall and sin. Thus, Zwingli can further say that the Providence of God also excludes human service. He shifts the problem from the dynamic relationship between grace and freedom to an abstract logical relationship between Providence and freedom.

In true Reformation thought the problem of the freedom of the will has to do with the guilt and corruption of man. We observe this most clearly in Calvin. When we recall how uncompromisingly Calvin taught predestination and the invincibility of Providence, we might expect that his protest against the idea of the freedom of the will would be a logical deduction from his God-concept, wholly apart from sin and guilt. Actually, however, Calvin considered the freedom of the will extensively in connection with the historical fall, in the second book of the *Institutes*. After pointing to the judgment which came upon humanity through the fall of Adam, he showed that man, after the fall, was divested of his freedom and subjected to a wretched servitude. Calvin's entire view of the bondage of the will is dependent on this. Human will is fettered in the slavery of sin and, hence, cannot move toward the good. "We must therefore observe this grand point of distinction, that man, having been corrupted by his fall, sins voluntarily, not with reluctance or constraint; with the strong-

A THIRD ASPECT? 151

est propensity of disposition, not with violent coercion; with the bias of his own passions, and not with external compulsion: yet such is the depravity of his nature, that he cannot be excited and biased to anything but what is evil."[27] Calvin approaches the whole question of the freedom of the will from the conflict between sin and grace. He speaks of the impotence to which sin "necessarily" leads and which has its origin in man's subjection to the lordship of the devil. "Hence, therefore, the corruption with which we are firmly bound. It originated in the revolt of the first man from his Maker."[28] This is the manner in which Calvin opposes freedom of the will. It leaves him innocent of determinism.

It is characteristic of determinism with its absolute causality to relativize all events and actions. It cannot embrace responsibility within its system and in principle it cancels all creaturely freedom. Determination and freedom of the will are mutually exclusive. This is why Divine determining is utterly different from what is generally understood by determinism. It is not that there is a material similarity between the confession of God's Providence and determinism and that the only difference between them is the formal difference that in determinism the first cause stands at the end of the series of causes, while in the confession of Providence *God* stands there. Since we have to do with the Providence of *God*, everything else, including planning, determining, and acting, is different. This is why we never find in the Scriptures either the rigidity or the violence typical of determinism. In the confession of God's almighty power, the personal, living God is confessed. Responsibility is not crowded out by His power; neither is the meaning of guilt and punishment. We are deeply conscious of the impossibility of our discerning the relation between the Divine activity and ours, but we are able to see in Scripture that the incomparable enterprise of God is in its

---
27. J. Calvin, *Institutes*, II, 3, 5.
28. *Ibid.*, II, 5, 1.

Divine character so great and majestic that it can embrace human freedom and responsibility within itself without being thereby assaulted or even limited. The essential error of identifying the Providence doctrine with determinism is the de-personalization of the God-concept. God is looked on as the beginning of a sequence out of which all things emerge.

The Reformed confession of Providence does not reason from the idea of causation. It simply recognizes the invincibility of God's sovereign activity. Hence Augustine's opposition to Pelagius, the reformers' conflict with Rome, and Luther's debate with Erasmus were not motivated by a cosmological theory, but by religion and, thus, by the honor of God in His sovereignty and grace. These men did not exclude human merit by causal logic, but rather from the religious relationship of man to God. They contested freedom of the will from *this* cause: *corruptio naturae*. They did not attack the creaturely freedom which God had created in human life, for this creaturely freedom did not compete with the omnipotent activity of God. Erasmus's idea of the freedom of the will did compete with God's activity, since it sought in man that which only God can give. But true creaturely freedom is such that it can be given its place within the activity of God without its contesting God's prerogatives. This is why it is so very important to keep aloof from determinism. We may not involve the Providence doctrine in any offence other than the *scandalon* of the Gospel, the offence to the natural man who does not understand the things of the Spirit of God.

Many still look on Divine Providence as being on the same level as the determinist system. God, they reason, occupies the top rung of the causal system, but the fact of His being there does not essentially change the system itself. All is determined in any case. What they forget is that *the nature of the personal living God absolutely defines the nature of the determining.* The Church has always seen this, though it

A THIRD ASPECT? 153

has not always taught it with such clarity that everyone could see immediately that "Christian determinism" was a contradiction in terms.

This sometimes becomes apparent in pastoral work. A person may know well enough (from school or catechism) that God's Providence does not take away our responsibility and yet not be free from the oppressive fear that, in the light of God's absolute determination, all our willing and working, all our prayers and decisions are meaningless. Such an essentially rationalistic line of thought, misunderstanding the essence of the truly personal and Divine determining, may frustrate pastoral exhortation: everything is determined anyway, arranged just as it is causally determined by God. And the result is that man's acts and all history are relativized and no longer taken seriously, as the Scriptures take them seriously (cf. Matt. 18:7). The pastoral answer usually given — that both lines in Scripture, Divine determination and human responsibility, must be recognized and held — is Scripturally quite responsible. For there are here not two competitive exclusives, as determinism would have it, but a Divine activity over and in the creaturely activity of man.

* * *

It is remarkable, in this connection, that Scripture itself never presents Providence in its relation to sin by way of a theoretical argument, but always in the historical actuality of the invincible power of God and our continual responsibility. The enmity of man — the cross of Christ! What consonance! This profound concord becomes perceptible in the prayer of Acts 4:27, 28. God's enemies are portrayed as enterprising, but not able to escape the supremacy of God. Even in his most apostate acts man cannot break out of the sovereign concern of God. Divine revelation does not let us penetrate the mystery of this consonance, this harmony. The living God rules here! We cannot explain the sequences of history with an all devouring system of causation, nor by a theory of Divine influx. The Scriptures show us God's work. Then, in history, we are shown how unparalleled that work is. It is striking, for example, that Scripture does not speak of God as being at work in leading Judas down the road to the act of betrayal. It says that Satan filled Judas' heart. He who sees this well will not look on this work of Satan and Judas' betrayal as one side of a dualism, independent and detached from God's work, but will bow before the power of God which is present even in the acts of extremest sin, and will stand speechless at the wisdom and mystery of His ways.

* * *

We have already discussed the much used distinction between first cause and second causes. This distinction is always in the background of every discussion of concurrence and has played a large role in Reformed theology. It is only fair to acknowledge first that by this distinction it is not intended to posit God and man as comparable magnitudes by bringing them both under the common denominator of causation. The idea in presenting God as first cause was doubtless to put all the accent on the word *first* and thus to honor the uniqueness of God's greatness. It was not intended to involve God in a system of causality to which He would then be subject and in which He, like man, was just another cause, though the *prima causa*. On the contrary, the purpose of the distinction between first cause and second cause was to avoid any pantheistic notion which might identify the two, making God a part of the causal system of nature.

But, though we may respect the intent, we must realize that this distinction has not brought the Church essentially further in her reflection; in fact, it has more often obscured her insight into Divine Providence. This is partly due for one thing to the terms, especially the word *cause,* which were applied to God. We cannot invalidate the criticism brought against this merely by pointing to the good intention behind it. Even though it is not intended to involve God in interaction with other causes, the use of the terms first and second causes implies that God is only the most important cause among equal causes (*causa prima inter pares*). The manner in which the distinction is often employed reveals a danger that God be viewed as enclosed within a system of causality, a system in which the causal chain extends through this world in one unbroken line to God. The threat to our thinking here is the same as that posed by the ancient emanation theory, though this brings God even more definitely and less disguisedly down into the world-process. The terms, by their arrangement (first-second), nevertheless suggest a causal circle in which God and man alike are involved.

He who may think that this is a mere terminological difficulty should consider the role that this distinction has played in Roman Catholic thought, particularly in the so-called causal proof for the existence of God. Here it becomes clear how this distinction leads to a singular and stubborn staticizing of the God-concept, in which God is conceived as first cause or first mover. This also blasts any notion that this is a Reformed distinction. It is far more typical of and legitimate in Roman Catholic thought, the natural theology of which allows for a God-concept that is to a certain extent empty. Catholic thought insists that rational thought, by reasoning from creation, can obtain a certain knowledge of God, that is, of God as first cause. All things must have a cause. A rose garden in summer bloom must be caused to blossom. There *must* be a cause external to the thing itself; and this "law" does not lose its force at the boundaries of the cosmos. Scholastic thought attaches a transcendental value to the principle of causality. Natural reason, in its highest flight, discovers the mystery of the world's origin. This is, admittedly, not sufficient for salvation, but neither is it of small significance. Natural reason discloses a first cause, or a prime mover, or a Being that exists in itself and by virtue of itself, and this Being is, in reality, the Christian God. Man can know this first cause outside of revelation through the exclusive powers of natural reason. The distinction between first and second causes is, then, quite emphatically propounded by Rome.

It is, in fact, often argued against the Reformation that the reformers did not do full justice to second causes. Przywara argues that the Reformation had a principial and consistent disrespect for second causes and that therefore neither the Church nor good works could be given an essential place in Reformation thought. The Reformation concept of an exclusively active God occasioned a disregard for Divine immanence. He maintains, then, that the distinction between first and second cause is a specifically Thomistic teaching. We may, indeed, agree that this distinction did not originate in Reformed thought. It was worked out to finesse by Thomas. Przywara says, quite correctly, that in this lies "the essential Thomistic thought: in the question of second causes, in the question of the tension between the continuous activity of God and the unique act of creation."[28] Thomas says, for example, that things of nature possess their own energy (power of movement), though God is the unique and general active cause. God does the work of Providence "in which He guides and moves the energy of all things according to their own activity . . . and all self-generated power of the creature works in the measure that it is guided and moved by the Creator." One can say that in this Thomas argues against Aristotle much as the later theology directed itself against deism. But at the same time, it is apparent that his distinction gets us nowhere, though with it Thomas expected to make lucid the relation between God and the world. God becomes the first cause to which all causal chains in this world must ultimately lead. In this way it was thought that Providence as well as sin and grace would be made at least relatively transparent. The result was that both good and evil had to be deduced in the same

---

28. E. Przywara, *Ringen der Gegenwart*, 1929, II, p. 909.

way from this causality. The first-second cause relation was like a net spread over the whole world, catching everything, good and evil alike.

Consistently employed, the first-second cause distinction should be able to explain sinful acts, just as it should explain the sinful tendencies and disposition of the heart. Everything must be traced back to the first cause. The fact that men shrank back and reached for new distinctions, like that between the form and matter of sin, indicates pretty well that they realized themselves to be on the borderline of a danger zone. That they grasp at another distinction shows, at the same time, that the first and second cause scheme left them where they could no longer make clear that God was not the author of sin. As soon as man begins to schematize on the basis of causality, he immediately begins to grope in darkness, and creates an insoluble problem in the doctrine of sin. We cannot say that the mystery lies here. For this "mystery" is created by a universally applied rational system of causality. The basic error of this kind of reasoning is that an injustice is done to the incomparability of the Divine activity, which, though it may have been acknowledged theoretically, was sacrificed in practical thought.

The Scriptures approach the matter quite differently. We are unmistakably taught the absolute dependence of all creatures on the work of God. There is no terrain in which man can escape being defined by the activity of God. Our work does not limit the work of God. The prophet Isaiah speaks of God as "the first" (Is. 41:27; Is. 44:6) when witnessing to His absolute incomparability. But it cannot be alleged that the distinction between first and second causes is thereby implied. Consider the entire tone of Isaiah's speech. Compare the first-second cause distinction with the prophet's preaching of God's incomparability: "To whom then will ye liken me, that I should be equal to him? saith the Holy One" (Is. 40:25). Our eyes are directed to Him who created all things

(Is. 40:26) in contrast to the vanity of idols. And these idols are not only the images molded by the craftsman and guilded by the goldsmith. They refer to every image that is applied to Him: "To whom then will ye liken God? or what likeness will ye compare unto him?" (Is. 40:18).

Who does not sense that this "first" emphasizes rather than minimizes the incomparableness of Jehovah: "I am the first, and I am the last; and besides me there is no God" (Is. 44:6; cf. Rev. 22:13). We are on another level here than with the distinction between first and second causes. This *first* and *last* accents the majesty of God and lays the basis for the warning against comparing anything to Him. The word *first* points to the absolute Creator, not the first cause, of all things. He is the *last* as well as the *first;* when the last generation shall have appeared, He is still God. He lives beyond the duration of human history; always, He is the eternal God (Is. 41:4).

His being the *first* does not suggest a relation of first to second causes. It reveals His Creator-greatness, which is also the greatness and sovereignty of His Redemption as the King of Israel, Lord of lords, who establishes His eternal nation (Is. 44:6, 7). "Fear ye not . . . Is there a God besides me? yea, there is no Rock; I know not any" (Is. 44:8).

* * *

Do we stand, then, in the relation between Divine and human activity before an enigmatic paradox, an antinomy, which sterilizes our thinking? This would indeed be the case if the activity of God and man were viewed on the same level as comparable magnitudes. Then His activity would limit and annul ours, or our activity would limit His. But since the activity of God is preached to us in its absolutely incomparable character and as His Divine invincibility *in* our activity, there is a way for faith in God's Providence. Our "problem" is resolved in our listening to God's revelation. Listening and believing, we can confess this invincibility of God. We confess it through faith, which knows it has gotten everything from God's hand. We confess it in our working, in which God works according to His good pleasure. At the same time we confess our guilt and our responsibility, knowing that there is no unrighteousness, but only light, in God. Rational conclusions which staticize His activity, give way to a living faith in *Him*. We know that His hand is mighty, even in and over all the sin of humanity, in hardening and reprobating. We know it as we in faith pray that these evils may not come upon us (Is. 63).

Faith knows its boundaries. That which is intended by the distinction between the matter and form of sin is known by faith in confession of guilt and dependence. Faith does not flee from responsibility, nor does it explain guilt in any other way than out of man's own heart. In the temptation to deduce all things from the first cause and to remove all responsibility and guilt from man, we may make our stand in the reliable revelation which directs us to the historical course of God and, in all our musing over "God and man," brings us to rest in the Gospel of reconciliation through the cross.

In fear and trembling faith confesses God's Providence over the entire flight of history. Providence does not remove the seriousness of history; it charges history with responsibility. In history the freedom of creaturely will manifests itself in the ways of sin. History moves onward, not as though coerced, but in creaturely freedom and continually fresh decision. Meanwhile, the servitude of the will exposes itself in history by its slavish confinement in sin. But servitude of the will, in this Reformation sense, does not turn history into a frivolous marionette show. Encompassing creaturely freedom and servitude to sin, history is on the move toward God's future. He is the first and the last.

Faith knows of creaturely freedom and responsibility in history. It also knows of evil. For the history of evil advances in spite of all resistance; and God writes history with the acts of man. That is the terrible seriousness of history, that God works in it and that man is responsible for it. Behind all views of concurrence, first and second causes, matter and form, the *reality* of history must be seen. In history, always anew, the invincibility of the Divine activity shall manifest itself. There is a singular coherency of sequence in history: when unrighteousness increases, then the kingdom of God draws near; when the anti-Christ appears, then Christ comes; when the mystery of unrighteousness reaches its climax, then the hour of *parousia* strikes. And then the meaning of history will be revealed in the kingdom of God — in which no other light is necessary than the light of the Lamb.

But now we still see through a glass, in riddles, and our knowledge is made up in fragments. Now we are menaced by unbelief, doubt, and disloyalty. Temptation levels itself on the reality of our time, in which, however, the living God is at work. We cannot fathom it. We can only listen to the voice of the Word — listen, as it speaks warning and comfort.

After every pilgrimage of thought, we shall have to turn back again to the simplicity of undoubting faith — the faith which bends its knee and prays: "Who is a great god like unto God?" (Ps. 77:13). We shall know that God in His incomprehensible ruling is not a despot God, but the Shepherd of Israel; and we shall experience that the shepherd psalm of the Old Covenant (Ps. 23) still gives light for our darkness. Really to know this Shepherd of Israel we must go back again to the word of Christ: "My sheep hear my voice, and I know them, and they follow me" (John 10:27). And he who follows Him shall not walk in the darkness (John 8:12). To find this is to find the foundation of life. For the Shepherd of Israel is the God of Hosts (Ps. 80:1, 4).

CHAPTER VI

Providence and History

WE HAVE already discussed Providence as God's rule over all events of time, and thus over history. Nevertheless, a particular, persistently recurring problem in this connection demands our further address. Recall that the confession insists that *nothing* occurs apart from Divine Providence. This confession gives the believer a perspective of totality, of the whole, but it may be asked whether it does not level all events to one plane and partially blind us to the particular, the special events. All events, it would seem, receive equally ultimate significance, each of them alike being shaped by the hand of God.

Does this allow for distinctions within God's Providence over all things, for *special* leading in particular circumstances? Are there definite moments or phases of history in which not only the hand of God, but, so to speak, His finger, is evident? Are there not special events that rise as mountain peaks above the plain of history, in which God's leading is peculiarly significant? But our confession says that God leads in everything without exception. Do we not refute this by looking for extraordinary evidence of His leading? We know, for example, that God has led both in light and in darkness, in the Reformation and in the counter-Reformation, in the rise of capitalism and in the rise of communism, in Dunkirk and in Normandy. When then should we, besides confessing His hand in all of history, look for the *finger* of God in special events?

It is common, even among those who most seriously confess His rule in all things, to look for and see God's finger exceptionally evident on certain occasions. It is thought that there are situations in which the Providence of God takes on a unique and striking character, endowing His leading in these situations with singular lucidity. Simple believers have always testified to experiences of unmistakable and exceptional guidance in their lives. The Church, too, has always had her special "days of thanksgiving." There is a danger, however, that men subjectively and arbitrarily interpret history in the light of the extraordinary, that they seek only the special intervention of the finger of God instead of living with confidence in the hand of God which governs *all* things. For this reason, the question deserves our further attention.

* * *

Christians have often been too willing to capitulate to this danger. The so-called "German Christians" saw the special finger of God in Hitler's rise to power in 1933. The Church, it was said, could not without fault fail to recognize this providential sign. A fragment of history was in effect canonized as a new revelation. God's Providence was here setting Germany, after years of sorrow and misunderstanding, again on the way of blessing and greatness. In the background was Hitler's continual call upon "Providence," leading to the all too popular conviction that his was a "word of redemption."

This is a question of the interpretation of history, of whether we can comprehend the mysterious intent of God in a certain moment. The "German Christians" spoke of the "Lord of history" who was at that moment in Germany's history speaking in a clear voice. It led a group of theologians at Würtemburg to come out in 1934 with this statement: "We are full of thanks to God that He, as Lord of history, has given us Adolf Hitler, our leader and savior from our difficult lot. We acknowledge that we, with body and soul, are bound and dedicated to the German state and to its *Führer*. This bondage and duty contains for us, as evangelical Christians, its deepest and most holy significance in its obedience to the command of God."[1] Another declaration, in 1933, said, "To this turn of history (i.e. Hitler's taking power) we say a thankful *Yes*. God has given him to us. To Him be the glory. As bound to God's Word, we recognize in the great events of our day a new commission of God to His Church."[2]

Karl Barth, among others, offered memorable resistance to this interpretation of history. He saw it as an attempt "to bind the Church irresponsibly to a definite form of world history," and, with respect to the above resolutions, as "an unprecedented new confessional and normative principle," by which it was openly contended that "the new commission of our Lord to His Church was something to be found not in the Holy Scripture, but in the great events of our day."[3] But there were other, more moderate voices than those of the "German Christians," which nevertheless took issue with Barth. G. Kittel,[4] for example, said that he had prayed for years that his people might be saved from their distress and disgrace, and asked Barth whether this prayer, too, was heretical. If not, should he not then give thanks for what occurred in 1933? Was God in the time of Moses, but not in ours, the active God of history? Is it not an irrefutable Biblical doctrine that God is ever the same, in our times as in the past? Kittel agrees with Barth that God's work in the New Testament was soteriological and that this work was a "unique and unrepeatable . . . segment of history," but adds that there are also other works of God, and these too, must be interpreted, though *in the light of the work of redemption*. Therefore, says Kittel, the Church may still speak in a concrete historical situa-

---

1. Cf. K. Barth and G. Kittel, *Ein theologischer Briefwechsel*, 1934, p. 5. 600 ministers and 14 professors of theology approved this proposition.
2. Resolution of the so-called Dreimännerkollegium of April 28, 1933. Quoted by Barth in *Theologische Existenz heute*, p. 10.
3. Barth, *Theologische Existenz heute*, p. 12. Cf. also Barth, *Für die Freiheit des Evangeliums*, 1933, p. 7: "The freedom of the Gospel is dependent on this, that there is no other source for the Church's proclamation: no book of fate, of history, of nature, of experience, of reason, nor the currently so zealously quoted book of 'the hour of destiny.'"
4. Editor of the *Theologische Wörterbuch zum Neuen Testament*.

tion. Then Kittel gives a further interpretation of history: "If the decision of world history falls for a people between the Soviet star and the Germany of January 30 [1933], then the Church under the Spirit and Word of God is not so weak that she does not have the authority to speak out as to whether the decision of these days is from God or from Satan." Finally, in this connection, Kittel accuses Barth of a docetic ecclesiology.[5]

The entire debate illustrates the problem of the activity of God in history. The "German Christians" opened the eyes of many of us to the dangers of reading God's purpose from historical facts. Was it not possible for the Soviet Church to give a similar interpretation of history? Patriarch Sergius, in fact, spoke of Stalin as "the divinely appointed leader of our armed and cultural forces, leading us to victory."[6] Does not the phrase "divinely appointed" imply a summoning of Divine Providence for the justification of Russia's history? In fact, cannot everyone according to his own prejudice and subjective whim canonize a certain event or national rise as a special act of God in which He reveals and demonstrates His favor?

The problem is not unique to our age. Lactantius wrote in 314 *Concerning the Death of the Persecutors of the Church*, in which he tried to show that God obviously had revealed His retributive justice in the terrible deaths of those who had fought His Church. God's purpose, he said, was irrefutably demonstrated in the *facts of history*. Interestingly enough, Lactantius skips the years between 96 and 249, which include the emperors between Domitian and Decius, claiming that those years were years of peace. Undoubtedly the fact that the Caesars of that period did not meet disastrous ends and, therefore, did not fit into his theory, also influenced his work. This again shows the danger of going outside the sphere of

---

5. K. Barth and G. Kittel, *Ein theologischer Briefwechsel*, 1934, p. 11.
6. Sergius, *Die Wahrheit über die Religion in Russland*, 1944.

faith into the area of observation, letting the facts speak their own language and thus, render faith at least partly superfluous. It is not that the confession of God's Providence over all things is in question. We are only disputing the legitimacy of *interpreting* the ways of Providence on the basis of facts.

The problem arises especially when one's own land or people stand before a crisis. When the fall of Rome in 410 was attributed by certain Romans to the forsaking of the ancient gods and the adoption of Christianity, Augustine took it upon himself to interpret the catastrophe in another light. Thus, he wrote his *De Civitate Dei*. Augustine saw that the events leading to Rome's decline were not a series of accidents in which it was impossible to discern meaning or continuity. There was a discernible relation between Rome's fall and the special purpose of God. It was, he said, not the rejection of the state gods, but the moral impotence of paganism which led to Rome's destruction. Naturally, Augustine did not pretend to interpret all the secrets of Providence, but he did refuse to leave the events of the day uninterpreted.

Shortly thereafter Salvianus came with quite another interpretation of the same events. Salvianus explained Rome's catastrophe by the unrighteousness of the Christian believers in Church and society. The fall of Rome was, according to this interpretation, not a judgment on the heathen, but a judgment on the Christians. Such contradictions as that between Augustine and Salvianus can be expected to arise every time men try to interpret Providence on the basis of particular events. In fact, you find the same general form of contradiction in all such interpretations; judgment on the unbelieving world or judgment on Christendom — which is the meaning of a given catastrophe?

The proposal of such questions can be evidence of an awareness of God's majestic presence in history. Both Augustine and Salvianus, as well as Lactantius, looked at history far differently from either the earlier Epicureans or the later deists. But the interpretation of an historical event as a special revelation of Providence too easily becomes a piously disguised form of self-justification.

* * *

The Dutch statesman and theologian, Abraham Kuyper, whose views we have discussed in other connections, also spoke often of the leading of God in history. We read in the second article of the program of principles of the Anti-Revolutionary Party: "Neither in the will of the people nor in the law, but only in God, does [the party] find the source of sovereign authority. It rejects therewith the principle of popular sovereignty. On the other hand, it honors the sovereignty of the House of Orange as rooted, under the guidance of God, in our history."[7] Kuyper acknowledges such a "guidance" because he believes "the creation of great men is, more than any other, an immediate work of the Father of spirits." He honors the rise of such a dynasty as the House of Orange as "a gradual work of Divine Providence." It is clear that Kuyper's intent is not to place Scripture and history alongside of each other as independent sources of knowledge of God's purposes. He insists that "our situation is not something that can be arbitrarily created by us, but is the necessary fruit of the past which, independent of our desires and outside of our participation, is created by Him in whom we live, move, and have our being." He calls man to attend to Him, "whose holy footsteps can be heard upon the entire path of history," but at the same time protests that history is not to be coordinated with the demand of the Gospel. In the light of the Gospel, says Kuyper, we know of the one work of God which controls all history and, further, "that there is now no other cure for the ills of the European people than that found in the cross of the Man of Sorrows." In this connection, revolution is criticized as "an emancipation of the people from the

---

7. Cf. Kuyper, *Ons Program,* 1880, p. 21.

sovereign authority and jurisdiction of Almighty God."[8] This type of emancipation, according to Kuyper, found its first conscious expression in the French Revolution. Kuyper sought to judge such events *from* the norm of the Gospel. In any case, the point of departure for Kuyper is quite different than the simple canonization of concrete events as revelation of God's purpose. He accepts the Gospel as his determinative starting point, whose significance he then tries to find for all of life.[9]

It is quite another thing to perceive the finger of God in crucial events, to conceive of Providence atomistically as a fragmentary demonstration of power. God would in that case reveal His will by intervening in historical crises. His leading in history is then, as far as our knowledge is concerned, identified with His secret purpose. To assume this can lead, as it did in Schelling and, under his influence, in Stahl, to a romanticistic quietism. With this in mind, Dooyeweerd protests that God's leading in history is not "a sort of irrational activity external to human creativeness."[10] He suggests that Divine leading in history must be considered in its *normative* significance. By God's leading is not meant the actualization in world history of His hidden plan, for the realization of His plan embraces the universal scope of things, and this can never be either the normative measure for human action or the standard "for the judging of the course of world history." We are concerned more with a leading of God that has to do "with the results . . . of the incursion of the human 'shapers of history' against the normative principles, laid down by God as the meaning of history itself." God's leading is closely related to the fact that the formative process of history is not without law and to the fact that judgment reveals it-

---
8. Hence the name Anti-Revolutionary Party, the political party founded by Kuyper. (Translator's note).
9. For above citations of Kuyper, see *Ons Program*, pp. 20, 21.
10. H. Dooyeweerd, *Wijsbegeerte der Wetsidee*, 1935, II, p. 186.

self in history itself against, for example, every excessive and arbitrary presumption of power.

Dooyeweerd, thus, approaches the problem of the leading of God, not as a matter of striking and remarkable events in history, but as a matter of norm, defined by what Dooyeweerd calls the "law sphere of history." Thus, there are laws immanent in the formation of history, as there are in nature. Dooyeweerd does not define history merely as that "which has happened in the past." He is concerned with the meaning, the formative principle, or, if you will, the modal determinative of history. We can best understand the norm for the formation of history as the forming of a given historical tendency, structure, or situation, which does not develop by itself, but is proposed to man as a task, and is realized in "normative freedom" in the subjective development of what we usually call civilization. The actualization of this historical principle rests with the will of the human "shapers of history." Dooyeweerd speaks of man's responsibility to gain control over the "nature side of reality" as an historical norm, thus making a basic principle of man's responsibility to form cultures. Every immoderate contention for power which negates the formal principle in the order of civilization runs dead against the higher laws which God has established in the sphere of culture. And this, according to Dooyeweerd, suggests the Christian idea of the leading of God in history. History reveals God's leading in connection with and in the light of the norms which God has set down, within which history must run its course.[11]

Dooyeweerd, then, means something else by God's leading in history than the Divine rule over all events. He is primarily concerned with the important problem of historical norms, that is, with the idea that history, like nature, does not operate without basic laws. The difficulty is that it is possible for man to transgress these laws and that, therefore,

---

11. *Ibid.*, pp. 217, 218.

we can hardly speak of the judgment of God upon excessive contention for power as a "leading." We are at the moment, however, primarily concerned with the rule of God over all things, which, indeed, excludes "lawlessness" in the development of history, but in which, on the other hand, disobedience can manifest itself with great historical significance. This disobedience — under God's rule and according to His purpose — can, in turn, maintain itself in excessive contention for power over a long period of time. The relevance of Dooyeweerd's analysis to our discussion is its refusal to address itself to isolated events in history which on the surface seem to project themselves more or less irrationally into the normal course of events. Our concern, theologically, is with the designation of special, fragmentary events as the revelation of God's finger in history. The danger is that these events will be interpreted according to individual prejudice, while, as Dooyeweerd correctly observes, God's decree embracing all things does not provide man with a criterion with which to make arbitrary distinctions between special and normal events.

Those who see God's finger in history usually point to the surprising and portentous events in which God supposedly makes a special revelation of His favor or anger. The leading of God in history is narrowed to a special "Divine incursion" or rather — since His rule over all things is not usually denied — it becomes a matter of consigning these prodigious events to a special area of Providence. The normless character of this is obvious. While arising perhaps from a desire to understand God's leading in concrete events or to recognize God's sovereign power in actual occurrences, the selection of events which are revelatory and the manner of interpreting them is basically left to individual and subjective judgment.

* * *

On what grounds is it considered possible to perceive God's finger in special events in history? One usually answers that the very extraordinary character of certain occurrences cannot be explained other than as a special act of God. However, what appears at one time to be quite extraordinary and sensational may later be explained wholly from understandable relations of nature and history. In this way, whether or not God's finger has been visible in history is dependent — as in much of the Catholic approach to miracles — on the position of science in a given time. It may be said that no event speaks so clearly that we may conclude from it a certain disposition of God — as long as God Himself does not reveal that His disposition comes to expression in the given event. If events are to be thus judged, there must be a norm according to which the particular events are both selected for judgment and judged.

A subjective invocation of "special providence" in connection with very extraordinary events is actually worthless. This is particularly evident when men, as they often do, call upon the idea of "special providence" in order to involve God in the realization of their own dubious plans. It is relatively simple in this way to conclude the leading of God from historical facts. It then makes rather little difference *which* facts men use to prove the presence of God's special leading. A good many sincere Germans were convinced by the evidence that God's finger was directing the nationalistic movement of the 1930's. This is typical of the senseless impasse to which this type of reasoning may lead. And no people or nation is exempt from the temptation to so reason. The fact is that no one can recognize God's finger without knowing Him, and that facts and events as such cannot become revelation, but can only be seen and understood in the light of Biblical revelation.

What, then, about the unexpected and surprising acts of God in the history of Israel? Recall, for instance, the miraculous deliverances of the era of the judges, of God's path through the sea, of the victory of the angel over 185,000 Assyrians, and of the drought during Israel's apostasy in Baal-worship. It is clear that these are not subjectively interpreted facts, but events which are, in their deepest significance, revealed by God Himself. The Divine disposition is, indeed, revealed in these events. But it is the word of revelation which explains them as God's judgment and grace. The events speak only because God speaks first.

There is a danger that we subconsciously identify our own lands and peoples with Israel, in the sense that they too are specially chosen by God for a mission in the world. This probably lies behind the tendency to suppose that, as God's finger was evident in Israel's history, so it is (or has been) evident in that of ours. It is often forgotten that we have not been given a norm for explaining the facts of history, and that in the absence of a norm only an untrustworthy plausibility remains. Otherwise one must take refuge in religious intuition or divination, which, it has been claimed, is capable of discerning God's finger in the panorama of history. This would introduce a second source of Divine information, and, if one accepted it, he could hardly criticize such divination as it operated in Nazi Germany and in Stalinist Russia. Each divination would have to be held equally sacred and above criticism. He who sees the fallacies involved here can understand the dangers of a sort of "super history" construction, which, by the special significance given it, cuts off our perspective of God's *universal* rule.

* * *

The Scriptures, which witness to numerous extraordinary signs of God in history, earnestly warn us against drawing premature and rash conclusions from "facts." Recall the Galileans who had fallen victim to Pilate's unnatural savagery or the eighteen men on whom the tower of Siloam fell. The question Jesus asked about these extraordinary events is relevant to the interpretation of history: "Think ye that these

... were sinners above all [others], because they have suffered these things?" (Luke 13:1-5). These events had apparently been given this interpretation: God was so angry with these unfortunate men that He brought about their extraordinary death. This seemed particularly apparent in the case of the fall of the tower of Siloam where no "normal" factors seemed evident and where God thus acted without secondary means. But Christ exposed and rejected the assumption that God's purpose is thus to be concluded from even the most "unnatural events."

Being born blind was interpreted as having obvious connection with guilt (John 9). "Rabbi," Jesus was asked, "who sinned, this man, or his parents, that he should be born blind?" (John 9:2). Jesus again rejects the association of an event with "special providence." "Neither did this man sin, nor his parents: but that the works of God should be made manifest in him" (John 9:3). There *was* a Divinely intended relationship between Providence and this man's blindness, but a relationship quite different from that of simple causality, which self-righteous men had discovered. Not until the shadow of blindness had covered the eyes of the unfortunate man for many years was the Divine intent revealed.

Where fragments of history are not interpreted by God Himself, we are not permitted to explain them out of their entire context as though their meaning were intuitively and, hence, irrationally perspicuous to us. This is underscored by the fact that prosperity and success can never be confused with God's blessing, a fact which those who try to interpret God's intent in a given event often ignore. This actually raises an important question, a question for which light is often sought in the advice of Gamaliel to those persecuting the early disciples: "Refrain from these men, and let them alone: for if this counsel or this work be of men, it will be overthrown: but if it is of God, ye will not be able to overthrow them; lest haply ye be found even to be fighting against God"

(Acts 5:38, 39). It has been suggested that Gamaliel, a Pharisee and non-Christian, spoke as a Jew with some idea of God's permissive will in the world. Gamaliel was able to recall how, after the Pharisees had dethroned the high priest, Alexander Jannai, who had unlawfully set himself up as king, eight hundred Jews were killed on the cross as a punishment for interfering in God's purposes. He was now advising the Jews not to repeat such a mistake. The thought is that God may have willed that this new Christian sect should have its day in the world, and that therefore it was not for man to counter God's mysterious purpose. Apart from whether the Christians were good or bad, the Jews ought to have respect for God's will.[12]

The difficulty with such an interpretation is that Gamaliel's advice points to the dilemma: *from men* or *from God?* That Gamaliel here is not suggesting that it may have been God's will to allow the existence of the "Christian sect," appears from his allusion to the disappearance of the movements of Theudas and Judas. He is apparently suggesting that the Christian movement would likewise disintegrate. Actually, Scripture gives no hint as to the intent of Gamaliel. He appears in the Acts, not to show his sympathy or antipathy for the Christian Church, but because of the fact that he, through his advice, was used to make room for the progress of the work of God.

But apart from this, what about the worth of his advice? Kuyper concludes that Gamaliel's advice is bad. "It is not true," says Kuyper, "that God the Lord destroys forthwith that which is not from Him and crowns with success every endeavor of His believers .... How is it that Gamaliel's advice, so profoundly untrue, is repeated again and again in life? Could it not be just as well the other way around, that to have no success suggests virtue? Is not the Cross a mark of holy origin? Oppressed, downtrodden, molested — can

---

12. Cf. K. Bornhäuser, *Studien zur Apostelgeschichte*, 1934, pp. 56ff.

these not be signs that you are walking on the way of God?"[13]

Gamaliel's advice is based on the now familiar attempt to deduce God's special leading and intent from the course of certain events. The failure of Theudas' revolution is a proof that his movement was not from God. Its tragic end is presumed to be evidence of the "finger" of God; it is an independent source of knowledge of God's purpose. Such reasoning is basically fallacious and, in addition, causes an unnecessary offence because of its arbitrariness and simplicity. Christians cannot hope to answer the criticisms of those who see in this method an attempt to tyrannize over history. What is at stake here is not whether extraordinary events fall within God's rule or not, since even a sparrow does not fall outside of his will (Matt. 10:29). But what is at issue is the interpretation of these events as special revelations of God's will and disposition.

There are many events in the history of salvation whose immediate significance we can understand because they are Divinely explained. The death of Herod — deified by the people and thereupon struck dead by an angel — is directly explained, for example, by the fact that "he gave not God the glory" (Acts 12:21-23). God's Word itself explains this extraordinary event. This is far different from all such attempts as those of Lactantius, who set up his scheme for the interpretation of the deaths of the persecutors of the Church and thought he heard the voice of Divine interpretation in his own explanation. The recognition of history as the work of God, directed toward His purpose, His kingdom, does not include a detailed calculation of His intents.

In faith we know that God's rule goes out over good and evil, over the growth of the Christian Church and the amazing spread of Islam, over the rise and fall of civilizations, over West and East, but "there is no searching of his understanding" (Is. 40:28). All these fall under His unsearch-

---

13. A. Kuyper, *Revisie der revisie-legende*, 1879.

able Providence, but the confession of this does not allow us to pluck what for us are the extraordinary events from the entire stream of history. To do this must end in the reduction of the significance of Providence to occasional supernatural accomplishments, which are, in turn, selected for interpretation arbitarily and interpreted according to our own interests.

* * *

Does this mean that the simple faith which witnesses to God's leading in one's own life is illusory? Does not God's hand disappear from one's individual life when we are conscious only of a universal Providence and when every special intuition of God's presence is denied us? Was it possible only in the Old Testament to say: "Thou hast holden my right hand. Thou wilt guide me with thy counsel" (Ps. 73:23, 24)? Are our prayers and our thanks not to be directed to a very concrete and real Divine leading? The confession of Divine Providence is, in fact, not at all meant to be an abstract confession with no relationship to the concrete life of believers, of His people, or of the whole world; nor is the significance of this confession any less than when the believers in the Old and New Testaments spoke of the leading of God in their lives. All depends on whether or not this confession is really a confession of faith, a sincere confidence in the word of His promise.

When faith ceases to be a living faith, when the believer's walk falls out of God's path, the perspective of the working of God also disappears. Israel was often warned of this danger. We are reminded, in this connection, of the forceful appeal of Amos 9, which deals emphatically with God's activity in history. God's relation to Israel, His disposition in Israel's history is the subject here. Israel, however, assumes the self-evidence of a certain Divine disposition. She builds on patent, historical fact, in this case, the fact of the exodus. At least this fact, as such, seems to give proof of God's special favor.

But Amos reports God's answer: "Are ye not as the children of the Ethiopians unto me, O children of Israel? Have not I brought up Israel out of the land of Egypt, and the Philistines from Caphtor, and the Syrians from Kir?" (Amos 9:7). The uniqueness of Israel's exodus disappears as soon as she tries to use it as argument. The Word of God here, however, may seem to be an extreme case of historical relativizing. Does it not throw a truly unique event into the total maelstrom of historical sequence, there to lose its own particular significance? The Lord's question is the more disturbing since the exodus, more than any other event, is qualified in revelation as God's providential act for the redemption of His people.

What is the purpose of the remark? It becomes clear to anyone who reads the entire book that Amos is not inclined to deny the unique significance of the exodus and to place it on the same level as the histories of other peoples, of the Philistines and Syrians. The meaning is simply this: the *fact* of the exodus may not be used as basis, isolated from revelation and seen by itself, from which to draw selfish conclusions about God's disposition. The exodus as a naked historical fact gives Israel no prerogatives. The Philistines and Syrians are exodus peoples too. The crucial point of Israel's exodus is whether Israel views it in the light of God's work, His disposition revealed in mercy and challenge. As a mere historical fact, the exodus puts Israel on the same level with other nations. But accompanied by a proper faith in God, it constitutes a challenge and, given the proper response, further blessing.

This example of Israel's interpretation of the exodus offers important suggestions for the understanding of God's activity in history. The facts themselves — apart from revelation — do not speak the word from which man may draw final conclusions. To assume that they do have such a message is to be occupied with a neutral philosophy of history, and not with the service of God. Viewed from such an outlook, even such an extraordinary event as the exodus, accompanied as it was with signs and miracles, falls back into the milieu of all other historical events. The exodus was the work of the living God, a work of His mercy and holiness, from which it may not be abstracted. Not to know Him is not to know the exodus in its real significance. The fact needs faith for its real appreciation. Without faith, without constant listening to His explanatory Word, man is not able to distinguish basically between the exodus of Israel and the exoduses of Syria and Philistia. We are told here that we shall never recognize God's finger in history without first meeting Him in the fulness of His revelation. This denies us the luxury of simple conclusions, of the ability to perceive the finger of God in events which we arbitrarily select. We must constantly judge ourselves whether we are subjecting our thinking to the *norm* which is established for all explanation of all events.

This demand holds as well for our interpretation of the central fact of history, the cross of Jesus Christ. Even this event does not speak its own language, apart from revelation. This is God's act of redemption for the world, but it has been misinterpreted whenever it has been contemplated without faith, as, for instance, when Christ's call from the cross was interpreted as a call to Elias for help. One could conclude the impotency of Christ to "save himself." Or one could say, with the disciples going to Emmaus, "But we hoped that it was he who should redeem Israel. Yea and besides all this, it is now the third day since these things came to pass" (Luke 24:21). The word of revelation was ignored and, therefore, the fact misunderstood, its true significance lost within the stream of all events. Then Christ came; and their hearts were ignited, and faith recognized the Resurrected One. Divine action, even in Christ, was not understandable apart from faith and revelation.

When this danger is avoided, the very practical question of faith as to how the confession of Providence can take on concrete significance is answerable. The question is whether, since history — even personal history — cannot be considered a source of knowledge of God's disposition, all events which touch us must be seen as mere enigmatic sequences without any sign of the presence of God's hand and finger in the here and now and with no meaning other than that they all fall within the circle of God's mysterious almighty rule? In the first place, that faith confesses that the end of this mysterious rule of God is our good. The Heidelberg Catechism in Lord's Day 10 defines Providence as God's rule over all things. This is related to Lord's Day 18, which says that Christ is ascended into heaven "for our good," and to Lord's Day 19, which says that Christ rules at the right hand of God to "preserve and protect us from all enemies." It is faith which speaks thus and which sees all things in the light of redemption. It is through faith that we can relate all things to the leading of God. Faith sees the relation of which Paul speaks when he says, "And we know that to them that love God all things work together for good . . ." (Rom. 8:28). Through faith in Jesus Christ "all things" assume the form of a relationship in which the activity of God is not a mere stage play enacted for our observation, but is an activity in which we are intimately involved. This is the background of Romans 8 in which Paul exclaims that nothing either possible or conceivable can thwart the salvation of Christ.

It is possible to speak concretely about God's Providence only on the basis of the blood of the cross. Otherwise we will certainly fall into one of many possible arbitrary interpretations of history. Whim is excluded by redemption. Only faith furnishes the foundation for a vision of history's significance. That is to say, there can be no place for intuition alongside of faith and apart from the word of revelation. All events are embraced in the one work of God, which is explained for all time by His Word. Thus, there can be no proceeding from facts or events isolated from that revelation.

He who sees things this way will never succumb to the temptation to identify prosperity with blessing and adversity with curse. In faith, however, one can accept prosperity as the gift of God, and adversity as God's hand graciously leading him to greater faith.

All this touches on the life of a society or nation as well as on individual lives. If the faith of a people is real, and the Church more than a fallen power, the thankfulness for prosperity is more than a selfish interpretation of Providence. There *can* be a meaningful "Thou hast set us free." There can also be a jubilation that construes God's favor from a neutral fact, apart from faith and apart from "the service of the Lord." The success of the Normandy invasion in 1944, in and by itself, does not prove a special favorable disposition in God toward the West European people any more than the liberation of Stalingrad, in and by itself, proves a special favorable disposition in God toward the Russian people. The Providence of God included West and East, but everything depends, for both, on how the facts are understood. In the absence of true faith, liberation can be turned against a people, as Israel's resting its case for expected blessings on the mere fact of the exodus was turned against her. God's way with the world cannot be summarized with charts or statistics. Each of His acts, and his gifts, is charged with a new summons to obedience and new reminders of responsibility. Therefore the era after a liberation is as critical for a people, for East and West, as the oppression itself. We have seen shadows. Deeper shadows still can fall when after liberation the liberated people estrange themselves further from the service of God.

And without faith, life loses its perspective. It is thrown back into historical relativity. Israel is put on the same level as Philistia.

If ever, then certainly on national days of thanksgiving, God's holy providential command applies to the people: "O earth, earth, earth, hear the word of Jehovah" (Jer. 22:29).

* * *

As is well known, a distinction is often made in dogmatics, and in practical life, between *general* Providence and *special* Providence, and even *very* special Providence. It is a distinction which has in mind the objects of Providence: general Providence includes all creatures, special Providence embraces men, and very special Providence is limited to believers. Theologians do not mean by this distinction to divide up Providence into three separate acts of God. Special and very special Providence do not reveal a more powerful work of God than does general Providence. It is so, however, that the *love* of God is revealed particularly in very special Providence. We see in this that God's Providence is not only a matter of Divine invincibility and power, but of the invincibility and power of His *love*. This is not an anthropocentric narrowing of Providence. It is only a recognition of God's holy care, which in redemption becomes an irrefutable confirmation for all who love Him.

The idea of very special Providence is love's answer of confidence that in God's revelation love is both possible and meaningful. It is not, as it may at first seem, a projection of pride which sees the believer lifted above all others as a "special" object of Providence. Rather, it is ventured as a formulation of thankfulness and humility in the face of this gift of confidence. Such a confidence may seem impossible in this world. It may be, however, that it, better than anything, can illustrate the difference between the freedom from anxiety that a believer may enjoy and the despairing acquiescence in which life estranged from God often culminates. The word of Him who declared to us the God of Providence has relevancy within the infinite complexities of modern life: "Are

PROVIDENCE AND HISTORY 181

not two sparrows sold for a penny? and not one of them shall fall on the ground without your Father: but the very hairs of your head are all numbered. Fear not therefore: ye are of more value than many sparrows" (Matt. 10:29-31).[14] History thus loses its power to fill the believing heart with dread. This, in the face of actuality, seems like pious nonsense. Is this not pre-eminently the "age of anxiety?" In reference to this anxiety, Jesus tells us to seek first the kingdom of God (Matt. 6:33); which is to say that the peace of mind that the Gospel gives does not allow us to decline into the superficialities of comfortable bourgeois living. It gives us the calling to seek and work in the coming kingdom.

* * *

We are thus kept from looking for God's very special Providence only in our prosperity and in the better moments of our lives. God's leading directs all things with a view to the coming of His kingdom and not to our individual lives. It can hardly, then, be identified with prosperity. The author of Hebrews writes about the chastisement of the Lord: "My son, regard not lightly the chastening of the Lord, Nor faint when thou art reproved of him; For whom the Lord loveth he chasteneth, And scourgeth every son whom he receiveth" (Heb. 12:5, 6). Chastisement and the love of the Father are closely associated. Over against the identification of very special Providence with continual prosperity, the writer says, "God dealeth with you as with sons; for what son is there whom his father chasteneth not? But if ye are without chastening, whereof all have been made partakers, then are ye bastards, and not sons" (Heb. 12:7, 8). The chastening, however, is for our own good, to the end that we may share in His holiness (Heb. 12:10).

---

14. Cf. C. S. Lewis, *Miracles*, London, 1948, pp. 208ff. (Appendix B, "Special Providences").

Chastisement — proof of God's love! Chastisement — proof of sonship! This has significance for the understanding — in faith — of the facts of our lives. The facts themselves seem to speak another language at times: "All chastening seemeth for the present to be not joyous but grievous . . . ." (Heb. 12:11). Apart from faith, then, these hard and bitter facts can never be rightly understood. Through faith, it is possible to see the purpose and sense of painful chastening.[15] Without minimizing its severity, we may believe that pain and sorrow, the chastening of the Lord, can lead to their Divinely intended purpose — the sanctifying of the soul. The believer can encounter God's hand, and His finger, precisely in the distress of life, so that he, in the discipline of adversity, may see God. But the first thing necessary is that a man know God as Father, if he is to recognize His hand in his suffering.

Scripture never offers an interpretation of facts apart from faith. It speaks of the finger of God in history, but in quite another sense than that of much human speculation about His special interventions. The Scriptures do not connect the finger of God simply with extraordinary events which men find hard to interpret naturally. For instance, we read of the heavens as the work of God's fingers (Ps. 8:3) and of the two tables of stone written with God's finger (Deut. 9:10). Pharaoh's magicians also associated God's finger with something extraordinary. Upon seeing Moses's miracles, they called out: "This is the finger of God" (Ex. 8:19). A kind of contest of extraordinary phenomena took place in Pharaoh's court between Moses and the Egyptian magicians. As Moses' works were equalled by the magicians, they were all on the same level in Pharaoh's view. So, he hardened his heart. When the magicians failed to match one of Moses' wonders, they interpreted it as the finger of God. This, how-

---

15. Cf. Eccles. 3:10-12 and Deut. 8:5. We meet the same words in Jer. 2:19 as in Heb. 12. Heb. 12 also quotes the LXX version of Eccles. 3:10-12.

ever, had nothing to do with an acknowledgment of the true God of the miracle. It was only a way of saying that their intelligence could not account for a new phenomenon. At the same time, Pharaoh's heart was again hardened (Ex. 8:16-19).

The exclaiming of "This is the finger of God" ought not, then, lead to the rash conclusion that God is thereby acknowledged. This illustrates again that the way to the knowledge of the true God does not run from observation of facts to Him. It illustrates also that man can harden his heart in the very face of "irrefutable" facts. He who wishes to speak responsibly about the finger of God may well ponder the vigorous words of Christ: "But if I by the finger of God cast out demons, then is the kingdom of God come upon you" (Luke 11:20). But we read in Matthew, "But if I by the *Spirit* of God cast out demons, then is the kingdom of God come upon you" (Matt. 12:28). This is the invincibility of God's kingdom in Jesus Christ. And he who would understand and recognize the finger of God must know that there is only one way: the way of the kingdom, the way of salvation in Christ, which is known only through the Holy Spirit.

* * *

Finally, we must consider one important question which has bearing on the final coming of the kingdom of God. Having seen that we are not able to conclude from fragmentary facts and extraordinary events in history that God is leading in a particular direction with a particular purpose, we still must recognize that the Scriptures themselves point to certain events which are signs of the return of Christ. The Bible speaks emphatically about portents of the end. The question of the interpretation of history arises from Scripture itself. We are not concerned with eschatological problems here, but we must take note of the so-called signs of the times, since our expectation of Christ's return is connected here with the understanding of extraordinary events in history.

Scripture warns us to be discerning of the times, to be analytical, to attend in faith to God's conducting of history. Christ once chided the crowds that while able to discern the signs of change in the weather, that is, to discern the earth and the heavens, they were not able to discern the time (Luke 12:54-56). As there are connections in nature (clouds: rain; southwind: heat) so are there discernible connections between events in history. Christ did not summon the hypocrites to discern the times in the sense of scientific investigation; He reminded them of the approach of the kingdom of God. The times of the action of God are always charged; but these men did not sense it. They could not perceive that the times of the prophecies were being fulfilled before them, that the terrible time of which Mary had sung in the *Magnificat* was now upon them, that God was busy in the time of salvation, that God's salvation was on the streets and in the houses. They could not see this, though they could discern the face of the heaven and the earth. And Christ rebuked them.

But we are told also to be alert to the omens of the future. Prophecy sheds its light, not only on the time of Christ's life on earth, but also on the future. There are portents of the end. We are not given the magic word of prediction. We recall that only Christ may open the book of history, that His day is unknown, that He shall come as a thief in the night (Rev. 5:5; Mark 13:32; I Thess. 5:2). But nevertheless a specially directed attentiveness, a listening concentration, is demanded. There are moments, fragments of history, which must be interpreted from the standpoint of revelation. This interpretation, however, is not meant to be a time-table, a speculation, an historical prediction. It is rather a testing and hoping examination of history for signs of the approach of the returning Lord. The portents of the end are all connected with a radically religious illumination of history. They have to do with events which have their coherence in the salvation of Christ. The preaching of the signs of the end is introduced by Christ Himself in the focal message concerning His person. When the disciples asked Him on the Mount of Olives for signs of His coming, He first warned against temptation: "Take heed that no man lead you astray. For many shall come in my name, saying, I am the Christ; and shall lead many astray" (Matt. 24:4, 5). Regardless with what pretentions and authority, and with what miracles, they may come, "Believe it not." "Behold, I have told you beforehand" (Matt. 24:25). The norm for the interpretation of the future lies in His person, in the salvation which is exclusive in Him. There is one great danger for the Church on her way to the future: to be deceived, to be led away from this salvation of God.

In this connection, Christ has qualified certain definite striking events of the future as augurs of the end, as signs of His coming. He speaks of the things that are certain to come: wars and rumors of wars, famine and earthquakes, oppression and persecution of the Church, false prophets and love waxed cold, increasing unrighteousness, and the preaching of the Gospel over the entire world as a witness to all peoples (Matt. 24:6-12). The warning for the Church to be discerning of the times is included in all this. Watchfulness is demanded, and attention to events. Again Christ draws the parallel between discerning the times and understanding nature: "Now from the fig tree learn her parable: when her branch is now become tender, and putteth forth its leaves, ye know that the summer is nigh; even so ye also when ye see all these things, know ye that he is nigh, even at the doors" (Matt. 24:32, 33). All this stands under the guarantee of Christ's holy witness as He says, "My words shall not pass away" (Matt. 24:35).

* * *

We are perhaps not given historical laws, which could be presented as a scientific formula: if A appears and B follows, then C must also come. But Christ does say quite clearly, that if *this* occurs then the end *is near*. This must be a matter of faith combining historical events on the ground of concrete prophecy. We are not to draw charts. We are to remain in expectation of His approach. Thus the accumulation of events, with their religious background, can shed light on our daily lives. In the growing tension we are more keenly aware that we have here no abiding city, that we are to live in God's salvation lest the day of the Lord catch us unprepared. Here lies the believing interpretation of history. It is not a task of observing the extraordinary events in which God's immediate activity supposedly substitutes momentarily for natural law. It is the illuminating of Christ's approach through providential events. These events must then direct our attention not to themselves, but, by their character and nature, to the coming salvation.

Divine Providence and history!

The line of events climaxes in the kingdom of God. This is not proven by natural reason. War can be viewed strictly in its military or economic aspects, earthquakes as movements of the earth's layers, famine as an economic and social problem, and the increasing unrighteousness as natural moral decadence. But in the light of revelation the course of history can also be seen from the one all determinative religious perspective. Then, though there have always been wars, earthquakes, and pestilences, these will be recognized as signs, as portents of the end, when the powers of sin are overcome and God's judgment flashes. In the increasing chaotic senselessness of life, man can lose all perspective for the meaning of history and sink under the hopelessness of life. Or, conceivably, prompted by idealistic and optimistic motives, he could work for a reconstruction of culture. But the Gospel sheds aside both pessimism and optimism and directs us to the meaning of history contained in the kingdom of God. The complexity of events does not present us with a spur to doubt or suspicion, but to more faith. Only thus shall the believers be able to stand in the day, which is "nearer to us than when we first believed" (Rom. 13:11).

The central, religious aspect of history is here touched upon, as is apparent from one of the signs: the preaching of the Gospel to all the world (Matt. 24:14). The portents of the end find in this their centrum. The consummation of history is approached in the light of this preaching. The signs of the end are not mysterious events, but simply the maturation of unrighteousness (II Thess. 2:7) and the execution of judgment on the last "powers" of evil. And ". . . when these things begin to come to pass, look up, and lift up your heads; because your redemption draweth nigh" (Luke 21:28).

CHAPTER VII

Providence and Miracles

A STUDY of God's Providence would be much impoverished if the relation between Providence and miracles were passed by. Anyone at all acquainted with the theological history of the last few centuries knows how prominent miracles have been in all discussions about the reality of God. The possibility and reality of miracles have been increasingly disputed, particularly under the powerful suggestion of modern science. Just as it had rendered expendable the "hypothesis" of Divine Providence over all things, the scientific method relieved many persons of their sense of need for the possibility of extraordinary Divine interventions into the normal course of things. With the scientific method applied universally and with no fields impervious to its advance, a world sealed by mechanistic, natural causality was taken more and more for granted. Divine intervention was not only unnecessary. It was impossible.

With the inner causal relationships of nature, if not understood, at least understandable, the Church's doctrine of miracles seemed an expendable remnant of the old supernatural view of the world. It was assumed that the Church considered miracles as an incidental disruption of natural law, as though a miracle meant something that God did in opposition to nature. This concept of miracles was, of course, according to the dogma of natural causality, quite impossible. The facts which disproved miracles were considered so irrefutably obvious that no one with an honest conscience could avoid them. Even in orthodox circles men were often ready to capitulate by adjusting their concept of nature to render a *new* view of miracles possible.

Nineteenth century Calvinism has also been charged with thus surrendering to natural science, there being, it was said, a notable difference on this score between Calvin and the so-called neo-Calvinism of Abraham Kuyper. The difference allegedly was that original Calvinism had a supernaturalistic, and neo-Calvinism a naturalistic world and life view. Supernaturalism meant the recognition of an intervention of supernatural powers into the natural course of things. God's acts and natural events are, thus, independent of and, at times, even opposed to each other. Naturalism, on the other hand, taught a fixed order and denied the incursion of supernatural powers. The accusation was that neo-Calvinism, in contrast to original Calvinism, taught naturalism, that it accepted the world and life view of the contemporary nineteenth century mind and built its house on the foundation of natural science. This, it was claimed, did not occur merely by way of a few concessions and tendencies. In its view of man, nature, and history neo-Calvinism had, as it was said, "with admirable brilliance and consistency exchanged the old life and world view for the new."

This idea is easy to refute, but it raises a question with wide implications. We are not now interested in the relation between Calvin and Kuyper, but in the larger problem posed here, that is, the problem of supernaturalism. This criticism of neo-Calvinism was occasioned by Kuyper's strong protest against a certain form of supernaturalism. The question is whether such criticism of supernaturalism actually involves a capitulation to naturalism and to the life view of modern natural science.

Nineteenth century modernism certainly was guilty of submission to natural science. As Scholten, one of the fathers of modernism in the Netherlands, said, "The newer theology does not speak of a God who is outside of and thus separated from nature or, what is the same, from the world . . . [He is] not a Being who intrudes into the natural interdependence of phenomena . . . God's activity is not outside of, much less contrary to, nature, but natural, for the simple reason that the word nature is used by science to indicate the totality of all activity in its interdependence. His activity is one with nature, which, in turn, is the totality of God's activity." Naturally, the new theology, on this basis, rejected miracles as well as every form of inspiration given mechanically, as it was said, from the outside. Modernism's controversy was with the supposed dualism of supernaturalism. And with its rejection of supernaturalism, modernism also had to revise its concept of Divine Providence.

The movement of modernism was in the direction of monism. It rejected deism, which set God apart from the world, and elected a conception of God which reveals itself and works itself out in the whole of existence and events, as they unfold His true essence in the visible realities to which He belongs, but with which He does not entirely coincide. It is a view that has more affinity with pantheism than with Christian theism, which modernism accused of proclaiming the autocracy of God as though it were a human despotism in inflated proportions.

Not everyone, however, was willing to accept the full consequences of this monistic view of the world. This was illustrated with particular clarity by Allard Pierson, the *enfant terrible* of modernism, one of the few who accepted the practical consequences of modern thought. He resigned his ministerial office, saying that his rejection of supernaturalism made it impossible for him to work within the Church without sacrificing his honesty and integrity. It was, he thought, impossible to construct a Christian theology on the modernistic assumption of a world closed to miracles. Pierson questioned whether modernism could honestly claim for itself the name of Christianity. He applied the consequences of modern thought particularly to the Providence doctrine. If, he reasoned, everything must have a natural cause, man can no longer believe in Divine intervention.

Further, granted an uninterrupted natural interdependence between all things and the absolute dominion of the law of cause and effect, there can be no place for miracles, no hope of Divine interference. The new theology taught that God never acted immediately, that all His acts were bound by the logical, mutual interdependence of natural things. Pierson concluded, "Though it may be desirable to speak kind and pleasant words from the pulpit to attentive audiences, it is better to be silent when these words have meaning only in a world which is no longer and can no longer be ours." Thus, compromise was unthinkable. And, since prayer for a pure heart is as supernatural as prayer for a sound body, the logical and unavoidable climax was Pierson's departure from the Church.

Most modernists did not follow him. By one means or another they avoided the proper wages of modernism. A place, somehow, was reserved for the reality of religion. The attempt to save religion was a part of another battle, the struggle to release human personality from the grips of mechanistic, natural cause. The more generally the scientific method was applied, the less place there was for free human personality. Boasting that everything could be resolved in quantitative and discernable relations, the scientific method gravitated toward a materialistic psychology.

When things had gone this far, even non-theological resistance stiffened. We may recall the defence that certain neo-Kantians like Rickert and Windelband put up against the universal pretensions of natural science. Natural science had, through its universal dominion, all but ruled out the significance of human individuality, and against this Rickert urged: "There are sciences which do not establish natural laws, which are not based on the idea of the universality of a general concept, and these are historical sciences in the widest sense of the term."[1] In this way Rickert tried to resist the exclusive domination by natural science. While not concerned about the possibility of miracles, many modern thinkers became insistent about the limits of natural science. They, like Rickert, attempted to maintain the peculiar character of psychology and, therewith, the individuality of the human soul, along with human freedom and responsibility.

Occupied almost exclusively with man, his life, his soul, and his freedom, modern thinkers were not concerned about the activity of God. Some modern theologians, however, attempted to draw conclusions for religion from this non-religious resistence to natural science. It was said that a purely monistic explanation of reality ignored certain facts of human experience. Monism may fascinate for an evening but when morning comes it leaves man unsatisfied. Human experience encounters everywhere a duality between what is and what ought to be, between the real and the ideal. It was this duality that monism mistakenly ignored. Windelband called it the "duality of values and reality." Others spoke of two worlds. Besides reality "sensitive to feeling as to sight," there is another world, a "higher" world of values. It is true that man is bound to the laws of empirical causality, but there is also a possibility of break-through. There is an element of irrationality in life, an interaction between two worlds — to put it religiously, between man and God.

This raised the question of whether Biblical miracles could again be accepted by modern man. The answers to this question were very cautious, hemmed in with many reservations. The absolute monism of natural science was broken, but this, while expanding the concept of causality, did not mean that any arbitrary break in natural law was considered possible. There was talk of "conservative modernistic" supernaturalism, but this had reference only to the spiritual life and had no bearing

---

1. H. Rickert, *Kulturwissenschaft und Naturwissenschaft*, 1921, p. 60.

PROVIDENCE AND MIRACLES 193

on the broad expanse of history. No general consequences could be drawn from the interaction between individual life and the higher world. Room was made for spiritual life, for encounter with God, for something new, unexplained by the law of cause and effect, but this incidental break-through had nothing to do with Biblical miracles. There was only one kind of miracle, that of the religious life. This was the only door open to the world for God.

Here, then, is an attempt to reserve a small place in the world for religion. In all such attempts we touch upon the heart of the modern problem: "nature" and God, the question of supernaturalism.

* * *

It is necessary to point out, perhaps with some emphasis, that the ideal of the universal dominion of science is still common, its influence still considerable. The absolutism of natural science was the rock on which anti-supernaturalistic monism rested. Its influence has more recently been demonstrated in theology by the "de-mythologizing" of the New Testament. Behind the modern terminology, one can recognize in this a motif similar to that of the nineteenth century anti-supernaturalism. Bultmann, for instance, repeats the old arguments in new form, speaking of the mythological character of the Biblical view of the world. The controlling idea of the Biblical view is that this world is the theater for supernatural powers. Demons invade the cosmos. Satan, sin, and death wield an influence on the world. The world, in turn, is headed for a cataclysmic end: the coming of the heavenly judge, resurrection of the dead, judgment, salvation and perdition. The reporting of the sacred events accords with this mythological view of the world: God sends His pre-existent Son who suffers and dies on the cross, then arises and ascends to heaven, promising to return for us. Modern man, says Bultmann, finds this mythological construction wholly untenable.

"Worldly knowledge and forces are so highly developed in science and technique that no one can and no one does seriously hold the New Testament view of the world. What meaning can 'descended into hell' or 'ascended into heaven' have for modern man? . . . One cannot use electric lights and radios, call in modern medicine and clinical methods in time of sickness, and still believe in the New Testament world of spirits and miracles."[2] Behind these ideas lies the same overestimation for science as that which in the nineteenth century led to the denial of miracles.

Miracles are rejected in proportion to the extension of our knowledge. As nature becomes more transparent the possibility of the Biblical miracles fades. This forms an important point in modern thought. Certainly, our insight into nature is amazingly extended in all directions. Bavinck, in his time, said, "The extension of our knowledge of second causes, the insight into the dominion of the law of causality, the deeper psychological and historical studies of phenomena have, as it were, alienated God from us. It is as though nature has intruded itself between God and us. He seems to be nowhere immediately present and directly at work. His activity is universally mediated by nature and history." God is farther from the consciousness of modern man than from the consciousness of former generations who thought they could perceive His hand directly in many events — events which since then have been explained by natural causes. In former days many phenomena could be explained only by a special Divine interference which are now no longer mysterious. The idea of miracles has become superfluous now that man knows that it is law which controls nature and history.

How must we answer the claims of science? Bavinck rejects the notion "that faith in the existence and Providence of God is built on gaps in our sciences, so that we need be in

---

2. R. Bultmann, "Neue Testament und Mythologie" in *Offenbarung und Heilsgeschichte*, 1941, pp. 27ff.

continual dread that with the progress of research and with the solution of more and more problems, faith must sacrifice its territory." Bavinck did not feel that the extension of our knowledge of nature created a sort of competition between natural forces and the activity of God. The repudiation of this competition idea is of fundamental significance for the correct approach to the problem of miracles.

Kuyper agreed with Bavinck, and refused to accept miracles as an incidental intervention into an otherwise hermetically sealed nature.[3] He opposed supernaturalism, but his opposition was wholly other than that of modernistic anti-supernaturalism. Kuyper's resistance to supernaturalism wore its own color, intending in no sense a limitation of the absoluteness and power of the sovereign activity of God. On the contrary, he pointed out that he was in full accord with supernaturalism in so far as it meant that God transcended nature. But his objection to supernaturalism was that it posited a false system, "as though nature is a power that stands over against God with its own forces and laws, under Him, to be sure, in that He hinders it from doing anything against His will, but possessing with its powers and laws a certain independence beside, under, and over against God. And that is not a pious but an ungodly conception, which we deeply abhor and which poisons true supernaturalism." As for miracles, supernaturalism saw them as an occasional intervention of God in the customary process of nature. Everything normally runs according to fixed law and order "but a mysterious hand appears now and then, interfering with the gears so that suddenly the machine works differently than is normal." According to this, nature was a sphere that is essentially independent of God through which God occasionally breaks to perform a miracle. "The error of supernaturalism is corrected only when every thought of such an independent and permanent existence of nature is plucked out at its roots and we understand that

---

3. Cf. A. Kuyper, *E Voto*, I, pp. 238ff.

nature with all her powers and all her laws is nothing in herself, but is what she is from moment to moment through the command that proceeds from God's mouth. They are all, O Lord, nothing but Thy servants."[4]

Kuyper refused to consider miracles against the background of a mechanistic, monistic concept of nature, the abstraction of a rationalistic natural science. He unmasked the irreligious character of this concept of nature and rejected it. His rejection of supernaturalism was not from a naturalistic design, but from a desire to maintain the Divine transcendence over (super) all created reality. A miracle, thus, is no *occasional* intervention by God into the course of natural things, "for nothing operates through any power apart from God." A miracle "means nothing more than that God at a given moment wills a certain thing to occur differently than it had up to that moment been willed by Him to occur."[5]

Kuyper certainly did not deny miracles. He simply refused to confront the idea of miracle with an abstract concept of nature and insisted on considering miracles in their inseparable connection with the universally effectual activity of God. "He speaks and it exists; He commands and it is done. Nothing withstands His will. For Him there is no miracle .... The manna that rained in the desert is not more miraculous than the grain that grows through His will and power. The miraculous element lies in our consciousness, in our eyes." Again, a miracle is "exactly the same as an ordinary work of nature, for in a miracle there are two elements, the command of the Lord and the work of His servants — the elements and powers of nature."[6]

Kuyper sharply distinguished miracles as works of God from the works of a magician "who performs now this and now that trick to display his skill." Not the whim, but the will of God

---

4. *Ibid.*, p. 239.
5. *Ibid.*, p. 240.
6. *Ibid.*, p. 241.

stands behind miracles. Miracles are not occasional interferences by God in a fixed order of nature. They are new, extraordinary ways of God's rule over all things. Summarizing, Kuyper's objection to supernaturalism arose from a religious protest against its concept of nature as being generally independent of God, but subject to occasional Divine interference by way of miracles.

He also spoke of the persistent tendency of believers to construe God's government of the world as an occasional or atomistic affair, a tendency that also appears in practical life. When in difficult circumstances we are provided an escape, it says more to us than "years of God's fatherly care." This is partly because the causal connection goes unnoticed in such special cases. But basically it arises from unbelief. "It is almost impossible for us to recognize and praise God in the common course of life." It is necessary to warn against seeking material for faith only in the extraordinary, for with this mystical notion of faith we pave the way for unbelief. Otherwise it may occur that "as soon as one comes into more knowledge, he is captured by brazen unbelief." Our life must be not occasionally, but continually, pious, that is, our whole lives must be lived in fellowship with God.

It is a serious failing of many that they "have no eye for the presence of God's power in the ordinary course of things." He who does have an eye for this sees things differently and is never afraid of science. As Kuyper wrote of the Reformed people, "they always went along with science; they were never afraid lest something new be discovered or explained."[7] This, of course, has nothing to do with naturalism. It arises from a resistance to an absolutizing of nature, as is apparent from Kuyper's insistence that a miracle is not something *contra naturam*. Scripture, he said, would have us understand miracles as "phenomena whose natural relationships, whose inward workings, cannot be understood by man." In any case,

---

7. A. Kuyper, *Dietaten Dogmatiek*, "Locus de Providentia," p. 209.

Kuyper placed miracles on another level than that of a "break through" of a causally sealed nature.

* * *

Perhaps the most discussed problem in the matter of miracles has been the idea of miracles as being *contra naturam*. Described as *contra naturam,* miracles are considered from one definite aspect, their relation to sealed-in nature. This idea has played an important role in the theology of miracles. Augustine, however, considered miracles as in contradiction, not with nature, but with nature as understood by us.[8] Miracles cannot be contrary to nature, for God's will defines the nature of every creature. There are potentialities in nature that we know not of, said Augustine. If we should ever know everything, the idea of *contra naturam* would of itself disappear.

In Roman Catholic theology the full accent is laid on miracles as contrary to nature. This means, especially for Thomas, not that God interferes with natural law, but that in a given instance He suspends it. When does this occur? The God-given laws are arranged for the achievement of the natural purpose of the world. But when God wishes to achieve a supernatural purpose, He uses supernatural means, that is, miracles. There is a distinction between supernatural and natural effects. "A miracle," says Pauwels, "is a fact, discernible by natural means, which deviates from the customary order of nature and has God for its proper cause."[9] Divine intervention is possible because God can suspend the activity of things or replace one by another, without destroying the proper nature of things. In any event, a miracle is an event that cannot be explained by natural causes and transcends the order of created nature. God is the immediate cause of a miracle.

---

8. *De Civitate Dei*, XXI, 8. "Portentum ergo fit, non contra naturam, sed contra quam est nota natura."
9. C. F. Pauwels, *Apologetiek*, 1948, p. 157.

This is worked out in various ways by Roman Catholic theology, but the distinction between miracles and nature is always the decisive point of departure for this concept of miracles. There are two forms of reality: the reality of ordinary nature and the reality of miracles. This is characteristically supernaturalistic. Only now and then is there an incursion into natural reality made by the supernatural reality of miracles.[10] This view is faced first of all with the formal problem of nature and of the possible place of miracles in nature. Though it is asserted that miracles are no violation of the laws of nature, the contrast between nature and miracle is always evident. The question of the *possibility* of miracles controls the entire line of thought, whether one speaks of miracles as an exception to or a perfection of nature. The uniformity of nature defines what a miracle can be: "even a conceivable point of intersection of the supernatural with the natural must in any case be proposed as something great."[11] In many discussions of miracles, this "point of intersection" gets the major attention. The formal consideration of the break-through seems to be the important thing, and, though the content of the miracle is not wholly without significance, it is considered only after the miracle is formally defined as a "break through," a "suspension" of nature — in short, as something more or less *contra naturam*.

As the hold of natural science on the modern mind became stronger, the problem of the relation between miracles and natural law was increasingly accented. Nature was considered as normal and miracles as abnormal, and thus the problem of miracles became a problem of contingency. The concept of miracles, then, became very formal and empty, and theologians were forced to the apologetical position of trying to reserve a place for the mere possibility of miracles on the basis of

---
10. Thomas, *Summa Theologica*, I, qu. 110, art. IV. "Miraculum est praeter ordinem totius naturae creatae."
11. H. Thielicke, *Theologie der Anfechtung*, 1949, p. 96.

causality. Under the impression of the new knowledge of nature and the presumed absoluteness of natural law, miracles were either strictly limited or wholly denied. Thus, miracles became a problem in modern theological thought. A deep uncertainty and inward doubt knocked at the door and was often admitted. The joy of the Lord, who alone works miracles, was stifled. The mere conceivability of miracles became the point at issue. The "possible" of God, of which the Scriptures speak so plainly, was refuted by the certainty of science with its monistic outlook on life. The consequence was a severe anti-supernaturalism. It was not only denied that miracles *now* occur, but the conquering crusade of natural science also absolutely rejected the Biblical miracles. The discovery of the sealed-in causality of nature worked with retroactive effect. Even the new Testament had to be "de-mythologized."

* * *

In this crisis, apologetic attempts were made to maintain the possibility of miracles. But in all these attempts one uncovers very little that is of value. We may consider, for example, the many attempts to secure a little space for "the intervention of God" by limiting the concept of natural law or causality. We can respect the good intention of this argument but must, nevertheless, say that by using this kind of apologetic one has already capitulated to a non-Biblical mode of thinking. The limits were set by posing the correlation: natural law — miracle. It was meant to show that — on the basis of the position of natural science — natural law did not have the absoluteness that had previously been ascribed to it. While previously the absolute validity of natural law threatened the conceivability of miracles, it was now thought that a more relative view of these laws would make room for miracles as a fragmentary intervention by God. Natural laws were considered as a "generalization of a number of particular natural laws" which allows for exceptions and is subject to error.

It is now claimed that modern natural science no longer believes in a fixed regularity "which is settled in the world, uniform for all time." Our concept of the world is infinitely richer than that of the nineteenth century. This touches on the possibility of miracles. Every incident that we study is of such bewildering complexity that many more possibilities are conceived of now than in the nineteenth century, when the manner of considering possibilities was too confined. It is said that "we possess no universally uniform natural law. We cannot say any more that these laws are always absolutely valid within perceivable limits."[12] Many physicists speak much more qualifiedly than previously about natural laws and causality, and from this it is thought possible to create a better relationship between religion and science. The current position of natural science invites this. "Even on the basis of the quantum theory, the possibility appears that the opinions of the causal connection of natural laws will have to be completely altered."[13] Thus, room is created for miracles because the statification of the "eternal laws of nature" has come into disrepute. In contrast to the standpoint of immanence, "which would view our entire world as a completely sealed-in system," there is granted the possibility once more for "interventions of Divine power in our world." Some theologians now believe that various modern scientific researches are of significance for faith and for the "conceivability" of miracles. Men are asking whether natural science's attack on faith has come to an end.

In the light of quantum theories and atomic research — and now that scientists hazard to speak only of probability where they used to speak of certainty — should not a new relationship exist between science and faith, especially between

---
12. A. Titius, *Natur und Gott*, 1926, p. 582.
13. *Ibid.*, p. 584.

science and faith in miracles? Has not — one may ask — a new gap been discovered in the former concept of mechanistic, deterministically sealed-in reality? Does not the "latitude for movement" theory, as it may be called, contain the promise that the offense that miracles constitute for modern man is at least partially removed? Are miracles not more possible now that men speak of "the impossibility of an objective description of nature"?

When one considers this apologetic approach, he is struck by the suggestive power that the old deterministic-mechanistic concept of the world has exercised on theology. The enthusiasm with which theologians currently make use of new researches in order to demonstrate the possibility of miracles is striking evidence of how they have been influenced by the old natural science theory. Usually this enthusiasm is not over the increased modesty that is evident among the scientists, but over the newly apparent "latitude of movement" for faith. Miracles seem to be made possible again only by the grace of science. Their possibility is a fruit of the problematic character of our time. The evident enthusiasm of theologians about Planck's quantum theory and Heisenberg's "relation of inaccuracy" is in itself symptomatic of a vitiation of faith in miracles. This does not mean that miracles had been sacrificed but that, under the menacing shadow of natural science, they had become matters of concern. And now, happily, there appears to be room and possibility for miracles again, thanks to the relativizing of natural law. Miracles are, thus, as far as method and apologetics go, approached from the standpoint of the structure of reality. At bottom, men feared natural order and natural law as a threat to the sovereign and free activity of God. And when natural science manifested doubts about the absoluteness of natural law, some theologians rejoiced. He who rediscovers room for the activity of God in a crisis of natural science, however, has already implicitly relativized and limited this activity and has posited it over against a natural order seen as a self-existing reality. In this way, the question of miracles will always be involved in the problems of natural science. And for the most part the Biblical manner of speaking about the activity of God in this world will have been abandoned.

This type of apologetics is rightly rejected by many modern theologians. Paul Althaus, for instance, writes, "Faith should under no circumstances seek to profit from a particular scientific position in physics . . . . The current thesis of atomic physics can one of these days be replaced by a new strictly causal physics."[14] Althaus warns against making faith dependent on natural science. He who ties the conceivability of miracles to a hiatus in the results of natural science can wait for the further development of science only with fear and trembling. And he may be forced to capitulate to a subsequent withdrawal of the "latitude of movement" which current science affords faith.

The Scriptures have quite another approach to miracles. They put the emphasis, not on the possibility, but on the reality of miracles. Furthermore, they do not consider the reality of miracles as a "break through" of the laws of nature. As Eichrodt has said, "Old Testament saints do not in the least consider a 'break through' of natural law as a *conditio sine qua non* for the miraculous character of an occurrence."[15]

It has become customary, because of the modern opposition to miracles, to speak of the primitive character of the Biblical viewpoint. This is understandable — on the basis of modern thought — since the Biblical faith in miracles has much more in common formally with the so-called primitive apperception of God and the world than with the secularized thought which brands miracles as impossible. Actually, however, the primitive concept of miracles and the Biblical miracles are

---

14. P. Althaus, *Die Christliche Wahrheit*, II, 1948, p. 73. Cf. E. Brunner, *Offenbarung und Vernunft*, 1941, pp. 292ff.
15. W. Eichrodt, *Theologie des Alten Testamentes*, II, p. 84.

not comparable, since the Biblical miracles cannot be considered merely in their formal characteristics; they are always miracles of Israel's *God,* who alone does miracles. Nevertheless, the Biblical concept of miracles does stand in opposition to the antithesis proposed by modern thought: miracle vs. self-contained nature. Only in this sense is the Biblical idea of miracles akin to the primitive concept of the miraculous.

The Holy Scriptures open another perspective for us. They see no antithesis between the activity of God and a self-contained world. Rather, they see all things without exception as lying each instant in God's hand. There is no talk of any self-sufficiency in nature. The Scriptures focus our attention not so much on the "point of intersection" of the supernatural with the natural, as on the content and purpose of God's activity in the world.

The Biblical miracles have to do, first of all, with a *new and surprising* mode of God's activity. Consider what God says in Ex. 34:10: "And he said, Behold, I make a covenant: before all thy people I will do marvels, such as have not been wrought in all the earth, nor in any nation; and all the people among which thou art shall see the work of Jehovah; for it is a terrible thing that I do with thee." (Cf. Num. 16:30; Jer. 31:22; Is. 48:6 ff.) In this element of novelty we are not faced with an abstract nature problem, but with the mighty historical activity of God in love and mercy. The element of newness is directed to His own work with the elect people. It is *His* act, not to be deduced from this world or from the people of Israel. The activity of God is not problematic, but almighty, Divine reality. His activity intersects all human expectations. From the limited human perspective, the activity of God seems sometimes to be impossible. Sarah's laugh at the promise of motherhood finds its answer in the word of the Lord: "Is anything too hard for Jehovah?" (Gen. 18:14). Over against what seems impossible to human conception stands the ability of Divine might. In His novel activity, God leads history on its way, in the establishment of His people and in the powerful defence against her enemies. What is impossible in human life, is possible with God.

There is not talk of a sealed-in world or of iron-clad laws which must be broken through. There is — in the nature of the case — nothing problematic in the activity of God, who does new things on earth. Out of death comes life through His act. Scriptural miracles are not products of an immature naive concept of nature, the mark of insufficient enlightenment; they are revealed as acts of God. Israel is acquainted with the ordinances of God, with His injunctions and His servants. He has fixed the limits of the sea, that the water may not trespass His commands (Prov. 8:29). He has arranged places for the waters by the mountains and in the valleys, fixing a boundary which they cannot pass over (Ps. 104:8, 9). He closed the doors to the sea as it came seething from its womb. "Hitherto shalt thou come, but no further; And here shall thy proud waves be stayed" (Job 38:11).

But these are His boundaries that are visible here, and they must never, though for an instant, be absolutized or abstracted from Him, the Lawgiver even of *these* servants. He is not the prisoner of His own servants. He works and goes *His* way. With whom shall we compare Him? The Scriptures nowhere present the miraculous activity of God as the problem of the *contra naturam*. This sort of problem abstracts nature from God and breaks the unity of Divine activity. There is neither limit nor problem to His activity. In the surprising and unexpected He goes trustworthily on His way into ever new historical situations. This is how Israel sang and worshiped Jehovah. He is great in might in the common things of life, but it is especially in the unusual deeds, the miraculous signs, that He arouses the attention and amazement of His people and shocks Israel's enemies with the invincibility of His works. Israel, therefore, honors Him as God, who stands alone in the working of miracles (Ps. 72:18). The surprising and extraordinary become, in the midst of ordinary life, a sign of His power and love. "Thy way, O God," sings Asaph, "Is in the sanctuary: Who is a great god like unto God? Thou art the God that doest wonders: Thou hast made known thy strength among the peoples" (Ps. 77:13, 14). "Thou art great and doeth miracles, Thou, O God, alone" (Ps. 86:10). "Praise Him, who doeth great wonders" (Ps. 136:4).

Impossibility disappears in the face of the limitlessness of His benevolent power, for impossibility means an absence of ability and might. Miracles have to do with the revelation of the power of God, for which all things are possible in the possibilities of His justice and His love. This Divine activity is no arbitrary or demonic power whose whimsical irresponsibility pervades the world. It is the personal ability of God, who acts in wisdom and love — and in judgment. It is the might of the Lord, the God of Israel, revealing himself ever in new ways in miracles. The nature of these miracles comes out startlingly evident and irrefutable, giving them the character of signs. "O Lord Jehovah, thou has begun to show thy servant thy greatness, and thy strong hand: for what god is there in heaven or in earth, that can do according to thy works, and according to thy mighty acts?" (Deut. 3:24). This activity is incomparable — historical and purposeful from beginning to end. For *His people* it is a sign. He gives manna, "which thou knewest not, neither did thy fathers know" (Deut. 8:3). The significance of miracles does not lie simply in their miraculousness, but in their redeeming and informing and instructing content.

They are not important as instrumentless activity *contra naturam,* but as saving, revelatory, admonitory, and comforting activity. Nowhere do we notice a tendency to preserve the miraculous by eliminating agents or instruments from Divine activity. It is calmly reported that the *wind* divided the waters of the Red Sea (Ex. 14:21). But the miracle of the

Red Sea is robbed of none of its miraculousness by the use of this means. Neither does Scripture ascribe miracles exclusively to God, without man having a role in them. We read that God sent Moses to do signs and miracles "in the land of Egypt, to Pharaoh, and to all his servants, and to all his land . . ." And it was Moses who showed the "great terror . . . in the sight of all Israel" (Deut. 34:11, 12). We read of miracles done by Moses, Elijah, and Elisha, by the apostles in the time of Christ and after Pentecost. There is no inclination at all to see every miracle as an immediate act of God, without use of means. This is because, without exception, none of the agents which He uses are competitors of Him who alone works miracles. For in their working of miracles these agents point in faith to God's miraculous power. "Take the rod, and assemble the congregation, thou, and Aaron thy brother, and speak ye unto the rock before their eyes, that it give forth its water; and thou shalt bring forth to them water out of the rock; so thou shalt give the congregation and their cattle drink" (Num. 20:8). The miracle is executed in correlation with faith and obedience. (Though this does not mean that miracles are never performed in unbelief and disobedience.) Therefore, Moses and Israel, even though it was Moses who stretched his hand out over the sea (Ex. 14:21), sing only to the Lord: "Who is like unto thee, O Jehovah, among the gods? Who is like thee, glorious in holiness, Fearful in praises, doing wonders?" (Ex. 15:11). And so, in memory of the water that flowed from the rock, the miracle-psalm of Israel can sing: "Tremble, thou earth, at the presence of the Lord, At the presence of the God of Jacob, Who turned the rock into a pool of water, the flint into a fountain of waters" (Ps. 114:7, 8).

* * *

Eichrodt once remarked that the singular significance of miracles is not "in their material element, but in their role as witnesses." This way of thinking does an injustice to a wealth of Scriptural considerations on miracles. True enough, there are miracles where the signifying of something is strongly underscored, miracles, or signs, through which God intends to impart knowledge of His will; but more often we observe that God, in working miracles, is active in the reality of His saving work. Restricting miracles to being informative or instructive symbols is hardly permitted. Israel sees God's mighty hand in His miracles, a manifesting of His magnificence and saving activity. "Thy right hand, O Jehovah, is glorious in power" (Ex. 15:6). Miracles are not only signs of His power intended to inform and to amaze the prince of Edom (Ex. 15:15) or to put fear in the hearts of the Moabites (Ex. 15:15). Israel's enemies are miraculously broken by the right hand of Jehovah; through miracles, Israel is liberated from the hand of Pharaoh.

The witness character of miracles is usually not dissociated from the historical effect of the acts of God: "Terror and dread falleth upon them; By the greatness of thine arm they are as still as a stone; Till thy people pass over, O Jehovah, Till the people pass over that thou hast purchased" (Ex. 15:16). Miracles penetrate into reality and, at the same time, signify something else, in Eichrodt's words, "as the outstretched finger of God's invisible power."

There is no contradiction for Israel between the witness and the effect of miracles. There is a profound interrelation in the miraculous activity of God, for it is directed at a purpose and thereby excludes all arbitrariness (Cf. Ex. 15:17, 18). There is a focus in this activity; He is on the way, through Israel and the nations, to the full revelation of His salvation. All miracles are coordinated in this perspective. In this activity He miraculously preserves His people against the superior power of their enemies, comforts them with His signs, and encourages them on their way. Miracles are never given to satisfy curiosity. Rather, they form a powerful appeal to

Israel's faith, love, and loyalty. Miracles are not a problem of *contra naturam,* but God's work in His people unto the salvation of the world. For the fulfilling of her calling Israel is brought under the impression of the unquenchable, benevolent, and powerful activity of God, which at one time takes this way and another time that way with them. His activity is not *contra naturam* but *contra peccatum.* The antithesis is not God and nature, but God and sin or God and perdition, and all the threads of miraculous events run together in the Messiah, whose name is Wonderful, that is, Miraculous (Is. 9:6).

This is why Scripture does not systematize its teaching of miracles. The nature and number of Divine miracles are determined by the historical situation as He guides it. We encounter in the turning points of the history of revelation a complete cycle of miracles, as, for instance, in the exodus and in the time of Elijah (the contest between Baal and Jehovah). Life is taken hold of in these miracles, and Israel's eye is fixed on the invincibility of Jehovah in His activity among His people. Miracles are not the intersection of the supernatural with a self-sufficient natural life, but with the life of sin under the influence of demons, and powers, and unbelief. God does not work against nature, but against presumptively autonomous life as it is fallen in sin and guilt.

* * *

We encounter the same construction of miracles in the *signs* and *wonders* of the New Testament (Acts 2:22, 43; 5:12; 6:8; 14:3). We think first of the miracles of Christ, which, far different from meaningless curiosities with only a bizarre impressiveness, are full of significance. They immediately affect the blind and the crippled, the sick and the dead, nature and demons. God works miraculously in Jesus Christ, His power being first revealed in the miraculous birth. The virgin birth is not presented in Scripture as a formal *contra naturam*. It is presented in the light of redemption and of the revelation of God in the flesh through the assumption of human nature. In the miracles following this one, miracles worked by Christ himself, we observe the powerful signs of the approaching kingdom.

The purpose of these miracles and signs is not at all to make faith superfluous. When the pharisees want to see some signs, disguising their unbelief in this desire, Christ unmasks the perversity behind their request (Matt. 12:38 ff.). In contrast to this, the true significance of faith is brought to expression. Faith is in Christ and His kingdom. When the disciples are helpless to do anything with a lunatic lad, Christ explains their impotence: "Because of your little faith: for verily I say unto you, If ye have faith as a grain of mustard seed, ye shall say unto this mountain, Remove hence to yonder place; and it shall remove; and nothing shall be impossible unto you" (Matt. 17:20). What occurs with the centurion occurs according to his faith (Matt. 8:13). Jesus recognizes faith and says: "Son, be of good cheer; thy sins are forgiven" (Matt. 9:2). Before the miracle of healing it is asked: Do you *believe* that I can do this? (Matt. 9:28, 29). In faith there is a looking to and a giving of the self over to the powers of the kingdom as they are revealed in Jesus Christ. "Fear not: only believe, and she shall be made whole" (Luke 8:50). In contrast, unbelief inhibits these powers, as it were, so that Jesus could do no miracles in Nazareth, for example, because of unbelief (Mark 6:5), and laid his hands there on only a few sick people. This relation between faith and miracles is so close that the Scriptures say that while nothing is impossible with God, they say also that nothing is impossible with faith (Mark 10:27; Matt. 17:20). There is no antagonism here. Faith is not an independently effective human power, but is entirely directed to the power and promise of God, and in them finds its ability.

This is why the miraculous power of the kingdom is not directed *contra naturam* but *contra peccatum* and against the horrible consequences of sin. God and nature do not collide in miracles; the kingdom and guilt, the kingdom of God and the kingdom of darkness clash. The devils are cast out by the Holy Ghost with the coming of the kingdom (Matt. 12:28). Unbelief absolutizes the world, making it autonomous and cut off from its origin. In faith man again sees the world as in the hand of God and is made a communicant in His redeeming activity. One realizes now how far the critics of "impossible" miracles are removed from what Scripture says about impossibility. If the critics of miracles say that miraculous activity is impossible, Scripture says that it is impossible that death could hold our Lord (Acts 2:24). The contrast could not be sharper. Impossible! this resurrection from the dead, say the critics. Impossible! that He should not break the bands of death, say the Scriptures. For the power of God raised Jesus from the dead (I Cor. 6:14), and Christ, the power of God (Rom. 1:4), lives by the power of God (II Cor. 13:4). Thus defined by redemption and the kingdom of God "impossibility" receives a totally new meaning. A miracle is not an abnormal or unnatural occurrence presupposing the normality of nature, but a redeeming reinstatement of the normality of world and life through the new dominion of God, which stands antithetically against the kingdom of this world. Miracles are not part of a supernatural order which intrudes upon an absolutized "natural" order of things, thereupon creating a tension between miracles and nature. They reveal the kingdom of God in opposition to the devil and his dominion. This accounts for the the amazement that God's miracles evoked as His acts of salvation spread their light over the world of the sick and the dead, over disrupted nature and men possessed of demons (Mark 5:20). When John the Baptist, languishing in prison, had doubts about the authenticity of Christ's Messiahship, Jesus said to

John's disciples: "Go and tell John the things which ye hear and see: the blind receive their sight, and the lame walk, the lepers are cleansed, and the deaf hear, and the dead are raised up, and the poor have good tidings preached to them. And blessed is he, whosoever shall find no occasion of stumbling in me" (Matt. 11:4-6).

Miracles cause surprise because life has become accustomed to the abnormality of sin and its curse of death and terror. The reaction to the irresistibility of God's saving power in Jesus Christ is sometimes so adverse that people plead with Him to leave their region (Matt. 8:34). Their hearts are filled with alarm — "It was never so seen in Israel" (Matt. 9:33) — and this dismay can lead to the honor of God (Mark 2:12) especially where He makes things well. The beauty of life, through God's mightiness of deed, breaks through darkness and death (Mark 5:42). Life restored through God's salvation in Jesus Christ — this is the meaning of miracles. This is why miracles are not merely extraordinary events, but saving acts. John hears not only that miracles are done, but that the gospel is preached to the poor (Matt. 11:5).

Thus, in the casting out of evil spirits and in the healing of the sick, the fulfillment of the words of Isaiah is accomplished: "Himself took our infirmities, and bare our diseases" (Matt. 8:17). The acts of healing must be seen in the light of God's salvation. There is no problem of might-in-itself which rages against other powers. This is the power of God in Christ unto redemption and restoration. This is how the words of Christ at the healing of the man with palsy must be understood: "Which is easier, to say to the sick of the palsy, Thy sins are forgiven; or to say, Arise, and take up thy bed, and walk?" (Mark 2:9). According to superficial, human viewpoint it is easier to forgive sins than to heal. But for Christ it is different; the mighty act of healing points, according to his express statement, to the Divine act of forgiving: "But that ye may know that the Son of man hath authority on earth to forgive sins, I say unto thee, Arise, take up thy bed, and go unto thy house" (Mark 2:10, 11). How different this appears from the opposition between miracle and nature, now that we can see the kingdom signified in His victory over the manifestly domineering kingdom of darkness. He destroys the power of the kingdom of evil. Satan's fall from heaven as lightning corresponds to the casting out of devils on earth (Luke 10:18). The Stronger One has come to strip Satan of his armor.

* * *

In faith, man looks to these signs. He who concerns himself only with the strange and unusual misses the significance of miracles and is likely to arouse resistance to this "might," which he fails to see as the power of Divine salvation. But it is also possible to see God's salvation *in* the signs. Thus John writes that a selection of Christ's signs and miracles were written up "that ye may believe that Jesus is the Christ, the Son of God; and that believing ye may have life in his name" (John 20:31). Thus miracles are not simply strange occurrences in the realm of "nature." They are acts of God which propose a decision — the decision that determines life. To believe this, to believe Jesus Christ as He revealed himself in signs and miracles — this is to have life in His name.

Peter, in his speech on Pentecost, spoke of Jesus the Nazarene as "a man approved of God unto you by mighty works and wonders and signs which God did by him in the midst of you" (Acts 2:22). His signs were instituted so that He would be recognized as the Messiah of the kingdom. They are His witnesses (John 5:36). Christ warns us against fixing our eyes on the signs as such, as facts abstracted from Him (John 6:26). The meaning of miracles lies in the kingdom of redemption; they direct us to the message of redemption which can never be understood except in faith and surrender.

In the first, foundation-laying days for the Church after Pentecost, signs accompany the preaching of the gospel. Many signs and "wonders" occur among the people at the hands of the apostles (Acts 5:12). With these miracles, we are told, the Lord certifies His word (Acts 14:3). God attests the proclaimed salvation through miracles and signs, even as through the giving of the Holy Spirit. The signs form, according to Calvin, an approbation of the preaching. They undersign the apostles' teaching with a special affirmation; they are the seals of the word. Calvin put special emphasis on the witness character of miracles. But it must be remembered that the sign is rooted in the reality — in the healing, in the raising from the dead, and in the restoration. This restoration and healing are, as realities, signs of the power of Christ and of the kingdom of redemption. It has often been pointed out that Christ did not heal nearly all the sick, but that only a few were restored or raised from the dead by His miraculous power. This absence of promiscuousness only accentuates the witness character of His miracles.

These miracles are presented us in the Scriptures without suggestion of anything problematic being created in the relation between God and nature. We are simply pointed to the invincibility of God for whom nothing is too miraculous. His deeds are always inscrutable, His ways unsearchable. But we are shown in miracles the unexpected and surprising, which, in turn, suggests afresh His Divine invincibility. It is not that in miracles a greater power is revealed than is present in the ordinary course of things. Everything that God brings into being is a work of His singular omnipotence. But in miracles God takes another way than that which had come to be expected of Him in the usual course of events. This "otherwise" of God's working is often discernible in Scripture and it lays the foundation for the witness character of miracles. This accounts for the arousal of amazement. The word *teras*, miracle, is used more or less synonymously with the word *thaumasion,* wonder (Matt. 21:15), that which amazes and astonishes. What occurs in Christ's miracles falls outside scientific norms and at the edge of man's reckoning. Man does not anticipate miracles. They take him by surprise — which in itself is something other than conversion. But in their surprisingness, miracles are means of Divine revelation. They are, at once, *reality* and *revelation.* One could say that man's amazement at miracles results from his living in and by this curse-affected world, where men, out of principle, assume the invincibility of death. Thus, when the kingdom of God in Christ victoriously invades this world, obtruding under the curse and its leaven, and death is subjected to Christ, then men are astonished. This reaction is far more significant for the understanding of miracles than is the approach to them as a problem of nature. In the latter case man is no longer taken by surprise. He simply declares miracles an "impossibility." This is why man's decision as to miracles is, in principle, his decision as to Christ. In Christ, King of the approaching kingdom, there is good reason to wonder.

Miracles are not proofs addressed to the intellect that thereby man should be convinced. They do not make faith superfluous. On the contrary, they summon men to believe. The witness character of miracles puts before man the decision which he must make as to Christ. He who views miracles from the standpoint of the antithesis, God — natural law, has ignored the deepest meaning of miracles. First, because he is not presented in Scripture with this antithesis, and, second, because, having turned natural law into something self-determinative and irrevocable, he has implicitly accepted a view of miracles which devaluates the "ordinary" work of God. The Divine act in miracles does not break any natural laws, as though they were absolute. Miracles are inscrutable acts of God, which can be accepted as acts of God only through faith. There can be no serious talk of a conflict with science. A conflict occurs only when man abstracts nature, as an absolute, closed system of natural causes from God's Providence, and considers the possibility of miracles as meaning the possibility of a supernatural breaking of natural law.

Miracles cannot be embraced by any one area of scientific activity. Each science has to do with a definite aspect of cosmic reality, while Divine miracles embrace the whole. Water at Cana's wedding becomes wine, sick are healed, demons are driven out, and the dead are raised. It is in these acts that the decision of faith falls. This is why theology (and exegesis) need not lend itself to a new notion of natural law in order that it might reach a synthesis with science. Neither does it have any need of rejoicing that concepts of causality and natural law have become less absolute, as though this may allow a little room for the possibility of miracles. To do this reveals a basic lack of faith in God's power, and only illustrates how the "amazement" of the New Testament people at miracles has been replaced by a dangerous concept of supernaturalism.

* * *

There is still another question which in our time has again become acute. It is the question of whether God still works through signs and miracles. Do miracles still occur, or must we say that the era of miracles is now closed, that we cannot and may not expect the occurrence of miracles any longer?

This question has, of course, practical significance for the life of believers. After all, we confess not only a general Providence, but that God's providential rule is directed concretely to all circumstances, and that God is the hearer of prayers.

The Roman Catholic Church gives a positive and affirmative answer to this question in keeping with its entire concept of miracles. This concept still lends to miracles a specific apologetic function. The Council of Trent declared: "If anyone says that Divine Revelation cannot be made worthy of belief through external signs, let him be anathema." Miracles according to Rome still function as proofs and witnesses. The Church itself, by her miraculous growth, sanctity, and fruitfulness is held to be a "miraculous sign" in the world and an irrefutable testimony to her own Divine commission. And in the same way, there are signs in and around the Church that add credibility to Divine revelation and demonstrate God's almightiness. Indeed, they form proofs of revelation. A miracle, according to Roman Catholic apologetes, is a fact, discernible by natural means, which departs from the usual order of nature and has God as its peculiar cause. Miracles, as special interventions of God, can occur on behalf of individuals or of institutions. This Divine intervention is deduced whenever a given occurrence cannot be explained by natural causes.

Miracles are understood here, first of all, supernaturally, which means that all attention is given to the point of intersection between God's activity and nature. Miracles are not approached first by way of Word and revelation, but are established by way of natural, scientific analysis of facts and circumstances. As one Roman Catholic apologete writes: "A better understanding of natural occurrences, a better insight into the play of natural forces and into the possibilities enclosed in nature makes man rightfully more critical and less disposed to believe in an excessive abundance of miracles without, however, undoing belief in the possibility of their occurrence."[16] The possibility of miracles is related to their natural discernibility. We need not, it is said, think immediately of miracles when we hear of unusual phenomena. We may only conclude a miracle if every natural, causal explanation fails. The healing powers of the "ordinary" water of Lourdes is a case in point. The question of whether miracles of heal-

---

16. C. F. Pauwels, *Apologetiek,* 1948, p. 150.

ing actually occur at Lourdes depends on exact research. Since there is a gap in the natural explanations of the healings, it must be concluded that God, as "first cause" of these events, has worked a miracle. And thus, the cures of Lourdes become, among other things, "the unavoidable testimony of God that Mary is the Immaculately Conceived Mother of God and that the Catholic Church, which has declared and defended this doctrine, speaks the truth."[17]

How remote this is from the Scriptural presentation of miracles. How "indirect" faith in miracles thus becomes. Miracles are always dependent, in their discernibility, on research and science, which makes it possible that what is now called "one of the most beautiful miracles ever to occur at Lourdes," may appear upon later research to have been no miracle, but a cure which did not at all transcend the powers of nature. Miracles become thus pure "points of intersection" phenomena with no essentially religious stamp. The research that must, in the nature of the case, be relative to the development of science, determines the definite qualification of an event as a miracle.

This is at bottom a kind of competition between the natural and the supernatural worlds. It is unavoidable that natural science with its continually growing knowledge of nature will also continue to set more limits on phenomena which have God as their peculiar cause. Things which previously — because of a more primitive understanding of nature — could not be explained from natural causes and which thus were called miracles, may now have a natural explanation and have to be declassified as miracles.

Through this formal approach to miracles, by which God's act becomes a plug for the gap observed in natural causes, the question of certainty necessarily becomes acute. The great

---

17. Pauwels, *Het Wonder*, (no date), p. 128.

difficulty for the Roman Catholic apologete lies in the fact that we are never absolutely certain of what nature can or cannot do. And no amount of reassurance can give certainty. This is what happens when men begin to conceive of miracles formally and abstract them — as far as knowledge of them is concerned — from Christ and His salvation.

The Scriptures speak differently about miracles and our knowledge of them. Recall, in connection with Roman Catholic miracles, the healing of the man born blind (John 9). The unaccountability of the healing plays a noteworthy role in this story. No one can deny the fact that he was healed, so the whole controversy centers about the basis underlying the fact. There are the Pharisees, first of all, who bring up the matter of the Sabbath (John 9:16). Others remark, "How can a man that is a sinner do such signs?" The Jews try to avoid the embarrassment of the miracle by asking the parents, " . . . how then doth he now see?" (John 9:19), and by demanding of the healed man, "What did he to thee? how opened he thine eyes?" (John 9:26). The man who was cured is still confused: "Since the world began it was never heard that any one opened the eyes of a man born blind. If this man were not from God, he could do nothing" (John 9:32, 33).

But, not being able to deny the fact, they throw him out (John 9:34). Then Jesus comes to the healed man and asks whether he believes. In this way, the man comes out of his confusion and learns to worship. And Jesus says, "For judgment came I into this world, that they that see not may see; and that they that see may become blind" (John 9:39).

Everything in the story circles, not around a logical and natural deduction from a determined fact to God as "first cause" (cf. John 9:21: " . . . who opened his eyes, we know not . . ."), but around the meaning of the miracle, which culminates in salvation and which summons faith and calls to worship.

* * *

Roman Catholic apologetes speak confidently of "the evidential cogency of miracles." This evidence is "an attribute of miracles which is absolutely sufficient." The problem of the point of intersection is removed from the relationship of Christ's saving work in opposition to sin and the devil; it is broached on the level of natural discernibility and moved by way of the highest form of natural theology finally into the confession of Divine Providence. A miracle is a fact, discernible by natural human powers, though transcending the powers of created nature and performable only by God. Thus, phenomena like those of Lourdes become important for apologetics. When we register serious objections to this "natural" theology of miracles, it is not to take away anything from the overpowering activity of God, which guides and rules everything in this world. It is the complementing of nature by the supernatural that we must reject as a fundamental misconstrual of our knowledge of miracles and, by implication, of Providence. It is a misconstrual of our knowledge of miracles because, since it depends on natural reason for its discernment, it dismisses us, if only temporarily, from faith in Christ.

By rejecting this "natural" concept of miracles, we have not therewith settled the question of the possibility and the reality of miracles occurring in our time. It is possible that someone may insist on the basis of scientific observation that miracles no longer occur. He may exclude miracles from the world, saying that it *appears* as though God no longer works in such miraculous manner. This sort of position is, of course, basically irreligious and is little different from the opinion of those who say miracles are not nor ever were possible and that the Biblical miracles were not *real* miracles.

Even though one may accept the fact that miracles occurred once in the past, he may consider such miracles *now* impossible. This usually involves a deterministic outlook on the world which, though accepting the possibility of miracles in Biblical times, insists on their impossibility for today. It appears easier to accept the miracles that occurred long ago than to accept even the possibility of them for today. The present always seems to be wholly determined. The proposition that miracles can no longer occur can be the effect of a deterministic infection in the Christian faith, which thus no longer lives in the assumption that God is actively Master of His own house.

Others may take refuge in the purely "spiritual" or "religious" miracles, of which there was so much talk in the nineteenth century. These miracles are construed as having no consequences for "natural reality." Here, too, is a flight before the menace of natural science. In this way one unwittingly expresses satisfaction with a miracleless world, not realizing that he thereby commits himself to a modern construction of the problem "miracle vs. nature."

For him who approaches miracles from the Scriptures the question "miracles now?" arises on a wholly different level. He cannot for a moment consider miracles in themselves, apart from God's work of salvation on earth. He who sees the miracles of Holy Scripture inseparably connected with the saving and redeeming activity of God knows that there can be no talk of a decrease or diminishing of the power of God unto salvation in this world. One can only speak of the revelation of the power of God in the progress of His kingdom. The outlook on this Divine power is in no respect defined by the position of natural science. It is possible only by faith in the redemption of the world through the blood of the cross.

The question of whether miracles still occur in the world takes us back to the question of the reality of the power of salvation on earth. The question can really be formulated only as to the *nature* of the Divine activity on earth. As the saving work of God proceeds on earth, after the outpouring of the Holy Spirit, it becomes clear that the era of the last hours, then rung in, is defined by the decision which fell with the completed work of Christ. The salvation of the Lord creates a new situation. And this new situation, inaugurated by the sending of the Holy Spirit, shall certainly not be poorer than the period when astonishment was aroused by the signs and miracles of Jesus' day. The poverty or wealth of the Church of Christ are not dependent on the *manner* of God's activity on earth. It is dependent on that activity itself — *contra peccatum* and *contra diabolum*. There is progress in the revelation that is given in Christ. The last days are the period of the preaching of the gospel, summoning men to believe. Christians had to live in this faith in the days after Pentecost, when the sword of persecution was raised over the Church and James was killed with that sword, when Stephen was stoned to death and the prison doors closed behind the children of God, and when John, without an intervention from God, was exiled on Patmos. There was no mention of a gradual recession of the power of God from earth after Pentecost. Paul speaks of an *abundance,* as he calls it, that we have received in the redemption through Christ's blood according to the riches of His grace, "which he made to abound toward us in all wisdom and prudence, making known unto us the mystery of his will . . ." (Eph. 1:8, 9). Rooted in the love of Christ, the believers together "with all the saints" were in a position to comprehend "what is the breadth and length and height and depth, and to know the love of Christ . . ." (Eph. 3:18, 19). The power of the kingdom was conclusively defined by this irresistible salvation, now preached to all creatures. And, until the return of Christ, the Church must live under Word and sacrament.

It is understandable that an analogy is often suggested between miracle and sacrament, since both are signs of the reality of Divine salvation. The difference lies in the fact that the sacrament creates nothing new and, as a sign, does not violate reality. It is wielded by the Holy Spirit merely as an instrument, as sign and seal, in utmost sobriety (water, wine, bread) to the strengthening of faith. The sacrament itself does not complement history, as the Roman Catholic doctrine would have it. It is, rather, a "remembrance" of the fulfillment of all history in Jesus Christ. The sacraments receive their function in Divine salvation only from the Word, of which they are signs and seals, arranged for by virtue of God's sovereign institution thereto.

As God's work progresses, miraculous signs give place to sacraments. It is not a drop from riches to poverty, but a rise from a wealth of salvation to a greater wealth in the knowledge of faith and the unction of the Holy Spirit (I John 2:20). Neither is it a transition from revelation to mystery, for the mystery is now revealed, "and by the scriptures of the prophets, according to the commandment of the eternal God, is made known unto all the nations unto obedience of faith" (Rom. 16:26). The progress of God's work is involved in this call to faith. And faith is directed toward the salvation which is exclusive in Christ. This is why the last hours since Pentecost bring no impoverishment, but furnish goads toward living in the fullness of wealth. When, shortly before Pentecost, the Emmaus travelers were talking with Christ, they recalled Jesus as a prophet "mighty in deed and word before God and all the people" (Luke 24:19). For them, this memory was aroused simultaneous with a sense of disappointment and impoverishment. But when Christ opened the Scriptures to them, their hearts began to burn with the Word that Christ explained. After the Savior had left them, they became aware that they had more than a fond memory. They became witnesses of His resurrection.

Even during His walk on earth, Jesus directed the attention of His disciples to the era when the Word would work through the power of the Spirit: "Let these words sink into your ears: for the Son of man shall be delivered up into the hands of men" (Luke 9:44). That is, so that you can stand fast when these things that I am now talking about come to pass, and so that in My words you may find support for your faith. They went into this era, this signless time, as sheep among wolves, before officials and princes to face hatred and persecution. But in this era, too, the power of God was to accompany them.

* * *

It is clear to us now, of course, that the special signs and miracles were not limited to the time of Christ's walk on earth. Scripture tells us of many signs in the days that followed the pouring out of the Holy Spirit. But it is everywhere evident that these miracles do not occur to provide the Church with a supernatural means of self-protection. They are aimed at the establishment and extension of the kingdom in the world. There are miraculous liberations. The prison doors swing open upon occasion (Acts 5:19). The apostles work miracles among the people (Acts 5:12-16). There is an activity of God which provides signs in the growth of the young Church in the world: the death of Ananias and Sapphira (Acts 5:1-10), the expelling of evil spirits (Acts 8:7), miracles of healing and raising of the dead (Acts 9:34; 14:19; 28:8; 9:40). The Name of Christ, which was the decisive thing during Jesus' earthly life (John 20, 31), is still among the people. (Cf. Acts 9:34: "Aeneas, *Jesus Christ* healeth thee.") Thus, God, even after the establishment of salvation in Christ, wills to go His way and to build the Church through signs and miracles. And we find nothing in the Scriptures to indicate a line that we can draw through a definite period to mark off a boundary between the time of miracles and the time of the absence of miracles. It is significant that this problem does not come up in Scripture.

The significance of this for us is that God's path through the world, in the building and gathering of the Church, is and remains inscrutable. The many signs that still appear after Pentecost should make us the more careful not to set limits, in our enlightened era, to the miraculous activity of God. There is not a single datum in the New Testament which makes it certain that God, in a new period of strengthening and extending of the Church in heathendom, will not confirm His message with signs, in holy resistance to the demonic influences of the kingdom of darkness. He who thinks that he can say with certainty that miracles no longer can occur may seriously ask himself whether he thinks in terms of God's power over the world or from a secret capitulation to determinism.

Perhaps the main issue in our time will be increasingly focused on this question. We must, in our faith, be once and for all freed from the fear of the difficulties posed by the "point of intersection." We must be able confidently to serve and respect science without fear of newly discovered facts. The way of the Church remains, just as it was for the persecuted congregations of Acts 8, the way of faith.

Miracles and signs do not decide anything for the Church, though they may propose a decision. This is illustrated in the parable of the rich man and Lazarus. In response to the rich man's request that a messenger from heaven go to his brothers, Abraham says, "They have Moses and the prophets; let them hear them" (Luke 16:29). But the rich man thinks that a resurrection from the dead has in itself power to convert. He is told, however, "If they hear not Moses and the prophets, neither will they be persuaded, if one rise from the dead" (Luke 16:31). Thus, it is not miracles, but the salvation of the Lord that is necessary for the well-being of the Church.

That men later began to yearn wistfully for special signs and new revelations of the Divine presence is indication of a serious devaluation of Word and sacrament and of an emasculation of the power of faith. Men often thought that a God without special signs was a distant God. They lost their perspective for the reality of salvation in Christ, yes, of Christ Himself. The reality of every day was no longer seen in the light of Divine salvation, and life in this world without supernatural signs became an impoverished experience, in which the austere signs of baptism and Holy Communion seemed to offer little relief. A complement was then sought for the spiritually impoverished world of reality. The "external" Word and the preaching of it were not enough; the Scriptures became a dead letter, the sacraments a silent tradition. Men began to listen for other, more articulate Divine voices, either in the external world or in the recesses of their own hearts. They wanted special signs of the providential rule of the Lord. Where these voices were not heard, there were only the silent spaces left by the Divine withdrawal. Existence was a desert with an occasional oasis provided by moments of special Divine revelation and leading. Such constructions, which were often absorbed into theological systems, betrayed a profound suspicion as to the constancy of the salvation and presence of the Lord. The roots of this suspicion lay in a theology which considered Providence as an occasional supernatural intervention of God into nature or our own lives, by means of a striking event or an inner voice. Adopting this point of view, one can easily lapse into a proud criticism of the "prosaic" life of a Church which has no eye for the contemporary miracle.

* * *

But we must not allow ourselves to neglect what the Holy Scriptures say to us about the power of the Lord's salvation. The Scriptures speak not only about the providential rule of the Lord, but, at the same time, about the faith which is directed to that activity. "If ye had faith as a grain of mustard seed, ye would say unto this sycamine tree, Be thou rooted up, and be thou planted in the sea, and it would obey you" (Luke 17:6). Was this not a strange answer to the request of the disciples for an increase of their faith? And does not Christ's answer indicate that working miracles is not a matter of great faith, but of faith as such — "If ye had faith as a grain of mustard seed"!

Perhaps we consider Providence too abstractly. Perhaps we do not live in faith that such great things can occur. One could from this standpoint significantly ask the question of whether miracles can occur in our time — not from the standpoint of a deterministic conception of nature or from that of the *poverty* of a world without miracles, but from the standpoint of the power of faith.[18] It is true that Paul seemed to minimize the significance of the big things in our lives, and, in the light of Jesus' appeal to faith, his expression was rather remarkable: "and if I have all faith, so as to remove mountains, but have not love, I am nothing" (I Cor. 13:2). But this necessary and serious warning takes away none of the significance of the power of faith. The Scriptures associate it with the power of prayer, which is able to do astonishing things (cf. Jas. 5:15, 16 and several passages in the Gospels). Is the seeming powerlessness of our time perhaps related to the weakness of our faith? Further, *must* not the confession of Divine Providence lead in the direction of idleness and lustreless acquiescence? The confession of God's Providence poses us here with a very important and practical question.

The mighty acts of faith in the New Testament are directed toward the *kingdom*. This implies a sharp criticism of every presumptuous attempt to assign to faith any power which is not inseparably bound up with the victorious revelation of the

---

18. Cf. Mark 11:22, 23: "Have faith in God. Verily I say unto you, Whosoever shall say unto this mountain, Be thou taken up and cast into the sea; and shall not doubt in his heart, but shall believe that what he saith cometh to pass; he shall have it."

kingdom. This all suggests the weakness of the rather strident claims of "faith healing." The error of such claims is not that they are in argument with natural science but that faith and prayer are considered able to determine the activity of God, without assurance that the things expected through faith and prayer are really serviceable to the kingdom of God. We have recalled that the healing power of Christ and the disciples was applied to only a few of the sick. The New Testament cases of resurrection as signs of His power to redeem and to save are even more exceptional. What is asked for in the so-called "faith healings" is even more than what Christ Himself did, and a universality is claimed for them for which there are no demonstrable grounds in the New Testament. The power thus claimed for faith and prayer is in contradiction to their very nature. There is in this sort of thing an impatience with the ruling of God, who employs His own criteria in determining what is necessary for the coming of His kingdom.

This has nothing to do with a devaluation of faith and prayer. It is intended to say that in faith and prayer we are supposed to accept the fact that God rules as He wills and that He alone oversees the progress of His kingdom. It is possible to hide behind this fact in order to conceal our own powerlessness. The disciples sometimes stood powerless against the forces of evil and then excused themselves from their own powerlessness. They asked, "Why could not we cast [the demon] out?" And Christ answered, "Because of your little faith" (Matt. 17:20). It is not an imaginary danger that, under the spell of the popular acknowledgment of a closed system of natural causes, we should hardly reckon anymore with the reality of the responsive activity of God. Prayer then shrivels to an expression of our inner lives, and the value of prayer is merely that of a psychological therapeutic. Prayer then no longer expects an answer from the Hearer of prayer, but becomes a functional release of subjective tensions. This kind of prayer can hardly be called a prayer of faith.

We should not, however, suppose that we can determine the progress of the kingdom of God or survey the manner of God's working. The world is no more closed now than it ever was. But the pattern of God's activity now is different than in the era of the Church's establishment. Human power over nature is enormously increased. All sorts of things that used to appear amazing and quite impossible are now included in the observable relationships of cosmic life. But the activity of God is not excluded from these. Nor is the necessity of faith diminished. God's answer to prayer can be just as real in medical therapy as in the sudden healings of the time of Christ and the apostles. Only the faith that desires special signs will fail to recognize and appreciate this relationship. God's activity is certainly not dependent on the position of science, but neither has our profounder understanding of nature occurred without His rule. And faith does not underestimate this. Faith is not primarily concerned with the extraordinary phenomenon resulting from God's activity, but with the invincibility of the activity itself. It lives in fellowship with God and does not yearn for signs. It lives under God's guidance and knows that His Providence surrounds our lives, knowing, too, that His kingdom — not our lives — is the final goal of His Providence.

Faith knows that unbelief also lives in this unclosed world and that it, within the limits of God's rule, exercises its own kind of influence. It is remarkable that Scripture speaks, in connection with the future, of signs and miracles which the anit-Christ will perform. We hear of a future *parousia* of Satan, of his working in power, in "signs and lying wonders, and with all deceit of unrighteousness" (II Thess. 2:9, 10). We hear of "spirits of demons, working signs; which go forth unto the kings of the whole world" (Rev. 16:14). Great miracles are foretold: fire comes down "out of heaven upon the earth in the sight of men" (Rev. 13:13). We also read that men will be deceived by these miracles (Rev. 13:14).

There is an interesting parallel between the miracles of the time of Christ and the apostles and those of the time of the end. The parallel is also seen in the astonishment[19] that the miracles arouse. But the parallel does not affect the absolute antithesis between the miracles of anti-Christ and those of faith. The miracles of anti-Christ are caricatures. How clear it now becomes that the decision of faith cannot lie in signs and wonders as such. In fact, it will be the striking signs and miracles in the end time that will provide the great temptation, which the Church will be able to resist only through the power of faith — faith not in miracles, but in God's salvation.

The confession of God's Providence and of the salvation included in it shall be put to the test by these striking signs and miracles — the anti-Christian caricature of the kingdom of God. The Church will know that the times of the kingdom are in the Father's hand and that her distress, symbolized by the souls pleading from their imprisonment under the altar (Rev. 6:9), does not diminish the reality of God's salvation nor of His certain purpose. And we shall, during our residence on earth, understand that the whole cosmos unfolds to the glory of the kingdom of God and we shall honor God's Providence in this. We shall not be entranced by this unfolding but shall be aided by it to understand life's distress and suffering. The Church will not see the development of things as competitive to God's Providence, but as a manifestation of it. The "miracle" of fire falling on earth will not interest the Church. But the fire that Christ will throw upon earth (Luke 12:49) will interest her, as does the unfolding of God's world, defined by His saving purposes. The Church will continually remind herself of this salvation, through the Word and the signs of the kingdom. The decisive question will be whether the unfolding of life occurs under the leading of faith or of unbelief, in service to the kingdom or in rebellion.

---

19. Cf. Rev. 13:3: " . . . the whole earth wondered after the beast."

We read in God's Word of signs and miracles in the future, but we read also of judgment (Rev. 19:1) : we read of the judgment of apostasy and of the marriage of the Lamb (Rev. 19:9) ! The Church must proceed in this perspective, like the Church at the time of John's exile on Patmos when her chance for escape seemed to vanish in the face of her distress. It is the joy of the Church, and will be till the end, that she does not live in wonderful signs, but in the salvation of God.

CHAPTER VIII

The Problem of Theodicy

THEODICY is a justification of God's providential rule. It attempts to prove that in spite of all enigmas and all criticisms God's governing of the world is holy, good, and just. Theodicy is an attempt to defend God against all complaints or accusations by demonstrating the meaningfulness and purposefulness of God's activity in the world and in human life. It presupposes the seriousness of all sorts of doubts and criticisms and assumes that there are empirical facts which cause tensions and pose problems in connection with the Divine rule. We find in every theodicy a consideration of such problems as these: human suffering, tragedy and misery, death, sin, and the numerous shocking events which almost daily bewilder us. Can all these evils — to our joy and comfort — be included in the whole of things, in a system in which all tensions are resolved and which affords us a harmonious perspective of and insight into the world? This question arises with particular acuteness in relation to our confession of God's Providence over all things. How is it possible to rhyme the frightening realities of life with the omnipotence of God over this world? Is there a demonstrable relation between God's omnipotence and His goodness? Questions like these theodicy attempts to answer.

Theodicy is an attempt to bring certainty out of doubt, confidence out of suspicion; its deepest motive can thus be pastoral affection. It assumes its apologetic stance in the midst of the distress of human reason which whelms up in the tensions that exist between the unavoidable facts of experience and the preaching of the Church regarding God. It reaches out from the midst of tragedy for an understanding of the truth expressed in Article 1 of the Belgic Confession: "We believe with our hearts and confess with our mouth, that there is one single and simple spiritual essence whom we call God: eternal, incomprehensible, invisible, immutable, infinite, almighty, absolutely wise, just, good, and an overflowing fountain of all good."

The word itself is interesting: theodicy, justification of God. When Kant wrote, in 1791, "Uber das Miszlingen aller philosophischen Versuche in der Theodicee" ("On the Failure of all Philosophical Experiments in Theodicy") he branded all attempts to arrive at a theodicy as "a pleading of God's case." One winces at these words. Can such a pleading of the case of the Divine government be the task of us human beings? Do we have a calling to defend God? Is it conceivable that, in the crisis and the incertitude about the Providence doctrine, God should entrust us with the task of defending His world government? Is it not more reasonable to assume that God reserves that privilege for himself? Is not the justification of His government clear in what is finally the irrefutability of His grace and judgment? Must not theodicy be replaced by the comforting teaching of the Gospel, the justification of the ungodly? Does not even the possibility of a theodicy suggest that the goodness of God's rule may be gainsaid? Can there ever be any other problem than that of the sinner and his distorted thinking?

In answer to such questions as these, the whole formulation of the theodicy problem has often been rejected as misleading. This is because theodicy usually involves an attempt to justify God at the judgment seat of human reason. We must, nevertheless investigate these important questions further. For the problem is not confined to scientific theological or philosophical discussion. It challenges every person who wishes consciously to take his place in God's ordered world, and it is a question that can disturb a man to his innermost soul.

When Pierre Bayle, at the end of the seventeenth century, pointed to the tension between faith and reason and then retreated to a basic dualism, it was not only the scholars who occupied themselves with this problem. Recall, for instance, how Queen Sophia Charlotte of Prussia discussed this and similar questions with the philosopher Leibniz before he, in 1710, introduced his theodicy in opposition to Bayle. This historical detail was typical. The magistrate and the man on the street, the scholar and the soldier, everyone could be entertained by the profound question of the reality of God's rule.

It is not surprising that the problem of theodicy arises irresistibly in times of severe crisis, depression, and extraordinary events. We know the role that the earthquake of Lisbon, in which sixty thousand lives were lost, played in the thought of the eighteenth century. This catastrophe occurred in 1755, and in that year Goethe was six years old. Later he wrote: "The boy was not slightly affected. God, the creator and ruler of heaven and earth, whom the declaration of the first article of faith presents as so wise and gracious, did not, when he thus sacrificed the just with the unjust, prove himself to be in any way fatherly."[1] Catastrophic events have always influenced thought about God — consider the earthquakes of San Fransisco and Messina in 1906 and the two world wars that lie behind us. And then if one considers the present technical development — climaxed in the use of atomic energy — and contemplates its possibilities, he can feel the question of the meaning of life and the goodness of the Divine rule rising in his heart. We spoke extensively in the first chapter about the crisis of the Providence doctrine in our century. Is it possible now, in this chapter on theodicy, to vanish all objections and protests? Is there a rational theodicy

---

1. In *Dichtung und Wahrheit*.

that can vanquish the "realism" occasioned or strengthened by this age of catastrophe? Can we prove God to be just and good?

* * *

It may be profitable, before discussing these questions, to consider certain forms of theodicy which, in the course of years, have been proposed to set human thought at rest. It is, of course, not our desire to give a complete history of each attempt. We shall limit ourselves to a brief survey of a few proposed theodicies.

1. *The dualistic theodicy.* The dualistic theodicy, observable, for example, in the Persian religions, is not concerned to justify the true God, the Father of Jesus Christ. But it is of interest because of its influence upon Christian thought. Zoroastrianism posits a living god, creator and sustainer of the world, source of all moral order. He will at one time appear as judge, to execute the resurrection of the dead and restoration of the world. Besides him there are six other gods. Over against these gods stand the demons, under the leadership of an evil spirit who is co-eternal with and, from the beginning, the enemy of god. He invades the creation of the good god by means of physical and moral evil.

This solution seems simple and clear. It is in principle dualistic, adamantly refusing to resolve the contradiction between light and darkness in an original monism. All that comes before the eye flows either from one or the other principle, and thus it will be until the ultimate triumph of the good principle. Evil, suffering, and darkness have their origin and explanation in the eternal evil principle, while all good is referred to god.

We meet this dualism also in Manichaeanism, which was influenced by Zoroastrianism and which also figured in the history of the Church, finding a principal opponent in its one time disciple, St. Augustine. Good and evil are ultimates in

Manichaeanism also, based respectively in the eternal principles of light and darkness. The solution is, as regards origin, dualistic. But as far as the future is concerned, it is eschatological: a time will come when light will triumph over darkness.

Dualism cannot be refuted by insisting on the monistic disposition of man. It is difficult, from the standpoint of human thought outside of Divine revelation, to choose between dualism and monism. And it is historically demonstrable that in the matter of origins, though not in eschatology, dualism can satisfy man.

Only Divine revelation exposes the basic fallacy of dualism. Every form of dualism that pushes the evil of the world back into an eternal principle in the end relieves the world and man of responsibility and guilt. A dualistic theodicy involves flight from reality and, usually, flight into eschatology. The eternal struggle between light and darkness has less human than cosmic significance. Man's personal guilt is relatively insignificant. The Scriptures, on the other hand, underscore man's personal responsibility. A theodicy which is ultimately dualistic is, from the vantage point of the Christian faith, to be judged a sham solution of the problem of evil. In resolving evil into an eternal principle, dualism only teases the mind away from evil's present grisly reality.

2. *The harmonistic theodicy.* Quite another explanation is offered by the harmonistic theodicy, which is perhaps best exemplified in Stoicism and in the philosophy of Leibniz. Leibniz "defended" God against the scepticism of Bayle, who had sought to demonstrate the bankruptcy of rational thought in matters of faith. In attempting, over against Bayle, to bring faith and reason into interdependence, Leibniz arrived at an unequivocally rationalistic theodicy. Following the line of Stoicism, Leibniz tried to demonstrate that ours is the best possible world. To understand that it is the best possible world we must first dismiss from our minds the fallacy that this is

an anthropocentric world; that is, that everything is created for man. We must view everything in the world as part of the whole, part of the cosmic unity. We shall then discover that there is in all things a pre-established harmony. Naturally, we shall still hear some dissonant notes within the harmony, but these are not essential. What Socrates said of Heraclitus, Leibniz would say of the cosmos: "What I understand, I like; I believe that I shall like the remainder no less, whenever I learn to understand it." If we keep the interrelationship of things continually before us, we shall, says Leibniz, learn to recognize God's goodness in creation. We shall then no longer allow evil and suffering to form a stumbling block to our faith in the righteousness of God's government.

Leibniz distinguishes between metaphysical, physical, and moral evil. Metaphysical evil is really imperfectness of development, physical evil is suffering, and moral evil is sin. Moral evil poses the biggest problem. First of all, Leibniz rejects the notion that Divine activity in human affairs is only general and mediate, that God gives power to His creatures by virtue of which they then can act without God's further immediate assistance. This, says Leibniz, is no solution, for God is continually cooperating, not merely in the maintenance of created substances, but in all human activity. He agrees with the philosophers and theologians who speak of continuous creation.

Leibniz turns to Augustine, who saw evil as a deprivation of the good. Says Leibniz, "The Platonists, St. Augustine, and the scholastics were right in holding God to be the cause of the matter of evil, which is something positive, but not the cause of the form of evil, which exists in privation."[2] God continually gives to His creatures that which is good and perfect: "every good and perfect thing comes from the Father of Lights; while imperfection and faultiness of works stem from an original limitation . . . God could not give them every-

---

2. G. W. Leibniz, *Die Theodicee*, Philos. Biblioth, 71, 1925, p. 117.

thing, or He would have made them Divine. He had to make material distinctions in the perfection of things, and thus imposed appropriate limitations according to the nature of the creature."[3]

"Evil corresponds to shadow, to relative absence of light. Not only ignorance, but error and deceit, are in a sense deprivation." Thus, sin becomes a matter of relative perfection or imperfection and loses its character as a radical rupture and derangement. By relativizing moral evil in this way, Leibniz arrives at his theodicy. For with moral evil, as well as physical evil, being at bottom a matter of incompleteness, all evil is really metaphysical evil. Metaphysical evil in turn is nothing more than the limitations peculiar to creatureliness. The evil in the world is explained, according to Leibniz, by the structure of creation. From metaphysical evil flows moral evil and from moral evil issues physical evil. A world without evil is inconceivable and impossible. Thus, God is justified: He has made the best possible world.

This theodicy rests principally on a relativizing of sin. God's goodness shines only as the grim clouds of sin and evil are dispelled. Leibniz carries the germ of the later evolutionism which considered sin simply as a moment in a developmental process. In this sense he is also a typical representative of the rationalistic *Aufklärung*, which also found a proper place for sin in the whole scheme of things and thus paved the way for the unfounded optimism of the nineteenth century. Recall, in contrast, how the Scriptures speak of sin as having "entered into the world" (Rom. 5:12), as "enmity against God" (Rom. 8:7).

The basic error of this theodicy is its fundamental assumption that reason can find a proper place for sin in creation. Evil, it says, is inherent in the nature and structure of this world. It functions as an accessory to the whole, as an atonality which is blended into the beautiful harmony of the cosmos. It is not

---
3. *Ibid.*

possible that this world be absolutely good; if it were, it would be Divine. To ask God for an absolutely good creation, is to ask more than He can reasonably give. It is to ask that He create another God. The entire problem of evil in the world arises from the original and necessary limitation and imperfection of creation. Within these limits, this world is the best possible world. This is Leibniz's "defense of God."

3. *Teleological theodicy.* The third form of theodicy, which we may call the teleological form, insists, in common with Leibniz, that evil be seen in its proper place within the whole cosmos. In this case evil is considered in connection with the purpose, the *telos,* of things. That which, when considered by itself, appears evil, takes on another color when one considers its results or the purpose to which it is directed. For example, one can look on the past war as an evil. But one can also see this evil in the light of the "good" that has resulted from it, for instance, the relief granted to the overpopulated world. Without denying the terrors of war itself, it is said that other perspectives open up as results of it: life becomes — through the death of many — more possible for others. There is also a perfecting of various techniques which, developed under the pressures of war, improve on the possibilities of life.

This teleological theodicy is limitlessly simple. One need glance only for a moment at the reality of suffering and death and then quickly take flight to its good end. We do not, of course, suggest that no good can ever be harvested from evil. The death of one is often the breath of another.[4] But this does not really explain the purpose of pain, nor does it establish a theodicy. The good that atomic energy may eventually do cannot in itself extenuate the sufferings of Hiroshima, anymore than Hitler's pogroms can be viewed simply as a step toward the solution of the problem of the Jew. God can bring good out of evil, as He in His mysterious ways has of-

---

4. The *dood* of one is the *brood* of another.

ten done (cf. Gen. 50:20). But Scripture never presents this as grounds for the construction of a natural theodicy. Barth once commented pointedly on this kind of theodicy: "It shipwrecks notoriously on every toothache, to say nothing of every serious consideration of the brutal, brazen reality that is present in every moment of the whole wide world of human affairs: birth, sickness, and death; hunger and war; human and racial destiny."

The distinguishing trait of this theodicy, like that of Leibniz, is a fundamental failure to appreciate the awful reality of sin, suffering, and death. Oversimplification typifies it, and the self-evidency of this oversimplification has contributed to modern man's profound distrust of every attempt at a theodicy.

4. *The theodicy of Wilfred Monod.* Wilfred Monod considers the attributes that traditional theological thought has ascribed to God as being the chief reason for man's refusal to believe in God. We have, says Monod, made a caricature of God. This caricature must be removed lest man continue to be offended by an idol. Monod imagines that God will at the judgment say to some atheists, "You have refused to believe in Me. Thank you, my son, for having had such a noble idea of the Father. . . ." The modern mind finds wholly unpalatable the traditional concept of God, in which all things — natural events, suffering, and joy — are ascribed to Him. Monod protests: "The Almighty leaves me cold. He offends me. I refuse to worship a God who is the responsible cause of reality."

Monod would rather preach *another* God, the Father God, Father of Jesus Christ, and thus rescue His *moral* character. To this end, he would divorce the Creator God (the demiurge) from the Father-Redeemer God who is revealed in Christ. Monod thus reveals his affection for Marcion, who likewise opposed the Father of Jesus Christ to the Old Testament Creator. The hour has come, says Monod, for Marcion's rehabilitation. With the traditional concept of omnipotence eliminated from our notion of God, a theodicy will be possible. Monod, confronted by grim reality, seeks to justify the Father in the face of it by saying, as did Marcion, that He had nothing to do with it. This theodicy justifies God by stripping Him of his full Godhead.

5. *The christological theodicy.* Finally, we must consider, though but briefly, the christological theodicy of Karl Barth.[5] Barth, it must be noted, does not speak of a theodicy in the usual sense of the word. The basic structure of his entire theology excludes and condemns the idea that man should justify the ways of God to man. In his *Credo* of 1935, Barth spoke of sin as the deed by which the creature, in spite of the sovereignty of God, assumes not only an independent reality but presumes an absolute autonomy, and thus sets himself up as God. Continuing, he considers the possibility of evil and death. He combines these questions with that of how the devil was able to become and remain the devil. We can say, reasons Barth, that God as Creator must conquer over these absurd, these "impossible possibilities," "but we can in no case say that God has willed and created these possibilities (to say nothing of the realities) as such." If we include these possibilities in the work of God's creation, we would — with Zwingli — make God an inconceivable tyrant. Dogmatics, according to Barth, must in the nature of the case, be logically *inconsistent* here. We cannot escape the frightening reality in and around us. But we may not consistently think through the problem of creation and the possibilities of evil. We must here refrain "from asking for the ground of their existence." We must be content to take these possibilities seriously as the "mystery of iniquity."

Since Barth expressly denies that God has willed these evil possibilities, he has already committed himself, in a sense, to

---

5. Cf. K. Barth, *Kirchliche Dogmatik,* III, 1, 1945, especially the chapter on "Schöpfung als Rechtfertigung."

a theodicy. While he speaks of the mystery of sin, he also insists on the latitude of freedom that was left to man. It is within this freedom that sin, suffering, and death originated. However, in his *Kirchliche Dogmatik,* which appeared later than the *Credo,* Barth brings the area of evil, sin, devil, and death within the sphere of God's will, since God's will is involved in *not* preventing evil.[6] The development of these thoughts is best observed in Barth's doctrine of creation.

Barth deals extensively with the problem posed by the reality of darkness within the created world and gives us an exposition concerning the goodness and the "justification" of creation. His point of departure is the word of Genesis 1:31, that God saw all that He had made, and "behold it was very good." This is not a description of the cosmos, as orthodoxy has constructed it to be. The orthodoxy of the sixteenth and seventeenth centuries erred principally in abstracting the phrase "very good" from Christ, the Word become flesh. Just as is everything else in the creation saga, the goodness of creation is related to Christ. The created world is good only because it is "the appropriate place, the appropriate implement, since man, in the midst of this created world, is the appropriate object of the Divine work which has its beginning, its means, and its end in Jesus Christ."[7] This is evident only to faith, through God's revelation; one cannot observe it by looking at the world about him. Barth is not talking about a world that was or is to come. He is not distinguishing between the world before and after the fall. He refers to this very concrete globe, as it now "groaneth and travaileth in pain."

Genesis 1:31 is not intended to stir a homesickness in us for "the original goodness of the existence of creation."[8] It means the creation as it exists *in* Christ. There is an "affirmation" of creation, heard only through revelation, which em-

---

6. *Kirchliche Dogmatik,* II, 1, 1940, pp. 670ff.
7. *Ibid.,* III, 1, 1945, p. 423.
8. *Ibid.,* p. 239.

braces the "shadow" as well as the "light" sides of creation.[9] The lights and shadows are not ignored, indeed revelation makes "evident the gladness as well as the sadness of existence."

Everything is created with an eye to Christ, to His death and resurrection. There is both a positive and a negative significance to every creature. The creature is "not nothing, but something on the brink of nothing."[10] In this way, both the joy and misery of creaturely existence are grounded in God's will. But God is not bound to this two-sided judgment of creation. The Creator has Himself become the creature, and therein the meaning and purpose of creation is unveiled. God has become "subject of both aspects of existence . . . Himself a participant in the glory and the fall of creaturely existence."[11] This is the revelation of the "perfection of existence." "Is there a more perfect world than that which in its imperfection is the theatre, the implement, and the object of this Divine activity?"[12]

Thus, justification is not merely a matter of a Divine word, a forensic declaration, which remains outside of creation and in spite of which everything in creation, at least for the time, remains the same (the pity of it!). No, death is vanquished. In Christ "the created world, here and now, is already perfect in all its imperfections." In this light, this world is "the best

---

9. *Ibid.*, p. 430. Barth best illustrates what he means by his interpretation of the creation story in his exegesis of Genesis 1:2: "And the earth was waste and void; and darkness was upon the face of the deep: and the Spirit of God moved upon the face of the waters." This has nothing to do with a "God willed and created primordial and formless condition of the world." It refers to the *possibility* which God passes by as He proceeds with the work of creation, just as a human creator in choosing a certain work passes by another possibility, perhaps many other possibilities, and goes on with his chosen task (*Kirchliche Dogmatik*, III, 1, p. 119). The "moving on the face of the earth" by the Spirit cannot, then, be a preparation for the creation that follows (p. 118). Cf. Barth's exegesis of the *Spirit* in verse 2, a good example of his entire exegesis of Genesis 1 and 2, in which all the texts refer to the redemption in Christ. This is christological theodicy *par excellence*.
10. *Ibid.*, p. 430.
11. *Ibid.*, p. 432.
12. *Ibid.*, p. 439.

of all conceivable worlds."[13] This is neither optimism nor pessimism. It is the perfection of creation which is seen only through faith in Jesus Christ. This, according to Barth, is God's *Yes,* spoken, in Jesus Christ, over His creation.

* * *

Barth's critique of Leibniz illustrates further his own thoughts. Like Leibniz, Barth proposes that this is the best possible and conceivable world. But Barth is eager to dissociate himself from Leibniz's optimistic rationalism. For Leibniz, too, it was possible to utter a positive *Yes* over the world. Leibniz did not mean that this best possible world was an absolutely good world, but his optimism was not dampened by this. Since Barth and Leibniz agree that creation here and now is good, what is the essential difference between them?

First, Barth criticizes Leibniz for rationalizing the "shadow side" of creation until it becomes a fringe of the light. Really, for Leibniz, there are no two aspects; there is no longing for redemption, since perfection already exists. The essential difference of the optimism of the Christian faith from that of Leibniz is that the Christian faith knows of "the perils at the borders of the created world; it knows of sin, death, and Satan."[14] Secondly, Barth says that the eighteenth century optimism of Leibniz is "a creature's judgment on itself and on the rest of the world." The perfection of creation is considered as though it were creation's own proper attribute, "immanent in itself and capable of being judged good by mere men."[15] Finally, though Leibniz's optimism seeks its basis in God, this God is really nothing else than the projection of human self-reliance. Leibniz's God was only "the mirrored image of the perfection that man first ascribed to himself."[16]

---

13. *Ibid.,* p. 442.
14. *Ibid.,* pp. 466, 467.
15. *Ibid.,* p. 469.
16. *Ibid.,* p. 473.

THE PROBLEM OF THEODICY   245

In view of all this, Leibniz's theodicy has nothing in common with the Christian faith.[17]

The radical difference is that Leibniz's optimism had no place for Jesus Christ, and Barth insists that that which is true in Christ is false and meaningless outside of Him. The justification of creation has meaning and is real only in the message of Good Friday and Easter. Leibniz tried to justify God's work without this gospel, and that was the weakness of his theodicy.[18] Only a christological theodicy can be a truly optimistic theodicy. There is an optimism outside of Christ, but it is an optimism without foundation; and, as eighteenth century optimism was almost shattered by the Lisbon earthquake, so will all such optimism be shaken — by an atom bomb or a toothache. But true Christian optimism is founded in Christ. Having in faith heard and understood God's affirmation, the Divine *Yes*, of creation, this optimism sees creation for what it really is: justified in Christ.

* * *

Within all the evident variations of the forms of theodicy which we have briefly outlined, we encounter certain central questions concerning the creation and the government of God. In theodicy the attributes of God are usually confronted with the experiential realities of sin, suffering, and death. In the light of these realities it is often suggested that the Church's confession of God's Providence over all things is an oversimplification. Thus, other more rational ways are found to square God with this actual world. There remains, however, after the most profound attempts to construct a theodicy, a feeling of uncertainty, a suspicion withal that the bruising reality of life cannot thus be justified. One feels

---
17. *Ibid.*, p. 474.
18. *Ibid.*, p. 475. At the close of his discussion Barth recalls an isolated instance in which Leibniz spoke of a *maxima ratio* which lies in Christ, the God-man. But, says Barth, Leibniz never saw the consequence of his own remark.

that theories of the pedagogical and teleological significance of suffering and death only muffle a protest that does not easily die. Does not an honest conscience, if not reason, forbid the preaching of an all-embracing harmony which takes black evil within itself and displays it as white?

Such a theodicy was, in the eighteenth century, still confidently sought. Reason was still trusted. Christianity, as the title of Toland's book had it, was "not mysterious." The world was all harmony, and God was to be found by only listening to the cosmic symphony. But much has happened since the eighteenth century.

The God concept that climaxed this beautiful structure has been unveiled in its emptiness and poverty as a human construction. God was a "machinist," as Leibniz once spoke of Him. He left the heart cold, and, in time, fell before new and crushing experiences.

Kant's critique of the rational proofs for the existence of God and his demonstration of reason's limits shook the foundation of traditional thought and, with it, the assurance that many a rational theodicy had brought. But experience has been even more severe with theodicy. Suffering, wars, Dachau, Hiroshima, dread, and the promise of more: this is life. Is this harmony? Modern man has reacted to his experience with a strong repugnance to all attempts to harmonize it all within a rational system. Many have chosen nihilism rather than bow their heads before *this* harmony.

This charges the Church with a weighted burden of responsibility. The crisis of the Providence doctrine brings a new task to the Church in her preaching of the Gospel. She must now preach to men for whom experience has made it obvious that God does not rule.

* * *

Must we conclude, then, that it is impossible to have a theodicy? Or is there an "authentic" method of justifying the rule of God in the world? The possibility of a *believing*

THE PROBLEM OF THEODICY   247

theodicy has been suggested, a theodicy which "is not philosophical, but theological, and posits over against rationalism the science of faith."[19] The purpose of this theodicy would be to hold high the righteousness of God and "to bring man to a recognition of it." Theodicy would belong to the prophetic task of the believer. But the question is whether this would be theodicy in the customary sense of the word, that is, a theodicy constructed on rational grounds.

The word theodicy suggests a man looking about in the world and coming to the conclusion that God's way with it is just. While it is not simply an attempt to summon God before the bar of human judgment and while it does not intend conscious rebellion, it does, nevertheless, mean that man proceeds from the facts of experience along the way of reasoned argument to demonstrate that God's rule of the world is just, to prove that experiential reality is not inconsistent with the righteousness of God. This is the way of the philosophy of religion or natural theodicy.

In theodicy one starts with reality, stands on the same level as all men, and then climbs up with them to the plane of God's righteousness. It involves a search for common ground with or a point of contact between the Christian faith and non-Christian thought. One tries, in theodicy, to open conversation within neutralized territory, in which, for the sake of the contact, he does not intrude the content of his own Christian faith into the discussion. Thus, putting aside the positive *declaration* that God is just, one seeks an independent area for a serious and unprejudiced conversation about reality, which it is hoped will form a common starting point for the recognition of God's righteousness.

This is the principal mistake of those who have attempted to construct a theodicy. They have abstracted thought from God's revelation. It has been assumed that the world and its events, apart from revelation, speak their own language and

---
19. A. Kuyper, Jr., *Theodicee*, 1931, preface.

that their speech can be understood and translated by our natural reason. God and His righteousness take their place, not at the *beginning,* but at the *end* of this process of thought. God is, as it were, the a posteriori conclusion of analytical thought. And, with this, the Divine revelation is in principle repudiated. It is denied, not in a purposeful disavowal, but implicitly in the structure and process of thought. It is not sufficiently recognized that this world cannot be understood without the word of the living God, that it will, at the most crucial moment, be misunderstood when God's revelation is not the determinative point of departure for analysis.

We may observe how the Scriptures protest against all independent analyses of the world which leave God, even though temporarily, in the shadows. The decision of faith, which knows from the start that any unrighteousness in God is impossible, is decisive for any consideration of theodicy. This is the way Paul speaks in the face of experiential realities that disturb him: "Is there unrighteousness with God? God forbid" (Rom. 9:14). This impossibility of unrighteousness is the converse of the a priori declaration that God is righteous. With this premise Paul can also appreciate God's ways in the world: "O the depth of the riches both of the wisdom and the knowledge of God" (Rom. 11:33). Even when considering the difficult fact that God sometimes hardens the heart of man, Paul maintains the righteousness of God: ". . . who art thou that repliest against God?" (Rom. 9:20). Contradicting all autonomy of thought, he reminds us that the living God is not to be subjected to the judgment of man and not to be grasped in the compass of experiential reality. Rather, all reality is to be seen as existing of, through, and unto him (Rom. 11:36), and to be understood in *His light,* the light of revelation.

This a priori does not prohibit reflection on God's work, nor on the manner of His activity. Paul himself, musing over the fact that Israel had not come to justification, raises the

THE PROBLEM OF THEODICY 249

question: Why? (Rom. 9:32). But an answer is possible only by way of revelation. The premise is not searched for as a conclusion. The righteousness of God is the *assumption* on which suffering and death, sin and guilt — and the rejection of Israel — must be discussed if they are, finally, to make sense.

This outlook is not peculiar to Paul, as though he had a unique theology of Divine sovereignty. "Far be it from God, that he should do wickedness," said Elihu in the Old Testament (Job. 34:10). Here, too, we have the assumption of the impossibility of godlessness in God, of any inner contradiction within Him.[20] Again, in the Psalms we hear the singer, after all his contact with life's reality, declare as an a priori that the Lord is just: "He is my rock, and there is no unrighteousness in him" (Ps. 92:15. Cf. Ps. 71:14-18).

* * *

Reality, including sin and death, evil and suffering can never be considered as having its existence in itself. Therefore, every time one proceeds from the assumption that reality is self-existent he proceeds from an abstraction. The basic problem of theodicy is defined by the manner in which one approaches reality. One cannot mount *from* reality to the righteousness of God, because reality can only be known through the explaining word of revelation. The Light that illuminates the world is found only in faith. Reality, isolated from this Light, remains, in the end, enshrouded in darkness. This is why all theodicy is principially unacceptable. What God said to Job is valid here: "Who is this that darkeneth counsel By words without knowledge? Gird up now thy loins like a man; For I will demand of thee, and declare thou unto me. Where wast thou when I laid the foundations of the earth? Declare, if thou hast understanding" (Job 38:2-4).

---

20. Cf. apart from his conclusions, what Bildad says in this same direction: "Doth God pervert justice? Or doth the Almighty pervert righteousness?" (Job 8:3).

True, this has to do with a complaint against God. But the earnestness of this Divine criticism applies as well to any attempt to approach God from the basis of empirical reality and thus — be it unintended — make His righteousness a *deduction* of human reason.

This makes all natural theodicy, in spite of its apologetic intent, worthless and unacceptable. Instead of preparing the way for fruitful conversation, instead of erecting a dam against the secularization of thought, theodicy only suggests that we try again to reach God by way of natural understanding. It is the ironic drama of theodicy that it actually abets the progressive secularizing of thought by insisting that man can understand his world without revelation. And the fact that one in theodicy usually concludes with an empty, abstract God concept is already a judgment against this method.

* * *

Natural theodicy always moves in a vicious circle. It is a line of thought that starts at empirical reality, runs through to God, and then comes back again to reality. It hopes thus to illumine reality with light of God, but its fallacy is that its God is, in the first place, a product of human thought. And this, in turn, is why it must always oversimplify reality. The view of reality that is abstracted from God must fall essentially short of reality as it stands in the full light of revelation. This is illustrated by the way in which Leibniz finally relativized the reality of sin and evil. It is made perhaps more clear in the modern philosophical analysis of the "phenomenon" of death.

The present interest in the phenomenon of death is not prompted by a desire to construct a theodicy. It is a part of modern analysis of human existence, an attempt to understand the meaning of death as a phenomenon of existence. Simmel sees death as the formative principle of human life; Heidegger sees it as an essential mode of existence; Jaspers as a border situation. In these and other constructions, death is characterized as something essential to life. This means that life can be truly understood and experienced only when death is comprehended. Thus, death is interpreted by way of a neutral analysis, which, nevertheless, is ruled by a definite a priori. This philosophy of death is another proof that the decisive step in any analysis of reality is taken at the very beginning of the way. There — at the beginning of the existentialist's analysis of death — the fundamental Biblical characterization of death is eliminated. This analysis of human existence brushes aside the basic relationship between sin, guilt, and death. Whether Divine judgment is manifest in death cannot be allowed to prejudice the examination of existence. That death could be the wages of sin is a standpoint that offers no useful data. In this way, modern thought seeks to operate only with its own resources. Certainly it would be illusory to suppose that this thought should lead to a recognition of God.

The same holds true of modern analysis of suffering. It was formerly observed that there is a universal law according to which natural life cannot exist except at the cost of creaturely suffering. The ancient religions, we were told, contained an understanding of the deep meaning of cosmic order, that life rises out of death as the wheat grows from the dying grain. From this, it was concluded that creation is so established by its Maker that natural life is based on the destruction of the organism. This explained the exalted significance of the eternal cycle of life-death-life. This kind of thinking illustrates the deepest tendency of theodicy. When analysis of the world, abstracted from revelation, becomes the basis of theodicy, man irrevocably arrives at an unacceptable and comfortless simplification. The existentialist philosophy of death has made short shrift of this "exalted meaning of life." Life has been reduced for many to an obviously meaningless fate.

Men have tried to make sense out of suffering in various ways. The meaning of pain has been sought in its pedagogical usefulness. Suffering has been "proven" unreal in Christian Science, for instance. This, too, is an attempt to construct a theodicy. The unsatisfactoriness of it, however, is self-evident. Furthermore, no reasoned, demonstrable connection between suffering and sacrifice or suffering and education can offer a solution which satisfies the mind. A neutral analysis of suffering always falls short of satisfaction.

Likewise, analysis of evil and, in particular, sin as a "phenomenon" of empirical reality, fails. The full reality and seriousness of sin are inexplicable, in fact, undiscernible, without the light of Divine revelation. A cynically critical tradition has grown up in Western thought in the last few centuries in regard to the Scriptural presentation of the origin of sin. The individualism characteristic of the recent past has occasioned the undermining and ridicule of the doctrine of original sin. Ironically, perhaps, it is the paradise story of the origin of human evil which best illustrates man in his flight from responsibility and the self-vindication which has been interwoven into human history and in which each has thought to have discovered his irrefutable alibi. Human thought, it seems, dedicated itself to the "explanation" of sin, to the vindication of man. Sin has been described evolutionistically as a "not yet" which would gradually be made good through human power. Or it has been seen as only the bad circumstances which have hindered the development of man's real inner humaneness. Even where the darkest shadows have fallen on humanity, man's own powers of resistance were deemed sufficient to extricate him from evil. Even when life has been portrayed in terms of guilt, sin, and tragic drama, the real significance of guilt was often disregarded; even when most realistic, man still was occupied in self-vindication. Again and again, analysis has run itself out in nihilism or absurdism. The illusion has arisen that the world can be understood in its deepest meaning and that reality is correctly defined by such concepts as fate, grief, "existence unto death," dread,

THE PROBLEM OF THEODICY 253

guilt, doom, and death. But the reality thus pessimistically construed is not the reality of God. The problem is incorrectly posed and therefore gets no solution. This type of analysis arises from secularized thought, from which is screened the only light which truly exposes reality. How, then, can this type of thought form a point of contact for the building of a meaningful theodicy?

This is not to deny the possibility of a believing apologetic. But an apologetic will have to begin with faith, not with uncertainty and doubt, if it is to be fruitful and a blessing to anyone. The apologete will have to advance into the struggle with modern thought from a position of faith, profoundly convinced that the logic of modern empirical thought, of neutral analysis and induction is the corrupted logic of sinful thinking. A true apologetic must begin with the awareness that unChristian thought involves an estrangement from the glory of God and suppression of the truth. "The fool hath said in his heart that there is no God," and all his analyses notwithstanding, he continually fails to understand reality in its deepest sense because his starting point has closed the way of his heart to this understanding.

When Christ's miracles were explained, though not denied, by the Pharisees — he casts out devils through Beelzebub — Christ rebuked their unbelief. But He also indicated the inner contradiction of their unbelief when He said that a house divided against itself cannot stand (Matt. 12:25). The basic fallacy of their construction was revealed by the manifest power of the kingdom of God. On Pentecost, too, the facts were not denied, but were given an invalid interpretation. The miracle of the Spirit was to the unbelieving mind, a sign of drunkenness: "They are filled with new wine" (Acts 2:13). In his Pentecost sermon, through which thousands were converted, Peter did not neglect to remind his opponents that their explanation was, in the light of the real facts, erroneous: "it is but the third hour of the day."

All this has significance for the problem of theodicy. Reality cannot be known, phenomenologically, in its deepest sense, apart from the light of Divine revelation. Theodicy is at bottom the fruit of the doctrine of "mixed articles." Natural theodicy must fall before the speaking of God, before the word of Him from whom and through whom and unto whom are all things.

* * *

Must we then, it may be asked, in the absence of a theodicy flee into the irrationality of a hidden God? Must we submit to the dreadful "sovereignty" of an absolute power, which, in Divine caprice, plays a ruleless game with man? Calvinism has sometimes been accused of seeking the solution in this empty concept of sovereignty "in itself," to which all things together are subject and to which man can only bow and submit. Christian faith, as was mentioned previously, is then mistakenly interpreted as Christian fate.[21] Christian faith could hardly be more grievously misunderstood. When this happens, it means that an abstract concept of sovereignty has replaced the God of revelation. God is construed as a "super power," a *potentia absoluta*, which is another God than He of Scripture. Sovereignty "in itself" is a compassionateless concept quite as inspiring of dread as is blind fate. Biblical thinking is always directed to the sovereignty of God, that is, to the real, the true, and living God, the God of revelation. It is to Him that all things are subjected and in Him that faith finds its rest and joy.

This God is precisely not the God of dangerous caprice, but the holy and merciful Father. We cannot accuse Him of arbitrariness, nor protest with a rebellious "Why?" We can

---

21. Cf. Thomas Aquinas, *Summa Contra Gentiles*, Chap. XCIII, p. 337 (Edition Leonina Manualis, 1934), and *Summa Theologica*, P.I., Qu. 116, A 1; cf. Augustine, cited by Thomas: "Si propterea quisquam res humanas fato tribuit, quia ipsam voluntatem vel potestatem fati nomine appellat, sententiam teneat, et linguam corrigat" (*De civitate Dei*, 5, Chap. 1).

THE PROBLEM OF THEODICY 255

only ask, "Show me thy ways, O Jehovah; Teach me thy paths" (Ps. 25:4). The Scriptures teach that God dwells in unapproachable light (I Tim. 6:16), and that "there is no searching of his understanding" (Is. 40:28). This incomprehensibility defines the limits, the nature of our knowledge. But what does this incomprehensibility really mean? It is not the incomprehensibility to which all religions in common testify on the basis of experience. The Scriptural idea of God's incomprehensibility cannot be identified with this universal concept. In Scripture we deal, even in respect to His incomprehensibility, with the true and only God. Even His incomprehensibility is apprehended only through revelation.

Israel often stood still before the riddle of God's mysterious administration. And repeatedly, in a variety of tones, she asked both God and men, "Why?" Sometimes her question carried an overtone of rebellion, impatience, or suspicion. But it was also at times meant as honest inquiring. "Why standest thou afar off, O Jehovah? Why hidest thou thyself in times of trouble?" (Ps. 10:1). "Wherefore doth the wicked contemn God?" (Ps. 10:13). This *why* suggests nostalgia for the assurance and the comfort of God. "Arise, O Jehovah; O God, lift up thy hand: Forget not the poor" (Ps. 10:12). This *why* implicitly admits the piecemeal nature of our knowledge (I Cor. 13:12). That it does not wholly silence the song of praise suggests that the incomprehensibility of God is quite different from the irrationality and arbitrariness of nominalism, in which God is a kind of "outlaw" to whose power alone one must capitulate. If the incomprehensibility of God were not wholly other than irrationality, His unsearchableness would be in the same category as the enigmas of fate or fortune. But, happily, all concepts of fate are poles removed from faith in the God and Father of our Lord Jesus Christ.

Thus, we can respect the limits of our knowledge and find peace within them — a peace which surpasses all knowledge.

He who has understood Christ's statement: "He who hath seen Me, hath seen the Father," possesses the sufficient knowledge that this sight gives. For him the struggle that remains is that against doubt, against the sinful distrust which seeks to implicate God in man's sin and which draws the curtain before God's glory. The struggle with doubt is the struggle against the protest of the autonomous man, who sees the limits which God draws to human knowledge as an outrage against his freedom and happiness. Through the sovereignty of His grace, this protest is withdrawn. But in the withdrawal of protest, worship is born.

* * *

It is necessary to reflect further on the nature of the limitation of our knowledge. We are not concerned with a formal problem of knowledge. That is, we are not dealing abstractly with the potentialities or restrictions of human knowledge in the face of the greatness of its object. We are concerned with the line drawn between us and God and with the light that this boundary may throw on the whole problem of theodicy. Three things will hold our attention as we investigate the limitations of our knowledge further: *God's wrath, man's guilt,* and *the Church's doxology.*

* * *

In theodicy one usually confronts the attributes of God with the existential realities of the world. But the confronting is often of a narrow and abstract character. This may be observed in the common failure to reckon with the real and concrete wrath of God, as it is revealed in Scripture. This, in turn, occasions a serious impoverishing of the holiness of God. Implied in the preaching of God's holiness is an earnest warning against every attempt to implicate God in the guilt and corruption of this world. Pure wrath needs absolute holiness.

This does not mean that one must consider God as standing outside of man's guilt, in the sense that He was taken completely by surprise or that He was suddenly encountered by an unexpected and unknown force that surreptitiously entered the world contrary to His intent. To try to vindicate God by placing His action dualistically outside of the sinful acts of man is to neglect much of Scripture. Revelation makes perfectly clear that God works sovereignly in the guilt of man. One need think only of the hardening of Pharaoh, the betrayal of Judas, and the contents of Romans 9-11 to see the fallacy of such dualism. God's inscrutable rule of the world realizes itself in His activity in and with man's guilty acts. God was active in the suffering and death of the Savior, in which man's guilt played a conspicuously historical role. "This is *your* hour, and the power of darkness," said Christ before His death (Luke 22:53). But in their "hour" and in this "power of darkness" God's own time was fulfilled and His own power revealed.

Nevertheless, the Church has, on the authority of the same Scriptures, always proclaimed and confessed that God is not involved in the guilt of the world, that is, that God is not the author of sin. By this seemingly inconsistent testimony the Church intended that God's action was not to be involved in guiltiness in the way that man's action was. The Scriptures teach as well that sin is not an isolated territory in which man held exclusive dominion and in which God cannot work except in reaction. But at the same time, they exclude a priori the possibility of darkness or guilt in God. And this outlook in the nature of the case precludes the possibility of man's calling God to account. The activity of God in sin is Divine activity and therefore is something different from man's subjecting himself in sin to God's will. That this idea should cause so much difficulty is the fruit of our applying the same measure to both man and God. This means that, to be logical, we must either make God the author of sin or, to save God from this stigma, set the world loose from Him and His rule.

The impasse is avoided only by listening to revelation. "And this is the message which we have heard from him and announce unto you, that God is light, and in him is no darkness at all" (I John 1:5). "Holy, holy, holy is Jehovah of hosts," sang the angels in Isaiah's vision (Is. 6). In revelation we are witnesses to the absolute blamelessness of God. No shadow from the world of sin can dim the light of His immaculate holiness. His holiness forms the spur to the sanctification of His people (Lev. 11:44; I Pet. 1:16). It is manifest in the holiness of Christ, the Holy One of God (Luke 1:35). The Spirit of God is the *Holy* Spirit. God's holiness is revealed in His holy law and in His holy wrath against the transgression of His holy law.

The reality of God's wrath underscores Scriptural insistence that sin may not be traced causally to God. Wherever the reality of Divine wrath has been minimized, the entire revelation has been affected. Apart from God's wrath neither His righteousness nor holiness, neither His love nor mercy can be understood; the whole Person of God is involved in His wrath toward the sinner. The threat of God's wrath reaches out over the universe of disobedience (Deut. 28:15). This is fully actualized and revealed in the day of God's wrath (Ps. 110:5). Wrath is the implication of God's holiness. It must direct itself against all evil.

Man has tried in various ways to avoid the reality of God's wrath. Theologians have often dismissed it as an anthropomorphic projection, saying that we must get rid of the idea of Divine wrath and, to do so, we must purge the entire concept of Deity of human images. But this idea thrusts inimically at the entire revelation of God. If the wrath of God were to fall, it would drag down with it the reality of forgiveness. The confidence of Psalm 90 in God's mercy and love (Ps. 90:14) is bound up with the recognition that He "turnest man to destruction" (Ps. 90:3). "For we are consumed in thine anger, And in thy wrath are we troubled" (Ps. 90:7). "Thou hast set our iniquities before thee, Our secret sins in the light of thy countenance" (Ps. 90:8). "Who knoweth the power of thine anger, And thy wrath according to the fear that is due unto thee?" (Ps. 90:11).

"Clouds and darkness are round about him: Righteousness and justice are the foundation of his throne. A fire goeth before him, And burneth up his adversaries round about" (Ps. 97:2, 3). He is a jealous God (Ex. 20:5) and an avenger (Nah. 1:2; Rom. 12:19; Heb. 10:30) and He "reserveth wrath for his enemies" (Nah. 1:2). "Who can stand before his indignation? and who can abide in the fierceness of his anger? his wrath is poured out like fire, and the rocks are broken asunder by him" (Nah. 1:6). God shows His goodness and forgiveness in this, that He does not keep His anger forever (Mic. 7:18). The question, "who knoweth the power of thine anger," is the converse of the question, "Who is a God like unto thee, that pardoneth iniquity . . .?" (Mic. 7:18). God's wrath is not arbitrariness, nor does it carry demonic evidences, as has been claimed. It is the exalted reaction of His holiness.

God's wrath is revealed in the New Testament as well as the Old. Moses' warning to the people that "Jehovah, thy God is a devouring fire, a jealous God" (Deut. 4:24) reappears in Hebrews: "for our God is a consuming fire" (Heb. 12:29). John the Baptist preaches of the coming wrath (Matt. 3:7). Paul speaks of it. Christ is the only Savior from it (I Thess. 1:10). This is the wrath that will be revealed from heaven against all unrighteousness and ungodliness (Rom. 1:18; Eph. 5:6; Col. 3:6). The impenitent treasure up wrath unto the day of wrath (Rom. 2:5). Paul defends the holy righteousness of God's wrath: "Is God unrighteous who visiteth with wrath?" (Rom. 3:5). Paul is so convinced of the rightness of His wrath that he adds: "I speak after the manner of men." In John's vision of the last day, the reality of God's wrath is very vivid: "for the great day of their wrath is come; and who is able to stand?" (Rev. 6:17; cf. Rev. 11:18; 19:15). What has been said of Luther could apply to the Scriptures: "His entire teaching would lose its form, if the wrath of God were removed from it."

Often the refusal to recognize the quality of wrath in God stems from the fact that God's wrath is judged according to the character of man's wrath, which is usually based on selfish claims and is therefore seldom capable of including sacrifice and forgiveness. The unfittingness of such a judgment appears most clearly in the revelation of the love of God in Christ, who bore God's wrath to the full and became a curse for us (Gal. 3:13). The total brunt of Divine wrath, climaxed in the forsakenness of the cross, was borne by Christ, whose "why?" gave only a hint of its terribleness.

Thus, it is everywhere evident that God's wrath is not the whim of a demonic power. The wrathful God maintains His righteousness but, in this jealous preservation, He gives His Son for the redemption of the world: God was Himself in Christ redeeming the world unto Himself (II Cor. 5:19). Following the "who could stand" of Psalm 130 is the confession, "But there is forgiveness with thee." In God's forgiveness, it is also possible to recognize His righteousness, His wrath and His holiness.

The limits of our thinking have practical significance for the problem of theodicy. Having received forgiveness, man can not possibly speak of God and the world in abstract categories. Theodicy has usually run aground in the shallowness of the human endeavor to find an *explanation* where only justification and forgiveness can provide a perspective. The problem of theodicy is at bottom the problem of man in his lostness, the problem of the prodigal son. A miracle was needed to get the son to think about his father's home. That is why the main role in the parable is played by the father — the man who let his son go, took him back again, and celebrated his return. This homecoming celebration stands at the border of our human thought. If we were not given the feast and the resurrection from the dead (Luke 15:32) in revelation, we would remain "critics" in our thought, untrusting and accusing. But in the feast the wrath of the Father is turned to joy. At that moment the conviction that God is righteous becomes an eternal premise. "As for me, I shall behold thy face in righteousness; I shall be satisfied, when I awake, with beholding thy form" (Ps. 17:15).

* * *

Secondly, we must consider human guilt as a limitation of our thought. Needless to say, this does not introduce a different limit, independent of that of Divine wrath. It is the same limitation seen from the point of view of our responsibility. Within the limits of the activity of God in all things and within the invincibility of His purpose, the Scripture also insists on human responsibility. This has inspired many charges of contradiction, a charge which has more than theoretic ramifications and which has often led to a denial of or emasculating of human responsibility. And with this, the problem of theodicy is intensified.

The Scriptures, however, never present human responsibility as a problem. Man in his guiltiness presents a problem, but his God-given responsibility is always an a priori postulate. The relation between sin and guilt and between sin and death is, thus, clearly revealed. This is not only the case in the story of paradise, in which the curse of exile is patently associated with man's fall and guilt. It is true of the entire Scripture.

Leibniz, as does all rationalism, traces evil to metaphysical evil (imperfection) and metaphysical evil to the necessary nature of God's creation. Thus, he views evil as an integral ingredient of finite existence. This determines his solution to the theodicy problem. Human existence is an essential component of this imperfect world. Consequently man can witness evil as David did while Nathan was painting the picture of sin to him. He can be an observer to evil, for he has not yet heard the accusation, "Thou art the man." Since evil *fits* properly into this world, which was intended as imperfect, it neither intrudes into nor disrupts man's existence. Man can take an interest in the problem of evil, as a philosophical or social problem. But his own personal involvement in guilt escapes him. He is unaware that his entire thought process on the matter is an attempt at self-vindication.

* * *

Man's persistent effort at self-exoneration is a contrast to the Biblical message of sin and judgment. God made the connection between sin and judgment clear to man before the fall. After the fall the preaching of it echoes through the entire Old and New Testaments. The Scriptures never analyze suffering and death apart from the relationship between sin and judgment. It is ever God who converts man, even to breaking him: "Thou . . . sayest, Return, ye children of men . . . For we are consumed in thine anger" (Ps. 90:3, 7). Paul, too, sees sin as a foreign element in the world and rejects the notion that sin belongs to the essence of created reality (Rom. 5:12). The relation between this foreign power and death is epitomized in the word *wage*: "the wages of sin is death" (Rom. 6:23). "For when ye were servants of sin, ye were free in regard of righteousness. What fruit then had ye at that time in the things whereof ye are now ashamed? for the end of those things is death" (Rom. 6:20, 21).

Scripture says at one time that God had given the heathen over to the lusts of their hearts (Rom. 1:24) but, at another time, that they have given themselves over to lasciviousness (Eph. 4:19). We are given an earnest picture of the results

THE PROBLEM OF THEODICY 263

of sin: vanity of the mind, darkening of the understanding, alienation from the life of God, and hardening of the heart (Eph. 4:17-19). Man, darkened in his mind, scattered in the imagination of his heart (Luke 1:51), lives in a world which, by his own choice, is subjected to corruption (Rom. 8:20). James, too, carries on the thought of sin as subject of wages, with death as the end of the process: "Then the lust, when it hath conceived, beareth sin: and the sin, when it is full-grown, bringeth forth death" (Jas. 1:15). This suggests that perhaps sin has an immanent force by which it is propelled out of inner necessity to its own appropriate end. But the Scripture also insists that God's judgment over man works *in* this immanent propulsion of sin toward its fruits. The entire process is the judgment of God on the vanity of this world for which man is held guilty. For this reason the blinds are drawn and the light extinguished. In the darkness of the world, with God's light rejected and with man loving darkness rather than light (John 3:19), the problem of theodicy arises.

Man has shown an almost unbelievable persistency in constructing a natural theodicy by means of unbelieving reason. It is the more amazing since the history of the continued failure in man's analysis of the world has only supported the Biblical testimony that human reason is darkened. Suffering and death are persistently explained either as the unavoidable realities of fate or, optimistically, as steps in the gradual ascent of humanity. In either case, there is a basic insistence that man is his own judge and that his trouble is his own problem. Existentialism is a good example of this. In it there is an analysis of life from which all relationship to God is cut off and which therefore has the pretensions of a judgment by man upon himself. "The humanism of Sartre is conceived as a creative humanism. Man creates himself and, therefore, his fate. Man is his own fate. He is the sum of his activity. His life is his judgment."[22] Since man, according to existentialism, is unrelated to God, he has no responsibility and, therefore, no guilt. The Scriptures reveal such ideas as attempts to flee, and it is the task of the Church to expose such flights as flights from God.

All forms of natural theodicy reveal something of a flight from Divine judgment. Dualistic theodicy, with its two eternal principles of good and evil, resolves man's guilt into an eternal principle over which he has no control and for which he cannot be judged. Teleological theodicy tries to assume God's prerogative of turning evil into a good end in order to attain His purpose. Therefore, there is no evil for which to judge man. Harmonistic theodicy accepts evil as a Divinely intended element of creation, thus excluding the possibility of a Divine judgment upon it. Monod relieves the world of God's judgment by acknowledging only a God who is unable either to create or to judge.

The christological theodicy of Karl Barth assumes a unique place and character among other theodicies. The starting point for the justification of the world lies in Barth's interpretation of *good* in Genesis 1:31. As we have noted, this text is interpreted christologically. But the basic problem in Barth's theology and, therefore, in his theodicy, lies in his teaching of the attributes of God. Barth considers the world not confronted by the righteousness of God, but enveloped by the love of God. In Barth's doctrine of the Divine attributes, the love of God dominates over His righteousness, His grace over His wrath. It would seem that he thus allows the gospel of grace, the Scriptural message of the love of God unto the salvation of the world, to come to its full expression. But the manner in which Barth speaks of God's *Yes* and *No* reveals a concept of grace different from that of the Biblical mes-

---

22. Egon Vietta, *Theologie ohne Gott. Versuch über die menschliche Existenz in der modernen französischen Philosophie*, 1946, p. 57.

sage. Barth conceives of a new order of grace, established in redemption and in the election in Christ, in which all men share. Unbelief is nothing but the nonsense of rejecting this irrefutable fact: the universal love of God.

With this universalism, Barth must interpret the love of God as embracing the entire world of pain and death and evil. At bottom, then, there can be no serious talk of a judgment of God in the world, because God's judgment was fulfilled in Christ. Whenever Barth speaks of judgment, it is always as the other side of grace. Barth's christological theodicy is thus closely related to his universalistic doctrine of election.[23]

Thus it is that, while Barth emphatically rejects all natural theodicy, he comes, because of his doctrine of grace, suspiciously close to Leibniz's view of this world as the best possible world. This exposes a certain speculative tendency in Barth's theodicy. It goes back to his view of Genesis 1:31 and his isolating of the theodicy problem from the historical fall. Barth sees God's pronouncement on His creation as good, as objectively true only in Christ. In Christ, therefore, this present evil world is "good."

The Scriptures, however, do not know of such an objectivized notion of the world in Christ. The gospel of redemption is proclaimed in the world as an appeal to faith. It is never a mere informing about a new state of affairs. Christ warns those who remain in their sins: the wrath of God abides on them (John 3:36). The gospel must go into the world which here and now lies under the bondage of corruption. It must not be objectivized into a proclamation that all is now right with the world. We cannot construe God's *Yes* and *No* as being in static relationship. Barth's attempt to do so in his theodicy, though he disclaims having a theodicy, is consistent

---

23. Cf. my *Faith and Justification*, Chap. VII.

with his entire dogmatics — with his doctrine of creation, of election, of redemption, of man, and . . . of eschatology.

* * *

The problem of theodicy is insoluble outside of a faith that knows the limits of human reason. According to revelation, the confidence of faith in God's holy direction of the world is possible only in the recognition of guilt. With the blessing of salvation, guilt is the more openly recognized and confessed. And in this confession it becomes possible to honor God's incomprehensible government of the world. Through our knowledge of Christ, who was sent from the heart of God to declare Him to us (John 1:18), we know of God's holiness and His mercy, of His righteousness and His grace, of His wrath — and our guilt. Being in fellowship with Christ, we can openly confess: "For now we see in a mirror, darkly; but then face to face: now I know in part; but then shall I know fully even as also I was fully known. But now abideth faith, hope, love, these three; and the greatest of these is love" (I Cor. 13:12, 13).

* * *

Finally, we must consider the significance of the Church's doxology. With this we deal with the profoundest point in all reflection on the problem of theodicy: is it possible to stand in this evil world and sing a doxology in the face of the incomprehensibility of God's world rule? We are not ushered by the Scriptures through the door of faith into a life of quiet and lusterless acquiescence. Nevertheless questions can and do arise which indicate that one does sometimes expect such a life. Is it not, after all, enough that the rebellion of the heart is silenced, that the clenched fist is relaxed, and that the mind, having surrendered to revelation, is illumined by the righteousness of God? Is the climax of our musing over God's ways and judgments already reached when we no longer sin

THE PROBLEM OF THEODICY 267

with our tongue and when we learn to guard our paths (Ps. 39:1)? The psalmist, silenced, comes before the Lord and sighs: "I was dumb, I opened not my mouth; because thou didst it" (Ps. 39:9). And, of Job, is it not more realistic that "in all this did not Job sin with his lips" (Job 2:10), than that a doxology should arise out of his distress: "Jehovah gave, and Jehovah hath taken away; blessed be the name of Jehovah" (Job 1:21)?

It is not as though the doxology is a special experience for natures peculiarly blessed with a deep insight into the goodness of God's mysterious ways. Praise is the gift of the simple. Doxology is the normal expression of the Church. The congregation of all ages has been roused to join the doxology, to come before His presence with joyful song (Ps. 95:1, 2), to "enter his gates" with praise (Ps. 100:4). One is sometimes surprised at the frequent singing before God in the Old and New Testaments. These songs do not arise from those who live without fear or misgivings, who escape all the shocks of life's experiences. On the contrary, doxology is sung when peril is near and fear possesses. It sounds above questions and cries. The remarkable fact is that all the questions that arise in Scripture around what we call the problem of theodicy have their profoundest and most definitive answer in a *Hallelujah*.

* * *

The normality of the doxology in the life of the Church does not mean that this Hallelujah is in the nature of the case to be expected. The doxology is born from the natural heart of man no more than is the shadow of death turned by our own power into the dayspring (Amos 5:8). It is impossible without faith to sing, or even to understand from afar, this Hallelujah. Satan misinterpreted Job's piety, explaining the "phenomenon" as an objectivized egoism:[24] "Doth Job fear God for nought? Hast not thou made a hedge about him, and about his house, and about all that he hath, on every side? thou hast blessed the work of his hands, and his substance is increased in the land" (Job 1:9, 10). Satan thus levels an indictment against all piety in the world: "But put forth thy hand now, and touch all that he hath, and he will renounce thee to thy face" (Job 1:11). The book of Job is the drama in which God's praise on earth is justified against this attack. The refutation of this "explanation" of piety is climaxed by Job's doxology. Satan, having had his word in the prologue, is silenced by the epilogue (Job 42). In fact, the entire Scripture refutes the psychological identification of prosperity and doxology. The wonder is that the paeans of praise arise so often in hard times, that the songs are heard so frequently from the shadow, and that the doxology is sung as the last candle-light of life's joy flickers.

On the other hand, as is known, religion in general and the doxology in particular are often explained as compensation for earthly distress, a projection of human wish into future fulfillment. This is another side to the same "egoism" from which all religion allegedly stems. This is the tendency — this looking to eternity when God Himself shall wipe away all tears (Rev. 21:4) — that the nineteenth century found so offensive. It meant, said the critics, that men lost their perspective for the actual, the biting distress of this life. They smelled this opium in Paul, too, for instance, when he said that the sufferings of the present age "are not worthy to be compared with the glory which shall be revealed to usward" (Rom. 8:18). The balm of the hereafter soothed the wounds of this world too much. The prophets of the revolution, misunderstanding its real message, raged against Christianity as

---

24. The explanation of all religion as a projection of egoism is not new with Feuerbach and Freud. We meet essentially the same explanation in Satan's criticism of Job.

THE PROBLEM OF THEODICY 269

the opium of the people. Marx and Nietzsche both protested against what they saw as a numbness and acquiescence which the hope of eternity inflicted on the people. They construed the praise of God as a flight from reality and Christianity, as Nietzsche called it, "Platonism for the masses." What they could not see and what they therefore really attacked, was the possibility and reality of a doxology in this bitter life.

According to the nineteenth century "realists," Christian worship is possible only because Christianity paints a rosy eschatology. But this opposition is inspired by a misunderstanding both of Christian eschatology and of the true nature of worship. The Scriptures do not portray what God will do when once His eternal light falls over human life as the fulfilling of man's bourgeois longings. There is no contradiction in the Bible between the glory of God and the joy which shall fill human life when it is overshadowed by Him who now sits on the throne (Rev. 7:15). Scriptural meditation on the future is directed not to man's achievement of the comforts of eternal prosperity, but to the glory of God and, by implication, to the salvation, the wedding of the Lamb. This is the theme of the last book of the Bible. And it is the norm for all doxology on earth: it is directed to God's salvation and is full of *His* glory.

* * *

The doxologies of Scripture are perhaps best epitomized in the august sentence of Psalm 22:3: "But thou art holy, O thou that art enthroned upon the praises of Israel."[25] Note the position of this verse. It is not set in a context of rest and security. Psalm 22 is the psalm of the terrible "Why?" — "My God, my God, why hast thou forsaken me?" This is how the psalm begins. "O my God, I cry in the daytime, but thou answerest not; And in the night season, and am not silent" (Ps. 22:2). Not till later comes the confession: "But thou

---
25. Alternate reading, American Standard Version.

art holy . . . Our fathers trusted in thee: They trusted, and thou didst deliver them. They cried unto thee, and were delivered: They trusted in thee, and were not put to shame" (Ps. 22:3-5). This is a psalm of suffering and a psalm of implicit trust, a psalm of struggle and trouble and a psalm of faith and thankfulness. The unity of the psalm lies in the rapturous: *Thou art enthroned upon the praises of Israel.*

The throne of God — we are reminded of the permanence of His rule. The throne of God — around it are clouds and darkness (Ps. 97:2). The throne inspires many descriptions in the Old Testament. Isaiah caught it in his vision high and lifted up (Is. 6:1) and later saw it based on righteousness and justice (Is. 9:7). Micaiah, oppressed by the throne of Ahab, visioned, in contrast, the throne of the Lord, surrounded with the heavenly host (I Kings 22:19). The magnitude of God's throne captures Isaiah: "Thus saith Jehovah, Heaven is my throne, and the earth is my footstool: what manner of house will ye build unto me? and what place shall be my rest?" (Is. 66:1) This is in criticism of a people who trust too much in the temple service, as though there they monopolize God, forgetting that God is everywhere. God's throne says to us that God is great; it is a "glorious throne, set on high . . ." (Jer. 17:12).

This helps us understand what the psalmist meant by God "enthroned on the praises of Israel." The grandeur of his power and glory is not a terrifying thing to which dumb acquiescence is the only fitting response. Rather, it inspires the hymn of praise.[26] It is not as though His greatness were comprehended. It is just that He — and His throne — is recognized as full of grace (Heb. 4:16). If His throne were

---

26. Naturally, the song of praise does not exclude the bending of the knee and the subjection of the soul. On the contrary, Psalm 95 says after praising His greatness and salvation: "O come, let us worship and bow down; Let us kneel before Jehovah our Maker: For he is our God, And we are the people of his pasture, and the sheep of his hand" (Ps. 95:6,7). Cf. Ps. 98:1-6,9; Ps. 138:1,2; and many other psalms.

not the center of grace and if the *Lamb* were not "in the midst of the throne" (Rev. 7:17), that throne would inspire only fear, a dread that would stifle every hymn. But, since His throne signifies *grace*, His holiness and power inspire the doxology. And His praises ring through all generations.

Can it be accidental that Psalm 22 is a messianic psalm, the psalm of Christ's bitter "Why?" the psalm of *His* terrible forsakenness, and, therefore, also *our* doxology?

The way to this doxology is the way of faith. The struggle of faith is the same striving as that of remaining in harmony with the doxology of the Church. The Scripture does not conceal our tendency to resist the call to praise. In this resistance the Church perpetually faces the temptation to estrange itself from its own *Gloria*. In such an estrangement the Church falls down into silence, into doubt, or, perhaps, into a dumb resignation, in which she submits, but cannot sing.

* * *

Naturally, the doxology gets a central place in the Scriptures. The life of the believers finds its appointment and fulfillment in God's praise. It is striking, too, that the doxology in the Scriptures is set within the paeans that arise both from nature and from angels. In the so-called nature psalms, creation is brought into the song: "The heavens declare the glory of God; And the firmament showeth his handiwork" (Ps. 19:1). The sun, moon, and stars — yes, everything in creation — are called to join in the hymn: "For his name alone is exalted; His glory is above the earth and the heavens" (Ps. 148:13). There is no nature theology here. Israel knows the Creator-God and so relates all creation to her Hallelujah. The center of things is God — the God of creation and of redemption. "He hath lifted up the horn of his people, The praise of all his saints; Even of the children of Israel, a people near unto him" (Ps. 148:14). Neither is salvation anthropocentric here. It is sincerely directed to the praise of God.

The angels also bless Him with praise. Isaiah hears their threefold "Holy" in his vision. There is joy in their life when one sinner is converted. Their song is the *soli deo gloria;* they sang it over the fields of Ephrata to honor the arrival of God on earth. But, can these angelic anthems have any significance to our problem of theodicy? There is a large difference between the angels and the struggling Church. The angels know no doubt, neither is their understanding darkened. They are, as a matter of presupposition, prepared for service, for the liturgy, at His holy command. It is this presupposition of their preparation that interests us.

All the questions about God's world rule are ramifications and implications of one question: the question of the human doxology. John's Revelation gives us the *magnificat* of the Church Triumphant. It is the new song: "And I saw, and I heard a voice of many angels round about the throne and the living creatures and the elders; and the number of them was ten thousand times ten thousand, and thousands of thousands; saying with a great voice, Worthy is the Lamb that hath been slain to receive the power, and riches, and wisdom, and might, and honor, and glory, and blessing" (Rev. 5:11, 12). The last book of the Bible is full of God's magnificence, even in its portrayal of the great judgment. The harps of God are played by the side of the sea of glass; but the sea is aflame (Rev. 15:2). The song of Moses is sung — and the song of the Lamb. The four and twenty elders cast their crowns before the throne of Him who is worthy to receive the glory, the honor, and the power (Rev. 4:10, 11). But what has all this to do with the Church on earth? This worship is in the sphere of eternity, beyond the region of doubts. What relevance can these last things have for the living, for those who still weep and struggle and still see as through a glass darkly?

The eternal light of God's righteousness radiates through revelation into time, into times of distress, hardness, and mystery. We can hear the benediction of those called to the marriage of the Lamb (Rev. 19:9), the *Gloria* of the dead who die in the Lord and rest from all their troubles. Eternity's light streams into the thinking and musing of the children of men, even into the problem of theodicy. This says repeatedly that there is also a way on earth through the struggle to the doxology — doxology for those still in the stark distress of earth, who possess only "the earnest *expectation* of the creation" as it "waiteth for the revealing of the sons of God" (Rom. 8:19). The way to this doxology is defined by its content: praise to Him who is "enthroned on the praises of Israel," and praise to the Lamb.

The knowledge of the Lamb is a contradiction of all natural theodicy. God is worshiped already on earth, as the prelude to the song of the Church Triumphant sounds below: "Thou wast slain, and didst purchase unto God with thy blood men of every tribe, and tongue, and people, and nation . . ." (Rev. 5:9). The Apocalypse speaks to us with assurance that only by our participation in this humble, yet jubilant, chorus can the oppression of anxiety and dread be lifted from life in this enigmatic world. Without this knowledge of the Lamb, without this knowledge of God, then, the problems are only multiplied. They become hopelessly insoluble, because they must then be wrongly proposed. We can attempt to resolve them only by summoning a rationalistically construed God before the judgment of human reason, or, in irrationalistic reaction, by submission to the arbitrariness of the whimsical god of fate, or, as a last possibility, by turning the critique against God around and setting up a proud judgment against man himself.

The distress and the suffering, the evil and the death, drive man continually to new questions, all without answers. This danger is not foreign to believers: "My steps had well nigh slipped" (Ps. 73:2), said the believing psalmist. When human thought is undisciplined by faith, when its pivot is not revelation, when it lacks the cohesion of purpose, when it does not recognize its rightful limits — then it is in danger. This is the thinking that seeks, but finds no rest. From this kind of restlessness we are called by a clear voice, the voice of the Good Shepherd, who taught us to pray: "Bring us not into temptation," and who showed us the final end of all thought: "For thine is the kingdom, and the power, and the glory, for ever and ever." This is the way of thought that ends in doxology, for it opens up perspective to the way of God — not to a projection of our vain thought, but to the God of righteousness, judgment, and grace: "By terrible things thou wilt answer us in righteousness, O God of our salvation, Thou that art the confidence of all the ends of the earth, And of them that are afar off upon the sea" (Ps. 65:5). Without this discipline all thinking comes under the judgment: "He shall die for lack of instruction; And in the greatness of his folly he shall go astray" (Prov. 5:23).

The struggling Church, then, still needs the Biblical warning: "Wherefore let him that thinketh he standeth take heed lest he fall" (I Cor. 10:12). Paul says this upon thinking about Israel's murmuring in the desert in revolt against God's way. Then, from this warning — a caution not to lapse into such a crisis of trust and confidence as Israel had experienced — Paul leads us to the Lord's Supper (I Cor. 10:16). It is in the supper — in the holy memory provoked by the broken bread and the poured out wine, in the participation in the body and blood of Christ — that the congregation is called back from murmuring to thanksgiving, from doubt to certainty, and from rebellion to doxology.

This is what the Church must experience and recall until the end, even when the vials of God's wrath are poured over the earth. In the judgment, too, the Church hears the song of the angel of the waters: "Righteous art thou, who art and who wast, thou Holy One, because thou didst thus judge" (Rev. 16:5). To recognize God's righteousness and justice, this is to bow before His goodness as well. The Church is called out of darkness — including the darkness of unbelieving thought — into the "glorious light" of His goodness. This call is a call to worship, and worship is possible only in the "glorious light." It is the light of the Sabbath: "It is a good thing to give thanks unto Jehovah, And to sing praises unto thy name, O Most High; To show forth thy lovingkindness in the morning, And thy faithfulness every night" (Ps. 92:1, 2). There is praise for the works of His hands (Ps. 92:4) and the depth of His thoughts (Ps. 92:5). This is the thankfulness which opens the eyes to the *throne* of God. The "glorious light" of this knowledge illumines the gray days of agedness, streaming through all the dimly understood experiences of life and through all the hard memories of barren times. "They shall still bring forth fruit in old age; They shall be full of sap and green: *To show that Jehovah is upright; He is my rock, and there is no unrighteousness in him*" (Ps. 92:14, 15).

"God is enthroned upon the praises of Israel." This is the beginning and the end of true theodicy.

INDEX OF PRINCIPAL SUBJECTS

angels, 113ff., 122f., 271f.
anthropomorphism, 26, 33f., 46, 73, 81, 237, 258
Calvinism, neo-Calvinism, 189ff., 354
causality, 144, 152
   neutral, 18, 87, 186, 188ff., 215ff., 228
   primary and secondary, 86, 125ff., 147ff., 194
Christocracy — see Jesus Christ and the state
Church, message of the, 8ff., 26ff., 31f., 34, 40, 48f., 54, 59ff., 68, 93, 105f., 110f., 115, 119, 121ff., 126, 130, 147, 152, 154, 156, 161ff., 173f., 179, 185, 188, 190f., 214, 217, 222, 224f., 230ff., 235, 245f., 256ff., 264, 267, 271ff.
civilization, 168, 174, 186
common grace, 42, 70ff.
creation, 37, 43, 54ff., 64ff., 235ff.
   continuous, 60ff., 237
death, 232, 239ff., 261ff.
deism, 25f., 87, 125, 129f., 156, 166, 190
demons, 8, 103, 114ff., 193, 209, 211, 225, 229, 235
demythologizing, 193, 200
determinism, 24f., 138, 141ff., 221ff.
dread, 12f., 22, 181, 246, 252, 254, 271, 273
elect, election, 75f., 265
Enlightenment (*Aufklärung*), 27ff., 238
Epicureanism, 25, 165
eschatalogy, 56, 183ff., 236, 269
   Israel's, 101f.
evil, 12, 33, 78ff., 140, 156ff., 235ff., 258, 261ff., *see also* sin
existentialism, 12f., 21, 251, 263f.
Exodus, the, 83, 88f., 175ff., 209
faith, 17ff., 31ff., 82, 98, 122, 126, 131, 133, 135, 142, 158ff., 165, 175ff., 195f., 201ff., 207, 210ff., 234, 236, 242ff., 247ff., 253ff., 265ff.
fall, the, 57, 68, 70f., 88, 140, 150, 242, 261f., 265
fate, fatalism, 16, 22f., 39ff., 85, 143, 147ff., 163, 251ff., 263, 273
freedom, human, 21, 24, 137ff., 159, 192
God
   arbitrariness in, 254, 259, 273
   as author of sin, 130ff., 157, 237, 257f.
   as first cause, 126, 144, 147ff.
   chastisement, 181f.
   eternal counsel of, 70ff., 169
   forgiveness of, 28, 258ff.
   goodness of, 232ff.,
   grace of, 14, 22, 26ff., 36ff., 56, 64, 69ff., 81, 85, 89f., 90, 98, 102, 107ff., 126, 148f., 171, 233, 236, 264ff., 270ff.
   holiness of, 69, 136, 140, 256ff.
   image of, 38
   judgment of, 69, 71, 73, 80, 86, 90, 94, 98, 101f., 138f., 167ff., 171, 186f., 206, 231, 233, 251, 262ff., 272f.
   justice of, 28, 37, 120f., 164, 206, 270, 274
   longsuffering of, 73ff., 117
   love of, 26, 28, 37, 47, 73ff., 120, 180ff., 204, 206, 258, 260, 264ff.
   permissive will of, 134ff., 173
   power of, 33, 37, 47, 67, 84f., 89, 97f., 106, 129ff., 141, 151ff., 180, 206ff., 221ff., 232, 257, 270f.
   reality of, 8ff., 32, 188, 234
   righteousness of, 140, 247, 260f., 266, 270, 272ff.
   wrath of, 26, 28, 29, 74ff., 256ff.
Gospel, the, 8, 152, 163, 166f., 181, 186f., 212, 214, 222, 233, 246, 265
guilt, 8, 79, 133, 136, 150f., 159, 236, 249, 251ff., 256ff., 261ff.; *see also* sin
history, 31, 35, 45, 47, 56f., 65, 70f., 76ff., 82, 84ff., 91f., 99ff., 136, 141, 153f., 158ff., 161-187, 205, 223
   interpretation of, 19, 161ff., 183ff.
   law (norm) of, 167ff., 185
   meaning of, 7ff., 70f., 160, 232
   optimistic view of, 7ff., 27, 186, 238, 244f.
   pessimistic view of, 7ff., 22, 186, 244
   "special" events in, 161ff., 208
Hitler, 45, 162ff., 170, 239
Holy Spirit, 183, 214, 222ff., 253, 258
humanism, 8, 21ff., 49, 146, 263
indeterminism, 24, 142ff.
Israel, 15, 48, 55f., 83ff., 97ff., 170f., 175f., 179, 204ff., 248f., 255, 270ff.
Jesus Christ, 11, 36ff., 43ff., 56f., 71f., 75, 76, 80, 84, 95ff., 137, 160, 171f., 177f., 183, 185f., 209ff., 242ff., 265
   and the state, 105ff.
   kingdom of, 105ff., 114ff.
   return of, 183ff.
kingdom of God, 84, 99ff., 117ff., 121, 124, 160, 174, 181ff., 210ff., 221ff., 253
knowledge, limits of, 255ff.
knowledge of God, 37ff., 42, 155
miracles, 170, 177, 185, 188-232

contemporary, 216ff., 227
contra naturam, 198ff.
of healing, 214, 228
modernism, 189ff.
monism, 190ff., 235f.
natural science, 18, 21, 31, 143ff., 170, 188ff., 215ff.
natural theology, 26, 35ff., 46ff., 59, 155, 220, 271
nature, 20, 35, 47, 52, 65, 67, 85, 87, 154, 163, 168, 188ff., 213ff., 271
nihilism, 8ff., 22ff., 37, 48, 246, 252
Noahic covenant, 69ff.
pantheism, 64, 125, 129f., 154, 190
parapsychology, 23ff.
Pentecost, 223ff., 253
Pharisees, 173, 210, 219, 253
prayer, 15, 17, 32, 47, 227ff.
Providence
  and concurrence, 137-160
  and history, *see* history
  and miracles, *see* miracles
  and redemption, *see* salvation, God's
  and theodicy, 29, 139, 232-275; christological, 241ff.; dualistic, 235f., 257, 264; harmonistic, 236ff.; Monod's, 240ff., 264; teleological 239f.
  as government, 50, 83-134, 233
  as sustenance, 50-82
  attacks upon, 17ff., 31, 33, 49
  definition of, 10f., 35ff.
  general, special, very special, 180ff.
  in 20th century, 7ff.
  knowledge of, 31-49
  purpose of, 67ff., 83-134
reality, knowledge of, 247ff.

reason, 38ff., 44, 47, 148f., 155ff., 163, 186, 220, 232ff., 246ff., 263ff., 273
redemption, *see* salvation, God's
Reformation, the, 29, 107, 129, 142, 147, 156, 161
Reformed theology, 10, 38, 42ff., 47, 60ff., 132, 137f., 142, 152, 154ff.
religion, 19ff., 191ff.
reprobation, 71ff.
responsibility, human, 79, 138ff., 153, 192, 236, 252, 261, 264
revelation, 16, 22, 36ff., 72, 74, 92, 97, 99f., 104, 141, 170, 171, 176ff., 184, 186, 209f., 215ff., 236, 243, 247ff., 266, 272f.
Roman Catholicism, 10, 36ff., 49, 124, 126, 155, 170, 198., 216ff., 223
Russia, 164, 171, 179
Sabbath, 54ff., 275
sacraments, 222f., 226, 274
salvation, God's, 34ff., 42f., 55ff., 63, 70ff., 81ff., 90, 97ff., 119, 123, 126, 130ff., 163, 174, 177ff., 208ff., 219ff., 230f., 264ff., 269, 271; *see also* faith
Satan, 37, 97, 136, 151, 154, 211, 213, 229, 241, 244, 267
scientific method, 18, 188, 191, 194, 217; *see also* natural science
secularization, 17ff., 23, 250, 253
sin, 13, 78f., 148ff., 157ff., 232, 237ff., 249ff., 257ff.; *see also* evil, guilt
substance, doctrine of, 50ff., 127
suffering, 12ff., 22, 43, 182, 232ff., 262ff.
supernaturalism, 188f., 211, 216ff., 226

INDEX OF AUTHORS

Aalders, G. Ch., 113
Althaus, P., 127, 139, 203
Aristotle, 156
Augustine, 40, 152, 165, 198, 235, 237, 254
Banning, W., 12
Barth, K., 28, 29, 36f., 42, 46, 55, 56ff., 107, 112ff., 139ff., 163ff., 240ff., 264ff.
Bavinck, H., 38ff., 54, 62, 64ff., 125f., 130ff., 194f.
Bayle, P., 234, 236
Berdyaev, N., 9
Berkhof, L., 133f.

Bornhäuser, K., 173
Brunner, E., 36, 110, 146, 148
Bucan, 136
Bultmann, R., 193
Calvin, J., 45, 54, 107, 112, 129, 131, 136f., 140, 150f., 189, 214
Cornill, 81
Cullmann, O., 110, 111, 112, 113
Damascene (John of Damascus), 40
Dooyeweerd, H., 51, 143, 167ff.
Ebrard, A., 138
Eichrodt, W., 88, 203,

207f.
Erasmus, 148ff.
Feuerbach, L., 19ff., 268
Freud, S., 19ff., 268
Goethe, J. W., 234
Hegel, G. W. F., 19
Heidegger, M., 12f., 250
Heim, K., 22, 60ff.
Heppe, H., 134ff.
Heraclitus, 237
Hodge, C., 64, 128
Hoeksema, H., 75ff.
Irenaeus, 40, 115
Jaspers, K., 250
Kant, I., 28, 233
Kittel, G., 89, 92, 113,

INDEX

163f.
Kuyper, A., 42ff., 62ff., 67, 70ff., 77, 80, 107ff., 117, 122, 132, 166f., 173f., 189, 195ff.
Kuyper, A., Jr., 247
Lactantius, 164f., 174
Leibniz, G. W., 234ff.
Lessing, T., 11
Lewis, C. S., 180
Luther, M., 65, 148ff., 152
Marcion, 240f.
Marx, K., 19f., 33, 269
Mastricht, 136
Monod, W., 240f., 264
Mussert, A., 46
Murray, J., 76
Nietzsche, F., 19ff., 269

Otto, R., 28
Pauwels, C. F., 198, 218
Pelagius, 152
Planck, M. K., 202
Przywara, E., 156
Rickert, H., 191f.
Ritschl, A., 26, 28
Salvianus, 165
Sartre, J., 143, 263
Schelling, F. W., 167
Schilder, K., 57f., 70f., 97
Schleiermacher, F. E., 28, 62, 127, 142
Scholten, J. H., 189
Sergius (Patriarch) 164
Simmel, G., 250
Spengler, O., 11, 22
Stahl, F. J., 167

Stauffer, E., 90, 95
Stephan, H., 127
Thielicke, H., 199
Thomas Aquinas, 156, 198f., 254
Titius, A., 201
Toland, J., 246
Toynbee, A., 11
Troeltsch, E., 19
Turretin, J. A., 136
Schopenhauer, A., 33
Tertullian, 40
Van Til, C., 74ff.
Vietta, E., 264
Voltaire, 28
Windelband, W., 191f.
Zahn, T., 58
Zwingli, U., 147f., 150, 241

INDEX OF SCRIPTURE

GENESIS
1 56, 58, 61
1:2 243
1:31 242, 265
1:31 264
2 56, 57, 58
2:2 54
6:7 69
6:8 69
8:21 53
8:21, 22 69
9:10, 12, 16 69
12 99
18:14 204
26:4 99
28:14 99
39 90
49:10 99
50:20 88
50:20 240

EXODUS
8:16-19 183
8:19 182
9:5 88
14:21 206, 207
15:6 208
15:7 89
15:11 89, 207
15:12 89
15:13 89
15:15 208
15:16 89, 208
15:17, 18 208
15:18 89

20:5 259
20:11 55
23:12 55
31:17 55
34:10 204

LEVITICUS
11:44 258

NUMBERS
16:30 204
20:8 207
24:17 99

DEUTERONOMY
3:24 206
4:24 259
6:4 49
8:3 85, 206
8:5 182
9:10 182
28:15 258
34:11, 12 207

JUDGES
4:23 86
9:24 92

I SAMUEL
15:2 92
15:6 92

II SAMUEL
23:3 100
7:12, 13 99
7:15, 16 100

I KINGS
11:29ff. 93
11:31 93

12:24 93
22:19 270

NEHEMIAH
9:6 51

JOB
1:9, 10 268
1:11 268
1:21 15, 267
2:10 267
5:10 52
8:3 249
9:17 15
10:9-11 87
26:14 54
34:10 249
36:29 53
37:5 52
37:6 52
37:10 52
37:15 52
37:18 66
37:23 52
38:2-4 249
38:8-11 52
38:11 205
38:12 52
38:25 52
42 268
42:5 17

PSALMS
2:10-12 106
4:6 15
4:7 15
8:3 182
10:1 255

10:12 255
10:13 255
12 182
17:15 261
19 54
19:1 52, 271
19:4 52
22 271
22:2 269
22:3 269
22:3-5 270
22:10, 11 87
23 160
25:4 255
29 18
29:7-9 87
31:15 85
33 54
39:1 267
39:9 267
40:26 52
42:4 32
42:5 32
42:10 32
46:9 27
65:5 274
65:6 66
65:9 54
65:11 54
71:14-18 249
71:17 87
72:18 205
73:2 14, 273
73:4, 5 15
73:11 14

INDEX

73:16	14	104:27, 28	53	40:27	99
73:21	15	104:29	52	40:28	174, 255
73:23ff.	17	105:40	89	41:4	94, 158
73:23, 24	175	105:41	89	41:27	157
73:23-26	48	106:14	89	43:15-17	89
74:12-17	54	106:29	89	44:6	157, 158
77:13	83, 160	107:29	52	44:6, 7	158
77:13, 14	206	110:5	258	44:8	158
77:19	83	114:7, 8	207	44:28	94
77:19, 20	89	115:3	136	45:1	94
77:20	84	121:8	85	45:4	94
78:11	86	125:2	85	45:5	42
78:15, 16	86	130	260	45:5, 7	94
78:33	85	136:4	206	45:7	65
78:47, 48	85	138:1, 2	270	45:9	141
78:50	85	139:13-16	86	45:12	66
80:1, 4	160	139:24	56	48:6ff.	204
86:10	206	145:16	51	48:13	66
89	54	146:10	85	51:13	66
89:11	66	147:4	52	54:5	90
90:3	259	148	54	55:8	83
90:3, 7	262	148:13	271	63	159
90:7	259	148:14	271	63:7	99
90:8	259			63:9	99
90:11	259	**PROVERBS**		63:15ff.	86
90:14	258	5:23	274	66:1	270
91:1	85	8:15, 16	115		
91:2	85	8:29	205	**JEREMIAH**	
91:7	85	16:9	88	1:3	93
92:1, 2	275	21:1	88	1:15, 16	94
92:4	275	21:30	88	2:19	182
92:5	275			17:12	270
92:7	77	**ECCLE-**		22:29	180
92:8	81	**SIASTES**		23:5	100
92:8, 9	77	1:4	66	23:24	54
92:14, 15	275	3:10-12	182	30:9	100
92:15	249	7:15-22	16	33:17	100
93:1	66	8:11, 12	77	33:21, 22	100
93:2-4	84	12:13, 14	16	33:26	100
95	58	**ISAIAH**			
95:1, 2	267	1:9	102	**EZEKIEL**	
95:6, 7	270	6	123, 258	20:12	58
95:11	58	6:1	270	**DANIEL**	
96:10	84	8:13, 14	30	2:29	103
97:2	27, 270	9:5-7	101	2:34ff.	102
97:2, 3	259	9:6	209	10:13	117
98:1-6, 9	270	9:7	270	12:1	117
100:4	267	10:5-13	95	**AMOS**	
102:25	65	10:15	95	5:8	267
104	54	22:13	158	9	175
104:3	53	24:21	117	9:3	54
104:4	53	29:8	48	9:7	176
104:5	53	32:17	73	9:11	100
104:8, 9	205	37:17	91	**JONAH**	
104:10	53	37:33, 35	91	3:10	80
104:13	53	37:36	91	4:2	80
104:16	53	40:11	99	4:11	81
104:20	53	40:18	158	**MICAH**	
104:21	53	40:22	66	4:7	102
104:24	53	40:25	157	6:4	89
104:25, 26	52	40:26	158		

6:5	89		
7:18	259		
NAHUM			
1:2	259		
1:3	81		
1:6	81, 259		
3:1	81		
ZECHARIAH			
9:9	101		
MATTHEW			
3:7	259		
5:45	75		
6:27	85		
6:33	181		
8:13	210		
8:17	212		
8:28-34	103		
8:34	212		
9:2	210		
9:28, 29	210		
9:33	212		
10:29	51, 174		
10:29-31	181		
11:4-6	212		
11:5	212		
12:25	253		
12:28	103, 183, 211		
12:38ff.	210		
17:20	210, 228		
18:7	153		
19:4, 8	66		
21:15	215		
22:42f.	103		
24:4, 5	185		
24:6-12	185		
24:14	187		
24:25	185		
24:32, 33	185		
24:35	185		
25:42, 43	135		
27:29	104		
28:18	105, 106, 112		
MARK			
2:9	212		
2:10, 11	213		
2:12	212		
2:27	55		
5:20	211		
5:42	212		
6:5	210		
10:6	66		
10:27	210		
11:22, 23	227		
13:32	184		

INDEX

LUKE
1	102
1:35	258
1:15	263
2	95
2:14	123
4:21	104
6:35	75
8:50	210
9:44	224
10:9	103
10:18	104, 119, 213
11:20	183
12:49	230
12:54-56	184
13:1-5	172
15:7, 10	123
15:32	261
16:29	225
16:31	225
17:6	227
21:28	187
22:53	257
23:2	104
24:19	223
24:21	177
24:26	96

JOHN
1:18	266
3:16	73
3:19	263
3:36	265
5:36	213
6:26	213
8:12	160
9:2	172
9:3	172
9:16	219
9:19	219
9:21	219
9:26	219
9:32, 33	219
9:34	219
9:39	219
10:27	160
11:47-53	96
11:49, 50	96
11:51, 52	96
18:37	104
18:38	104
20:31	213, 224
31:22	204

ACTS
2:22	213
2:22, 43	209
2:23	96
2:24	211
3:15	96
4:27, 28	153
4:28	96
5:1-10	224
5:12	209, 214
5:12-16	224
5:19	224
5:38, 39	173
6:8	209
8	225
8:7	224
9:34	224
9:40	224
12:21-23	174
14:3	209, 214
14:16	138
14:19	224
28:8	224

ROMANS
1	150
1:4	211
1:18	41, 259
1:18, 24, 28	79
1:24	262
1:24-28	139
1:29-32	78
2:4	74
2:5	259
3:5	259
3:25	120
4:17	64
5:12	238, 262
6:20, 21	262
6:23	262
8	46
8:7	238
8:18	268
8:19	273
8:20	263
8:28	178
8:31, 32	47
8:38, 39	121
9:3	97
9:11	217
9-11	217
9:14	248
9:20	248
9:32	249
11:11, 12	97
11:15	98
11:33	248
11:33, 34	84
11:36	51, 248
12:19	259
13	113, 114, 116, 118
13:1	116
13:4	118
13:6	120
13:11	187
16:26	223

I CORINTHIANS
6:14	211
10:12	274
10:16	274
13:2	227
13:12	255, 266
15	108
15:24	121

II CORINTHIANS
5:19	260
13:4	211

GALATIANS
3:13	260

EPHESIANS
1:8, 9	222
1:22, 23	105
2:2	121
3:18, 19	222
4::17-19	263
4:19	262
5:5	111
5:6	259

PHILIPPIANS
2:10-11	112
2:12, 13	126, 131, 135

COLOSSIANS
1:13	105
1:17	51
3:6	259

I THESSALONIANS
1:10	27, 259
5:2	184

II THESSALONIANS
2:7	187
2:9, 10	229
7:7	187

I TIMOTHY
1:15, 17	34
2:1ff.	116
2:2	121
6:15	84
6:16	255

TITUS
3:1	116
3:4	27, 34

HEBREWS
1	59
1:3	51
1:10	56
1:14	120, 123
4:3	57, 58
4:3-9	57
4:8	58
4:9	58
4:10	57
4:16	270
10:30	259
12	182
12:5, 6	181
12:7, 8	181
12:10	181
12:11	181, 182
12:29	259

JAMES
1:15	263
5:15, 16	227

I PETER
1:16	258
2:13, 14	116
2:17	116
3:20	73

II PETER
3:4	66, 82

I JOHN
1:5	258
2:20	223

REVELATION
4:10, 11	272
4:11	59
5:5	184
5:9	273
5:11	272
6:9	230
6:17	260
7:15	269
7:17	271
11:18	260
13	114, 117, 121
13:3	230
13:10	121
13:13	229
13:14	229
14:12	121
15:2	272
16:5	274
16:14	229
17:14	106
19:1	231
19:9	231, 273
19:11	260
21:4	268

www.ingramcontent.com/pod-product-compliance
Lightning Source LLC
Chambersburg PA
CBHW031251230426
43670CB00005B/140